GOOD SOIL

MANURE, COMPOST AND NOURISHMENT FOR YOUR GARDEN

TINA RÅMAN

EWA-MARIE RUNDQUIST

JUSTINE LAGACHE

F

FRANCES
LINCOLN

WHAT?! DID YOU SAY MANURE?

Manure is an odd, unsavoury subject that fascinates many people – head gardeners, commercial growers and garden nerds, of course, but we were surprised to find that its appeal goes further. The subject of manure is enough to make grown adults, even those who have nothing but one lonely geranium at home, get all excited about growing – and about pee and poo.

Manures and fertilisers probably aren't the most glamorous aspects of the garden world. They can be mucky, disgusting and smell like crap. The topic also involves quite a lot of chemistry. But in many respects, it's both important and interesting. Obviously, say the converted – the growing pros. We ordinary hobby gardeners often go all out on the plants and decorations, completely forgetting how important it is to build up a good, nutrient-rich soil so that our plants have the right conditions to achieve their full potential.

But standing in front of the shelves of fertiliser in the garden centre, it would be easy to think that using it is difficult. Or that you need to buy at least one bag of every expensive product to satisfy the specific needs of each of your plants. In truth, you can simplify the whole process by deciding to use one or two all-purpose fertilisers as a base, topping those up with something extra if you choose to. It doesn't need to be any more complicated than that, but if you really want to understand the way your garden works and become a real star of the flowerbeds, you have another 256 pages ahead of you.

The main challenge in writing this book was making the subject of manure as simple and comprehensible as possible, without being too superficial about it, and then presenting the information in an appealing way. Being able to wallow in manure has been great fun. We know a lot about gardens, but none of us is a qualified fertiliser expert, and that's why we sought the help of Karl-Johan Bergstrand, PhD in agronomy, from The Swedish University of Agricultural Sciences, who fact-checked everything we wrote. Thanks, Karl-Johan!

We hope you'll find this book useful in your growing attempts, and that manure will come to mean more to you and your garden. And that you'll be able to experience the huge difference the right fertiliser can make.

Tina, Justine and Ewa-Marie

CONTENTS

It's possible to live on love and air alone. Not for long, but for a while, at least. Then we start to lose our tempers and we droop, wilt and shrivel up. Once the nutrient reserves are empty, things pretty much come to a stop. Not even a head of cabbage can live on just love and air in the long run. Especially not a head of cabbage, come to think of it. All living things — just like love — need nourishment to grow. This is as true for plants as it is for people.

Nature solves its nutritional needs perfectly well on its own. The problem is that we upset the natural balance when we work the land, meaning that what we take from nature has to be repaid. Unless we provide nutrients, we break the natural cycle and the soil becomes depleted. It becomes drained of energy.

You can restore these nutrients in a number of different ways, taking advantage of what you have. And as a reward for taking care of the soil, fertilising it, you'll be left with a dazzling garden full of healthy plants in return. By adding a little nutrition to that romantic diet of love and air, you'll get much better results. In other words, you'll maximise your growing.

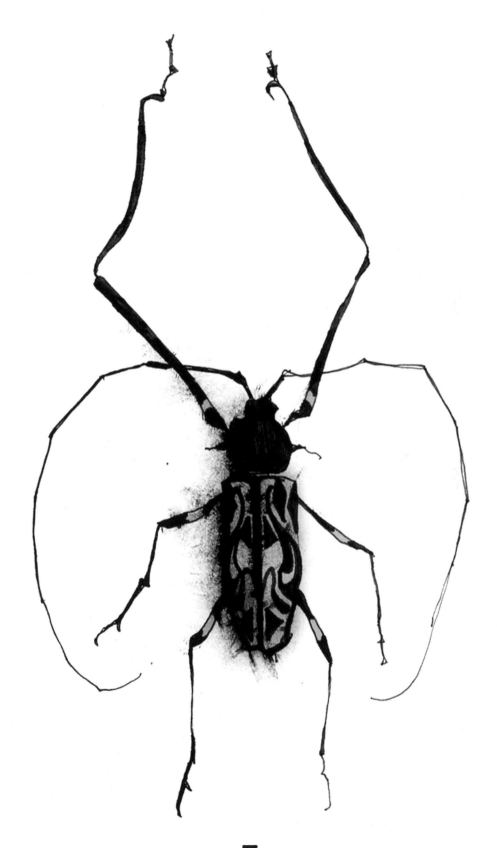

7

BIOLOGY

On the fundamental biological processes which affect the health and life of your plants. The magic which takes place without us noticing it — the wonder of nature.

A RETURN JOURNEY

'Earth to earth, ashes to ashes, dust to dust.' These words are, of course, about how the circle is closed when we die. This applies to all living organisms, plants included – they start and end with the earth. You don't need to be religious to realise that everything is connected – even if it is hard to understand quite how it works . . .

Any life that has ended decays and breaks down into the same constituent parts which once came together to build it. It makes no difference if this breaking down happens underground, in the sea or by fire. All matter is constant and will return to the earth in the end.

It might seem a bit heavy to be talking about the cycle of life and death already, at the start of this book, but it doesn't have to be sad. Not from a purely biological point of view, anyway. When the dear old apple tree finally croaks, that might give rise to a brand new tree.

All organic life is made of the basic elements found on our planet. The amount of this matter is constant – if we ignore any contributions from meteorites and other junk from space. It neither grows nor shrinks; the matter is just transformed and transferred. In other words, the basic elements are in an eternal cycle, regardless of our effect on them.

NATURAL CYCLES AND ECOSYSTEMS

There are a number of important natural cycles within nature: water, carbon, nitrogen and phosphorous, for example. These complex systems, which enable matter to be transformed, transported and eventually return to its original form, contribute to the exchange of nutrients and energy in all living things. It's a clever system, but it's also extremely sensitive if the circle is broken and the matter ends up in the wrong place, such as when phosphorous ends up in the sea rather than the ground, or when carbon ends up in landfill rather than our compost heaps.

Even the smaller natural cycles and ecosystems are important, such as those at home in your own back garden. The circulation of nutrients is a great example of this. If plant remains and household waste are returned to the earth as compost, and the plants absorb nutrients from grass cuttings, green manure and possibly even 'liquid gold' (urine mixed with water), the nutrients in your garden will be transported back and forth. In other words, you'll have created a nice little cycle within your domain.

But if those same nutrients are only given a one-way ticket away from the garden – if the bin men come to take away your rubbish and the only nutrients your plants get come from those plastic sacks from the garden centre – then no cycle is formed. Looked at from this angle, compost is something of a key player. Everything we take from the garden should be returned, once we have cleared, harvested and enjoyed it.

If we're aiming for a closed cycle, it's a matter of returning the resources we have in a smart way. That's exactly what nature does, after all! Plants sprout, grow, bloom, wilt and rot away to form humus in a constant cycle which creates the perfect conditions for new life and new growth.

That's nature's way – give and take.

NATURE'S MAGIC FORMULA

Every person on earth uses roughly a kilogram (2 lb) of oxygen every single day. We need a lot of other things too, of course, but in order to survive and not die within a few minutes, we need oxygen to breathe in and out, in and out. This oxygen is provided to us by plants, through a process called photosynthesis. It's an overwhelming thought, particularly for those of us who spent our biology lessons thinking about something completely different.

Photosynthesis: a fundamental requirement for us two-legged mammals. The really fantastic part is that this vital process takes place at home in your back garden, in the woods and in our parks, and all without us noticing it. It might even be taking place on the window sill in your kitchen.

Photosynthesis essentially drives all biological processes on earth. Using chlorophyll and light from the sun, plants convert water, minerals from the ground and carbon dioxide from the air into energy-storing carbohydrates. This magic process occurs in the plant's green cells, primarily in the leaves. The carbohydrates produced are then transferred to those parts of the plant which require nutrients. Oxygen is a waste product of this transformation, and an incredibly good one at that. The minerals found in the earth are, above all, nitrogen, phosphorous, potassium, sulphur and calcium. We'll return to these elements later on, because it is precisely these things which provide nutrition – or fertiliser – to our plants.

One very important and beneficial side effect of photosynthesis is that it binds the greenhouse gas carbon dioxide – the oxygen in this compound is released and the carbon fixed. When humans and animals breathe oxygen, we exhale carbon dioxide, but it is above all the burning of fossil fuels which has led to the amount of carbon dioxide in our atmosphere increasing and temperatures on earth rising.

Photosynthesis helps to lessen the greenhouse effect because plants reduce the level of carbon dioxide and simultaneously provide us with more oxygen.

More green on earth, more oxygen in our lungs, and less carbon dioxide leaking into the atmosphere!

CHLOROPHYLL – GREEN MAGIC

Chlorophyll serves a very important function within photosynthesis. It's chlorophyll which enables the plants' leaves to absorb light energy, like a satellite dish, and convert it into chemical energy. There are several different types of chlorophyll, and they collect light in different ways.

Chlorophyll also gives plants, or their leaves, that familiar green colour. The chemical structure of chlorophyll is somewhat similar to that of haemoglobin, which all mammals have in their blood. Haemoglobin contains an iron ion and chlorophyll a magnesium ion – hence red blood and green sap.

Chlorophyll is approved as a colourant in foodstuffs and is called E140. Usually, this uses extracts from grass or alfalfa.

CARBON DIOXIDE
WATER
+ SUNLIGHT
_____

OXYGEN AND
FRUIT SUGAR

WATER

Water is as vital to plants as it is to humans, a prerequisite for life. Roughly 90 per cent of the plant itself consists of water, and it's this water which gives elasticity to the flowers and leaves. A good watering should always be the first step in helping any plants that look sad or downhearted.

Water is also crucial in photosynthesis, enabling the nutrients to be released and transported to the plant, as well as for the growth of seeds and fruit. Another important function is the cooling and purifying effect water has on a plant's foliage.

When you water or apply fertiliser, plants aren't able to absorb everything in one go. They can't glug an entire watering can just like that. Or wolf down a helping of manure. As a result, one of the vital functions of soil is to store and portion out moisture and nutrients so that the plants can enjoy a snack every now and then.

It's also impossible for plants to absorb manure or fertiliser in solid form, meaning that they need water to act as a solvent in order to be able to assimilate the nutrients. 'Eating and drinking' primarily takes place through a plant's root system, and it is the root tip and the tiny, fine root hairs that are responsible for that process. Plants can even absorb a certain amount of water and nutrients through their leaves (through the stomata).

THE SOIL AS A LARDER

Soil is the nutrient depot for our plants. It contains a large number of cavities (pores) in which moisture, available nutrients and even vital oxygen are stored. Nutrients can also be fixed, when the mineral ions are latched on to the surface of the soil particles. The cavities, or pores, between the particles can differ in size, depending on the structure of the soil. A fine soil will have smaller cavities than a coarse soil, and the smaller the cavities are, the more effectively nutrients and water will be retained. Large cavities can mean that the water runs straight through, like in sand.

DRIED UP OR LACK OF OXYGEN?

Plants need both water and oxygen to survive. Oxygen is required for the plant's cellular breathing (respiration), so that it can take up water and nutrients. Without oxygen – no water. And without water – no nourishment. Roughly 70 per cent of a plant's oxygen intake occurs through the soil.

It's important that oxygen is present in the cavities in the soil, by the plant's roots. A loose soil containing humus will have good-sized cavities, meaning that oxygen uptake takes place as it should. In waterlogged soil, however, the pores will be completely saturated, meaning that the plant 'drowns' as a result of a lack of oxygen – the roots suffocate. The same phenomenon occurs if you overwater your pot plants. Watering too little is, of course, no solution to the problem. Under-watering will result in the cavities of the soil being filled only with air, which can lead to the plant drying up and dying instead.

BEAUTY SLEEP

Plants that grow in temperate zones are adapted to the four seasons. The time of year dictates their growth and maturation – their living conditions, in other words. In autumn, the plants start to make the slow transition into winter dormancy. The sun moves lower and lower on the horizon and the temperature falls outside. Above all, it is light and temperature which are responsible for regulating when the year's long beauty sleep begins and ends.

The process is equally magic every year, culminating in nature's brilliant explosion of colours in autumn, when the greenery transforms into a burning fire of yellows and reds. The cause of this colourful costume change is the plants' preparations ahead of their annual winter sleep.

The process gets underway when the leaves start to produce abscisic acid and the levels of chlorophyll drop off (in plants that are not evergreen). The energy used to produce chlorophyll is now needed for other processes, and as the green chlorophyll disappears, the yellow autumn colours start to emerge. They were there all along, but it's only now they become visible. The red tones come from the anthocyanins produced by the plants at varying levels during autumn.

Autumn colours vary depending on plant species and variety, and even depending on the weather. A mild, damp autumn will produce more yellow shades, while a dry, cool season will lead to redder tones. Either way, the process is beautiful.

What finally causes the leaves to drop is a series of changes in the leaf stem. The stem gradually dries out and a cork-like material forms until the leaves eventually drop, often during a cold snap or an autumn storm. You might have wondered why the leaves of certain plants take longer to drop than others, even within the same species? Access to light is the reason. Those plants which get more light often hold their leaves for longer than those standing in shade.

WINTER PREPARATIONS

As plants enter into dormancy ahead of winter, their nutritional needs drop off. The availability of nutrients actually declines as the temperature of the soil falls. During mild winters, nutrients will continue to be released, meaning that the natural balance can be upset. If the winter is cold, with ground frost, the nutrients remain locked up in the earth. A wet winter, on the other hand, can result in the nutrients being washed away by the rain and melt water, meaning that the ground itself becomes depleted.

As a result, it's important not to over-fertilise, and above all not to fertilise too late during the year. Nitrogen in particular stimulates growth, and would give the wrong signals to plants. Potassium and phosphorous, on the other hand, ensure that plants mature well, enter into dormancy ahead of winter, and that concentration of sugar in the cells increases, leading to better hardiness over winter.

Our plants are programmed for and adapted to the slow change of seasons. This means that rapid changes can lead to shock and damage. As good gardeners and proud plant owners, we should therefore try to prepare, protect and harden our plants ahead of each new season.

PLANTS' INTERNAL FROST SHIELDS

The cold tends to put a definitive end to our summer blooms' – or annuals' – lives. Perennials wilt down and overwinter below ground. Down there, beneath the soil, there are also tubers, bulbs and seeds. Above ground, woody plants such as bushes and trees are resting.

When these plants mature during the autumn, their composition changes in a number of ways. Their cell walls are strengthened with lignin, a kind of aromatic organic compound which stabilises the structure of the cells. The carbohydrate composition also changes, and the sugar concentration rises within the plant cells. These increased levels of sugar function in the same way as antifreeze in a car engine: the freezing point is lowered.

Those plants which originally come from warmer climates like the Mediterranean, for example, have weaker or non-existent internal shields against frost. Their cells can literally burst during a cold winter. As a result, they have to be protected, and possibly even brought indoors until spring.

BED DOWN AND TUCK IN

The soil will benefit from a little blanket during winter, made from leaves, straw or some other organic material. Adding this layer provides a certain level of insulation, and even a blanket of snow will do wonders. Covering the soil prevents ground heat from rising straight up out of the earth like it would if it was bare, and it also ensures that the chill from above is not able to penetrate as deep.

WINTER SLEEP PROBLEMS

Another reason to tuck in your plants is the spring sun. During late winter and early spring, the sun's rays can be strong, and temperatures can rise quickly during the day only to fall even more rapidly at night. Many plants, particularly evergreens, have trouble coping with these sudden changes. The internal frost protection within their cell walls can't keep up with the rapid temperature shifts, and the plant can suffer from frost damage. Covering plants with a fibre cloth, sackcloth or sheet can be their salvation. Even during autumn, when the first frosts arrive, this kind of protection can extend the life of delicate plants.

Another common winter problem is ground frost. If the ground around a plant's roots is frozen, they no longer have access to any liquid water. If light and warmth then cause the plant to reawaken above ground, it will need water. Protecting such plants from the strong spring sunshine is therefore beneficial. Doing so will mean that the entire plant – above and below ground – can come out of dormancy at the same time. Another idea is to try to thaw the ground using lukewarm water.

KEEP THE POT WARM

Plants don't generate heat in the same way that we humans do, not enough to be able to maintain a good 'body temperature', anyway. As a result, no matter how well we insulate our pot plants, it doesn't always help. Insulation can help to protect them against rapid changes in temperature, which can sometimes be enough, but it isn't a cast-iron guarantee against a really fierce winter.

If you can, it's best to bury your pots in the ground – in a flower bed, a compost heap or a pile of leaves. Otherwise, just do the best you can: insulate using polystyrene, foam peanuts, rag rugs, newspaper or leaves, and wrap your plants up in a 'packet'. To prevent your plant from rotting inside this packet, the air needs to be able to circulate. It's also a good idea to insulate your pots against the ground chill from below, for example by using a block of polystyrene.

It's important to remember that the cold itself isn't always the biggest villain during winter. Many less hardy plants suffer primarily as a result of damp soil. If that's the case, some kind of protective cover is a good idea – a winter umbrella made from a plastic box, for example, or a lid with a weight on top.

SOIL

On the actual living environment of the soil, where the majority of plants' nutritional uptake takes place. Each individual factor is important in the overall health and lift of the garden

COARSE-GRAINED OR FINE-GRAINED?

The soil types in our gardens vary, from fine-grained clay soils to sandy soils with a coarser structure. The properties of each differ, and they provide our plants with different living conditions. By getting to know your soil and understanding how it works, you can more easily improve it. And create a more comfortable environment for your plants.

In nature, soil comes from two directions: above and below. The lowest layer comes from the bedrock. Over millions of years, the mineral-rich primary rocks have slowly been worn away to form a much finer material. The upper layer of soil, the topsoil, has mixed with organic material from animal and plant life which has been broken down and transformed into humus.

The solid particles of soil consist, in other words, of minerals and organic material. Between these solid particles, the soil is full of pores, and it is here that the ground gas and liquid is found – in other words, the oxygen and water. The soil's pores are vital for retaining and providing moisture, nutrition and oxygen to the roots. An optimal composition would be made up of roughly half solid particles and half pores.

DIFFERENT PARTICLES

Rocks have slowly been broken down, eroded, into different sized particles. After stones come gravel, coarse sand, fine sand, silt and clay. In other words, the coarsest structures are stones, and the finest clay.

Soil types consisting of pure mineral earth are rare. The vast majority of gardens contain a mixture of some type of mineral earth and different types of organic material.

LABELS ON SOIL

It is useful to give your soil a label: 'sandy loam', 'clay loam', or whatever it is. That way, you know what you're working with down in the flowerbeds, which base ingredients you have. There are positives and negatives to each of the soil types, also depending on what it is you want to grow. If you know which type of soil you have, it's easier to take the right measures.

The most common definition of the soil types begins with pure mineral earth, and is based on the size of the particles. To avoid making things any more difficult than they have to be, we'll stick to that – in other words, the two extremes of sandy and clay soil, and then those in between: silts.

SANDY SOILS

Sandy soils have large particles, are light and porous, and they are easy to work with. Turning the soil after harvest in autumn is completely unnecessary, it's better to wait until after winter. This type of soil warms up quickly in spring, and it cools down rapidly in autumn. That makes it particularly suited to sensitive plants which need to go into dormancy early in order to survive winter.

The problem with sandy soils is that they are bad at retaining moisture and nutrients. They dry out quickly and need watering often. Nutrients are also quick to leach from the soil. As a result, it's important to apply fertiliser several times, and in smaller amounts, during the growth period. If you add more fertiliser than the soil can hold, it will just end up running away, contributing to the over-fertilisation of our waterways.

The best way to improve a sandy soil is to add organic material. Farmyard manure, compost and both composted peat and bark are fantastic. Covering sandy soils with organic material, rather than letting them lie bare, is also beneficial. This will contribute to increased humus content and a heightened ability to retain the moisture and nutrients in the soil.

SILT SOILS

Silt soil is an umbrella name for soils which consist of something between clay and sand. The group can be divided into coarse, medium and fine silts. The particles are medium-sized: finer than sand but coarser than clay. Coarse silt soils are porous and nutrient poor. Medium silt soils are made up of smaller particles and hold both moisture and nutrients better, but they can also form a hard crust which will need to be broken up. Fine silts have roughly the same qualities as medium silts; they are nutrient rich and retain moisture, which means that they can be incredibly wet during winter and take a long time to warm up in spring.

Silt soils can be improved using farmyard manure and humus-building materials. An easy way to prevent a hard crust from forming is to use organic matter, leaves or bark compost, for example, to cover the soil surface.

CLAY SOILS

Clay soils consist of small particles which clump together easily. The finest particles are found in 'heavy' clay soils which, as the name suggests, are difficult to work with. Clay soils are rich in nutrients and retain moisture well. Often, one application of fertiliser in spring will be enough. This type of soil is regarded as cold, which means that it takes them a long time to warm up and become cultivable in the spring. They also hold warmth for longer in autumn.

Clay soil is best dug over in autumn – once the growing season is over, in other words. Doing so will save both your back and your muscles. The high water content in this type of soil means that the winter's frosts will do the hard work for you – the cold will cause the lumps to crack, and in spring, all you will need to do is rake the soil.

One problem with clay soil is that it often contains too little air, which makes it sensitive to pressure. Make sure not to trample on clay soils!

The structure of clay soils can be improved with organic material, just like sandy soils. Composted bark is particularly good for this. Gravel can provide better drainage, but don't use sand. Adding sand will simply make clay soils even more compact. Leca balls and Perlite (volcanic matter) can be added to increase ventilation and drainage, but they are an expensive option.

MANAGE YOUR SOIL

All soil types can be improved. The aim is to increase the chances of retaining moisture, nutrients and air – in moderation. Consistently adding organic material and nutrients is good for all types of soil. Airing the soil by digging it over, not walking on the surface and 'cleaning' it occasionally is also good.

SOIL IN BAGS

The bags of multi-purpose compost you buy from the local garden centre can vary greatly in quality. You often – though not always – get what you pay for. A more expensive compost may contain better-quality peat, more and better nutrient levels, and even other additions like composted bark and lime. It won't sink down in the same way, like some kind of limp soufflé. One of the risks of cheap soil is that after a while, it will become so compacted that the roots suffer an oxygen deficiency.

A way to improve the quality of cheap soil is to mix in materials which will improve its structure in the long run, such as compost or composted bark. You could also add more farmyard manure – perhaps chicken or cow manure. That's a good cocktail for your soil.

Garden centres often sell soil for specific purposes, and these options are often of better quality than the cheap, all-purpose soil. You'll see sowing compost, rose compost, ericaceous compost, potting soil, etc., and these shop-bought soils might well suit your needs. Some of them have great compositions, even when it comes to the nutrient levels. Just remember that organic material is broken down and 'eaten up', and that the nutrients will eventually run out. This means you will have to continue adding nutrients to the soil. You can dig the soil from your summer pots into the garden once the season is over, for example. The nutrients will have already been depleted, but the soil still contains plenty of good humus-forming materials.

SOIL IN LARGE QUANTITIES

If you need larger amounts of soil, perhaps for a new flowerbed or an entire garden, you can order soil by the cubic metre (yard) or in bulk bags. You can pick them up yourself or have them delivered to your house. This type of soil is often called topsoil.

Depending on where you live and who you buy it from, the quality of this soil can vary enormously. Some suppliers will just scoop up some soil from the nearest field and then sell it on. Others will produce their own soil mix by ability and availability. Sometimes, the soil will have fertiliser added, other times not. Just make sure to check exactly what you are ordering, which is easier said than done. In practice, it can be difficult to make sense of the answers you get . . . Persist and be stubborn!

You can even mix your own nutrient-rich soil using the existing soil from your garden as a base. We've included an old gardener's recipe on page 197.

The optimal solution is for your soil to contain both mineral soil (ideally some clay, not just sand) and humus, but not too much peat; it should have a neutral pH, and have both slow-release (well-decomposed farmyard manure) and quick-release (such as chicken manure) fertiliser added. It should also be free from weeds which might spread through their roots.

THE SOIL TEST – ROLL, ROLL, ROLL YOUR SOIL

You can get an idea of what type of soil you have at home by carrying out a simple test. Take some soil (roughly 1 tablespoon) and start rubbing it between your palms. If the soil is very dry, you can add a drop of water.

If you can't roll it into a sausage shape, or even into a ball, you probably have sandy soil. The thinner you can roll your soil sausage, the more clay it contains. By thin, we mean down to 1 mm ($\frac{1}{25}$ in). If you can get it down to 4–5 mm ($\frac{1}{4}$ in), you probably have some kind of silt soil.

Take samples of soil from a few different areas and repeat the test several times. Doing so will literally give you a feel for the soil. You can also try to feel the grain of the soil. The coarser the grains, the more sand in the soil. Heavy clay soil is incredibly smooth (like a face mask).

SHADES OF BROWN

Soil often comes in shades of greyish-brown. When dry, clay soils are greyish, but when wet, they take on more of a graphite shade. Sandy soils are slightly lighter, often a warmer tone. The darker the soil, the more humus it contains.

The colour is also influenced by the type of rock the soil has originated from. In Scandinavia, the soil is often brownish because of minerals such as olivine (a green colour) and pyroxene (greyish-black) present in our rocks. Quartz is another common mineral substance which gives the soil a lighter colour. When soils contain high levels of iron, they can take on a variety of rust-coloured shades – like the red earth of Australia, for example.

If you take a good shovelful of earth, you can see the stratification of the soil, much like a cake with a number of clear layers. The cultivated top layer, the topsoil, is darker, airier and lighter. Deeper down through the layers, you come to the subsoil. It is harder, coarser, and often lighter/greyer in colour. The subsoil consists of leached mineral soil. Beneath this is pure, untouched mineral soil.

The nutrient value of the mineral soil depends on the rock type and how old the soil is (the nutrients may have leached).

Lars Krantz, Wij Gardens in Ockelbo –
a garden visionary with a feeling for soil

A feeling for soil

Tucked away behind the church in the town of Ockelbo, 120 miles north of Stockholm, are the Wij Gardens, surrounding the old Wij Mansion. The small town has become a familiar name among Swedes in recent years, first through head gardener Krantz and then through Crown Prince Daniel, who lived here. Walking through the gardens, it's clear that Lars Krantz is an important figure – everyone we meet says hello or gives a cheery wave as we pass.

Lars Krantz moved to Ockelbo in Gästrikland just over ten years ago. At the time, he felt he had achieved all he could at the Rosendal Gardens on Djurgården in Stockholm, having spent twenty years as coach and leader there. But his never-ending drive and enthusiasm led him to take on a new challenge, and the connection to Ockelbo of all places had long been there. Lars and his colleagues have, in a keen and sensitive way, managed to develop and interpret the soul and natural essence of the place. The inland climate in that area of Sweden certainly has its demands.

Naturally, the Wij Gardens have become everything Lars ever dreamed of or strove to achieve. In fact, the gardens have been voted Sweden's most beautiful park and awarded a national tourism award. Not that being given awards and honours was ever the aim. Lars' dream was more about creating an inspiring and creative meeting place for people, nature and culture. An aim which, in retrospect, can be checked off the list.

'Wow, a whole book about manure! Finally!'

Yes, Lars Krantz really is a passionate and inspirational man. His enthusiasm for soil, compost and manure is tangible.

'I have very strong feelings about manure', head gardener Krantz says with a shrewd smile, almost as though he was talking about some secret romance.

We assumed as much. Soil and manure are close to his heart. Lars talks about farmyard manure in terms of temperatures. Chicken manure is the hottest and pig the coldest. Sheep and goat manure is lukewarm, and horse and cow manure warm. At the Rosendal Gardens in Stockholm, they used horse manure from the Royal stables in their hot beds.

'It produced really good lettuce leaves in January,' Lars laughs.

It's early summer in the Wij Gardens, and the soil in the neat vegetable patches is rich and well-manured. The climbing frames and plant shields are in place, and the piglets are up to no good in a pen. The whole place looks like a table which has been set for a party, before the guests have arrived. But the plants are still small. Winter loosened its grip late this year, and spring was cold and rainy.

'Growing here is different to growing in southern Sweden,' Lars says. 'The plants are dormant for longer during winter and then the pace is quicker during summer. The long winter saves energy ahead of spring and then nature breaks free in a great crescendo of life, both in the plants and animals! To put it simply, it's a

'Once you've gotten to know your soil, you can adapt to its temperament more easily.'

shorter but more intense act of love in the North. The soil needs more here, not least in terms of fertiliser. That and the light give the plants inspiration and growing power. We're waiting for the soil to mature right now. And once the warmth comes, it'll show its fertility and the plants will quickly grow big and strong.'

Lars isn't an academic head gardener who spends his time leafing through books, checking values and using advanced instruments in his work. He follows his gut. It sounds so simple, free and wonderful. But behind that 'gut feeling' are, of course, many years of experience, not just an otherworldly sensuality and extraordinary gift. When Lars examines his soil, he uses his entire body, all of his senses. He can see, feel and sniff his way to a good soil with the right levels of nutrients. He has an innate sense of soil, to put it bluntly. Sigh.

'It takes time, trust yourself and follow your gut. If you've got the right passion, the knowledge and feeling will follow when you're ready for them.'

Krantz's education took place at Skillebyholm Biodynamic Garden School, in true anthroposophic spirit. What he learnt there is always lurking in the background, even if Lars does take a freer attitude these days. He calls himself a 'home anthroposophist'. That means, among other things, that he always keeps track of the moon. Right now, in the month of June, his focus is on the so-called 'iron nights'.

'When the moon is in one of the earth signs at this time of year, a little warning bell always starts ringing in my head', he says. 'It means you have to be on the ball with protective blankets and coverings. The consequences of one night of frost can be utterly devastating for the year's harvest otherwise.'

'Iron nights' is the name given to those nights in early summer where the temperature can suddenly drop below freezing. They usually occur around the start of June, but the time varies from area to area across the country.

Lars talks passionately about a gardener's relationship with the soil. He says that if you have a good relationship with the earth, it's easier to take the right measures, to improve the soil and apply fertiliser in the best possible way.

Lars divides soils with different structures into characteristic temperaments, something which isn't at all scientific, but based more on intuition and feeling.

'Clay soils are melancholy in nature. They're cold and introspective. A little bit sluggish and incredibly self-obsessed. They're sleepy soils which wake up late. Clay soils get ready for planting slowly, at their own speed. It's as thought they're saying 'the outside world need not apply.' Sandy soils are the opposite. They have a more sanguine character, they're extroverted and lively. Sandy soils are quicker, more alert, more fiery in nature. But they're also a little bit superficial, they don't have any real depth. I think sandy soils are the artistic souls among the soil types, the kind that trims its sails to the wind. Humus, that wonderful dark, beautiful soil, is lazy and comfortable; it has a phlegmatic disposition. It takes time to warm up in spring, and then lies there listlessly like a contented cat, happy to sun itself. It does hold water and nutrients very well, though.

'Once you've gotten to know your soil, you can adapt to its temperament more easily. You'll also find out a bit more about how it needs to be handled, how it holds water and nutrients, for example. How it wants to be showered with manure', Lars says, looking like the charmer he is.

'That's my best tip for all the gardeners out there. Get to know your soil, develop your sense of soil! That's the foundation for a long, fruitful relationship with all kinds of growing.'

'Winter gathers energy ahead of spring. If you take a handful of spring soil and compare it with autumn soil, you'll be able to feel the difference. It'll be rich and damp in spring, but in autumn it's more tired and worn out. A bit like us people, only in reverse.'

ACID, ALKALINE OR NEUTRAL?

THE MOOD OF THE SOIL

Different soils have different dispositions, just like us growers. Soil can be acid, alkaline or neutral, depending on the different compositions of acid or alkaline substances, and its pH level provides us with information about what the balance between the different substances is like. Most plants prefer a soil with a neutral or slightly acidic pH level. There are, of course, always exceptions to the rule.

The pH scale ranges from 1–14, with 7 the mid-value. This mid-point is called neutral, and means that the liquid in the soil contains an equal number of hydrogen and hydroxide ions. As the value sinks, the soil becomes acid, and as it rises, it moves onto the basic (alkaline) section of the scale.

Most plants thrive with a pH level between 5.5 and 7.5. The optimal pH is usually somewhere between 6–6.5, so if your soil measures above or below this, it might be a good idea to do something about it. This is because the pH level affects the nutritional uptake of your plants.

At extreme values, below 3 or above 8, the soil becomes an inhospitable environment for plants. The nutrients in the soil become 'locked' and cannot be absorbed. If this happens, it doesn't matter how much, or with what, you fertilise the soil. And it isn't just the release of nutrients that is affected, the pH level also has an impact on the structure of the soil and the life within it. In addition to this, a balanced pH level will also prevent dangerous heavy metals in the soil from being absorbed by your plants.

KNOW YOUR PH-LEVEL

The vast majority of plants are co-operative enough and will be content even when the pH level of the soil isn't quite right for them. But many plants will also reward you handsomely if you adjust it. First of all, you need to find out where your soil falls on the pH scale. There are a number of ways you can do this – using litmus paper, for example, or a lab-based soil analysis. The simplest method is to use a pH meter, which you can buy for a reasonable price from good garden centres. With some meters, you'll need to add deionised (or distilled) water to the soil. If so, buy battery water from the petrol station, or empty the condensed water from your tumble drier and use that.

Once you know the pH of your soil, it's easier to take the right steps to improve it. Generally, you can achieve a well-balanced soil by adding organic matter like compost or farmyard manure. Just be patient! Producing a good soil takes time.

CHANGING LEVELS
Lime is a quick shortcut to a higher pH level. Even fertilisers such as calcified seaweed can raise the pH, as can rock dust and wood ash. If you need to quickly lower the level, however, you can mix in a lime-free, peat-based compost. Most likely is that you want to raise the pH because chemical changes in the soil and acid deposits from the air have left you with a low pH.

THE PH LEVEL MOOD SCALE

Acid 1–6

Neutral 7

Alkaline 8–14

6.5

The optimal pH for the majority of plants is slightly acid: 6.0 – 6.5

HOW TO MEASURE THE PH

1. Take away the top layer of soil (roughly 3 cm/1 in) and dig down to about 20 cm (8 in). Dig several of these holes in the area you're interested in. You will need about 200 ml (6¾ fl oz) of soil.

2. Pour the soil into a large jar, cup or bowl with a lid. Add deionised or distilled water and stir. You should use two parts water to one part soil.

3. Put on the lid and shake for at least 2 minutes.

4. Allow the soil to settle at the bottom for at least 10 minutes.

5. Dip your pH meter (or litmus paper) into the water above the layer of sediment at the bottom. Follow the instructions on the meter.

6. Read and make a note of the results. Repeat this test in several locations if you think the results may differ.

DESIRABLE PH LEVELS

roses	6.5–7.0
lawns	6.0–6.5
brassicas	6.5–7.5
potatoes	5.5–6.5
leafy vegetables	6.5–7.0
raspberries	5.5–6.5
strawberries	6.0–7.0
berry shrubs	6.0–7.0
acid-loving plants	5.0
conifers	5.0–6.0

LIME

POWDER PUFF

What really contributes to the acidification of our soils are deposits of sulphur dioxide, nitrogen oxides and ammonia. Though emissions have decreased, acid environments continue to be a problem, even in our gardens. Liming is the most common way of raising the pH level and reducing the nutritional drainage.

First and foremost: don't lime the soil unless you need to. Too high a pH level is, just like a very low one, far from good. It encourages problems such as common scab in potatoes, for example. A good rule of thumb is therefore to always measure the pH (see previous) of your soil first, so that you know whether it really needs liming. Lime is good, but it is by no means a universal solution or magic fix.

A few decades ago, lime was added all over the place in spring, particularly to lawns. This was because it was believed that the lime would kill any moss growing in the grass. It's true that certain species of moss thrive in acidic soil, and lime does raise the pH level if applied in large enough quantities, but to get rid of moss it's better to clear it away manually and provide more comprehensive nutrition to the soil – enabling the grass to keep it at bay by itself.

That said, there are good reasons to lime your garden from time to time. Lime doesn't just raise the pH level of the soil, it also provides trace elements. The good nutrients in the earth become more accessible, and your plants will have increased difficulty absorbing the heavy metals from the soil. Clay soils in particular become airier, looser and an easier environment for roots to grow in.

LIME CONFUSION

So, what exactly is lime? Lime consists primarily of calcium and magnesium. It's easy to get calcium and lime confused, or to think that they're the same thing. But the element calcium (Ca) is an important nutrient for both plants and animals (one which even lime-shunning plants like rhododendrons need, just in smaller amounts). Calcium also appears in a number of different chemical compounds often referred to as 'lime'. All lime has an alkalising effect, meaning the pH level increases, albeit to different degrees.

It's important to know what you want when you add lime. Check the products/packaging to see what they contain and what effects they will have. Ask at your local garden centre! Try a different one if they don't give you the right answers.

LIME IN DIFFERENT FORMS

There are a number of different types of garden lime available. The products are made from minerals such as dolomite, limestone and chalk. Each consists of more or less pure calcium carbonate, and dolomite lime also contains magnesium.

In Sweden, we have products such as Turbokalk, which is dolomite lime that acts as both a fertiliser and a means of raising the pH level. Another, Algomin, is made from calcium-rich coralline algae, and is another such alternative 'combi' product. Even bone meal is worth a mention here.

The fineness (the degree of crushing and milling) of the lime differs. Ground limestone is the finest. Pelleted, or granulated lime, consists of finely ground limestone which has been treated to make it easier to handle. It doesn't cause dust, and dissolves quickly when added to the soil. You can also buy fine-ground chalk, which tends to be cheaper. This type of lime is more coarse and takes longer to dissolve in the soil. The finer the structure, the more quickly and efficiently a lime will take effect compared to coarser types. Ground limestone or pelleted lime is therefore preferable to crushed chalk.

THE RIGHT TIME AND AMOUNT

You can add lime at any time of year, but autumn and winter are best, when the rain and snow will help to wash the lime into the soil. If you apply lime at another point, you can dig it in to the soil or simply water it in if using ground limestone.

Often, you will need a large quantity of lime to be able to raise the pH level to the desired value. Clay soils tend to need more lime, sandy soils less. And since different lime products have different ingredients, you'll need to read the packaging carefully to make sure you're adding the right dose. Generally, you'll need considerably more lime if you're preparing a new area of a garden. If you're maintaining lime levels, however, you'll need much less.

'HARD-BOILED' LIME

Lime – and calcium – are not only found in garden lime – you'll also find them in bones, eggshells, mussel and snail shells, for example. Shells and bones are tough to digest (they take a long time to decompose), meaning they need to be finely ground or crushed if you want them to have any kind of effect in the near future. Eggshells consist of roughly 95 per cent calcium carbonate. Grind them down and scatter them among the roses. Use mussel and snail shells or pretty limestone rocks to decorate your flower beds. With time, they'll all add a little lime. They might also look nice.

LOVES:

lavender

roses

peas and beans

carrots

strawberries

cauliflower

broccoli

cabbage

DOESN'T LOVE:

hydrangea

blueberries

rhododendron

azalea

potatoes

heather

raspberries

A TYPE OF HUMUS

Humus-building materials help the soil to maintain a good balance of air, moisture and nutrients. On top of that, the humus also supports the insect and bacterial life of the soil and provides worms and other ground workers with good living conditions. One of the best humus-building soil improvers is compost, but composted peat, leaves and bark aren't half bad either. In fact, the structure of all soils can be improved with organic material!

Mull is the type of humus commonly found in cultivated ground. Other types of humus include mor, found in coniferous forests, and peat, which is found in bogs and marshes. Even the mud at the bottom of lakes is a type of humus. All consist of organic substances which have been created through the breaking down of dead plants and animals.

Mull, the type of humus we find in our gardens, consists largely (roughly 60 per cent) of carbon. Organic carbon increases the airiness of the soil and makes the transportation of water and nutrients to plants easier.

Mull is formed in your compost heap (read more about that soon). It has a higher nutrient and pH level than both mor and peat, meaning it is a better environment for micro-organisms. Those tiny little rascals help to stir the layers of soil, which is also good for oxygen exchange further down, by the roots.

PEAT HUMUS

Peat is formed of partly decayed vegetation from damp or oxygen-poor environments such as bogs and marshes. The lack of oxygen means that the decomposition process is extremely slow. It can take thousands of years for peat to form, which is why peat is currently classified as a slow-renewable resource. The cutting of peat, and above all when it is later burnt as fuel, releases carbon dioxide. This increases the levels of CO_2 in the atmosphere, and from an environmental standpoint, this is why it is better to improve your soil with composted bark or leaf mould and natural manures. Or compost – a natural process produced only a short distance from your garden.

Peat appears in the majority of commercially available soils, though the amount and the quality does vary, which can lead to the soil collapsing. The new soil can suddenly, perhaps as little as a year later, be as flat as a pancake.

Both white and black peats are available. Black peat tends to be chopped up into smaller pieces and is often called well-humified peat. It is this type which often leads to the soil collapsing. The black peat is cheaper and will give your soil a worse structure. The paler, less humified peat is has a more coarse structure and will therefore provide a better and more long-lasting structure to your soil.

Peat is a nutrient-poor soil improver with a low pH.

It is particularly good for improving the structure of sandy soils. Use unlimed peat if you want to maintain or lower your pH levels. Otherwise, use limed and fertilised peat. Remember that the peat will break down and need to be re-added regularly.

COMPOSTED BARK

The black or dark brown composted bark, consisting of composted or half broken-down bark from trees (usually spruce and pine) is a great structure improver – above all in clay soils. It gives a stable, long-lasting structure. Don't confuse composted bark and bark mulch, though – they are two different things with different functions.

Remember to add nutrients if you dig in a lot of composted bark, because the decomposition process will continue in the soil. The composted bark you buy from garden centres often has added nutrients and lime to compensate for this. Check the packaging. Natural composted bark has a neutral pH.

The advantage of composted bark over peat is that it breaks down more slowly. In addition, it contains more humus-building material than peat. In other words, you need to use less composted bark and you don't need to add it every year. You could still make your own mix, however – combine a little peat with some composted bark (and natural manure, which will improve structure and give comprehensive and long-lasting nutrients).

LEAF MOULD

Leaf mould, just like composted bark, is a great structural improver. It has a low nutritional content and a neutral pH level. If you have access to leaves,

Mull is great for soil

you can make leaf mould yourself. Simply cut the leaves up using the lawnmower in autumn, and leave them where they are, rake them beneath the bushes or scatter them wherever you need them. The worms in your garden will pull the leaves down into the soil, helping to create a wonderful mull humus. Make sure not to create too thick a blanket, on lawns, for example. Use any left over leaves as a winter cover for sensitive plants – or add them to your compost.

If there are still leaves left over after that, you can put them into plastic bags, store them in a dark corner somewhere, and leave them to break down. It will probably take about a year, depending on the type of leaves you have. Oak leaves take the longest to break down.

THE SOIL'S STOCK

Compost is as important to your garden as the stove is to your kitchen. The difference is that with a compost, you're creating goodies for your green and flowery friends. And the best thing about compost is that it virtually looks after itself. Like a rich, simmering pot of stock.

You've probably heard it all before. Compost is the black jewel to all gardeners, a miracle substance which brings incredible benefits to your garden, your pots or anywhere else you grow. It acts as an improver for all types of soil, from clay soils to sandy, but it can also provide valuable nutrients, depending on what it has been 'boiled down' from. One thing compost cannot do, however, is replace manure or fertiliser. But with the rich organic material it provides, it gives your soil a better ability to absorb and retain nutrients, water and oxygen.

Compost encourages the bacterial and insect life in the soil and helps your plants to become more resilient and healthier. Adding compost to the soil can even have a positive impact on the pH level. Then there's the environmental side of things. Creating a cycle of this kind is good in many ways. All 'rubbish' can have a positive impact if it's allowed to remain in your garden. It's cheaper, better and easier to make use of what you already have than sending your 'rubbish' to the tip and buying in something else to improve your soil. So, hallelujah. Here's to compost!

ENERGY BOMB OR DIET FODDER?

It's hard to work out the exact nutritional value of finished compost. For one, it depends on what has been composted and for how long – how much of the nutrients have entered the air or the ground through evaporation and runoff. Kitchen compost tends to have a high nutrient content, as well as lots of nitrogen. Garden compost has a lower nutritional value, but it still works well as a soil improver.

First and foremost, you should regard compost as a soil improver, rather than a means of fertilising your soil. You should add both compost and fertiliser/manure to your soil to guarantee the nutritional levels.

THE GARDEN'S TREASURE CHEST

Compost might not be the solution to all a gardener's problems, but it definitely helps to create the healthy soil we've been longing for. It's a treasure chest for all gardens.

There is plenty of information about composting out there, both in bookshops and online. Reading it, you might get the sense that establishing and taking care of your compost is a difficult task. But in truth, it's not that hard. In fact, it's almost impossible to fail – whatever you add to your compost will be broken down sooner or later. But in order to transform your waste into a rich compost more quickly than it would in nature, you need to keep on top of the balance of carbon rich material such as branches and leaves, and nitrogen rich materials like grass cuttings and food waste, as well as the addition of oxygen, moisture and warmth.

THE DECOMPOSITION PROCESS

What happens when you make a new compost heap is that bacteria quickly get to work, causing the temperature to rise – to somewhere between 40–70°C (100–160°F). This warmth will then gradually drop off. Different fungi will get involved in the process, eventually followed by insects and worms. Together, they all work to break down the organic material in the different stages.

The stages of composting are often referred to

as the mesophilic phase, the thermophilic phase, the cooling phase and the curing phase. The decomposition process slows down or comes to a complete stop during winter, but it will start up again once temperatures outside begin to rise.

The composting of nitrogen-rich food waste means that greenhouse gases (carbon dioxide, methane and nitrous oxide) are released when the temperature rises. Higher temperatures see more gas released. This isn't climate friendly, of course, and one way to regulate the process is to make sure the temperature doesn't run away and get too high. By ensuring a balanced mixture of food waste and dry material (nitrogen and carbon), and by making sure the compost isn't too wet, you can keep the temperature down and therefore reduce the amount of greenhouse gases which are released.

The best conditions for decomposition arise when the temperature is somewhere between 35–55°C (95–130°F). If the temperature is too low, the process will take considerably longer, and harmful maggots, eggs, seeds (from weeds) and illness-causing bacteria will be able to survive.

COMPOST × 2

It's good to keep two different compost heaps: one for garden waste and one for kitchen waste. The reason for keeping them separate is that the food waste needs to be kept in a sealed container to avoid an invasion of rats, mice and birds. That's guaranteed to be a party you don't want!

> Since this book is primarily about manure, we won't delve too deep into the subject of compost here. There are already so many good books on that, so if you're a beginner, we recommend you get your hands on one of those. Because even though it isn't especially difficult to produce compost, you're probably going to want to know more.

A practical location for your kitchen compost could be close to your kitchen. Your garden compost could be close to your vegetable patch – if you're lucky enough to have one of those. Otherwise, an out-of-the-way corner of the garden will work well, ideally beneath a tree or a bush for shade.

The better the conditions, the quicker the decomposition process will be, providing you with valuable compost in return. The process of decomposition can take anything from a few months to several years, but once the compost has cooled down and looks and smells like fine, dark soil, it's ready to use.

You'll get the best results by mixing the finished kitchen compost with decayed garden compost – roughly one part of the former to three of the latter. Kitchen compost contains considerably more nutrients than garden compost. Both are good, however, and important as soil improvers, so a mixture of the two is fantastic. If you only have one, that will still work very well.

GARDEN COMPOST

Choose a good location (never in direct sunlight) if you want to start a new compost heap. Then prepare your existing compost bin, buy a new one, or build your own. It shouldn't be too small - at least one square metre (yard), and it should have several compartments: three is usually a good number.

The compost should be in contact with the ground, so don't place it on top of flagstones, etc. - put it directly onto the soil. Use a biochar (or high-quality crushed charcoal) base and a layer of rice or some other loose material, to reduce nutrient leakage. Then, layer carbon and nitrogen-rich material so that the compost is ventilated and can get plenty of air. You should ideally chop any branches or twigs into smaller pieces - finely cut material will break down more quickly. Place any weeds you've pulled from the garden in the middle of the pile, where temperatures will be hottest, and then cover them with the rest of the material. Don't pack or compact the heap too hard - the decomposition process needs oxygen. Sprinkle a layer of finished compost, soil and/or natural manure onto your compost every now and then, to boost the process.

Try to keep your compost damp (not dry, not wet). The moisture content should be 50–60 per cent – something like a wrung-out dishcloth. Add water if you think the compost is too dry. Add absorbent, carbon-rich materials like sawdust, newspaper or straw if it's too wet.

Mix, air or poke holes in your compost using a pitchfork every now and then, particularly after winter. This will increase oxygen levels. You can even buy special compost aerators. It's a good idea to add a lid, a raffia mat or a layer of straw, for example, to reduce evaporation.

KITCHEN COMPOST

All cooked food waste, including vegetables and waste from animal products, must be composted in a sealed container to avoid any unwanted interest from animals. Raw vegetables, fruit, peelings and the like can simply be added to the garden compost heap. The balance between carbon-rich and nitrogen-rich material is equally important here, so layer your kitchen waste with things like newspaper, straw or leaves.

If you want your kitchen compost to keep decomposing over winter, you will need to insulate the composting bin or container. There may be regulations on storing kitchen compost where you live, so check with your local council first.

A compost bucket on your balcony still counts as composting.

OTHER TYPES OF COMPOST

You can compost virtually all kinds of organic material. Pine cones and needles take a long time to break down, but they will eventually produce a good compost with a low pH level that will be great for improving your soil if you have acid-loving plants. Even composting leaves will give you first-rate mix after a while. Oak and beech leaves are particularly slow to decompose. Bark can also be composted, and creates excellent compost. You can speed up the decomposition process by chopping up the material, with a lawnmower for example.

Adding bokashi (see next page) to a sealed plastic bag of leaves is another alternative. If you do this in autumn, your compost might be ready by spring if the winter isn't too cold. Then all you need to do is dig the material into your soil, or add it to your ordinary garden compost.

A compost bucket on your balcony
still counts as composting.

YES-YES IN YOUR COMPOST

◆ garden waste (preferably finely cut)
◆ kitchen waste (even bones can work)
◆ grass cuttings and turf
◆ wood ash
◆ charcoal residue (smaller amounts of FSC or SIS-marked coal)
◆ newspapers
◆ paper (corrugated cardboard, egg cartons, serviettes, etc. – printed paper should be recycled)

NO-NO IN YOUR COMPOST

◆ cigarette butts and tobacco
◆ vacuum cleaner bags
◆ inorganic material (plastic, etc.)
◆ medicines
◆ plant waste or leaves from unhealthy plants
◆ cat litter or similar
◆ lime
◆ salt
◆ fat

BOKASHI - JAPANESE COMPOST

Another way of breaking down waste into nutrient-rich compost is to ferment it. You can do this by adding lactic acid bacteria – similar to that found in yoghurt – and particularly efficient microbes known as EM (effective micro-organisms).

Bokashi is an anaerobic (doesn't require oxygen) composting method which was developed in Japan in the early 1980s, and which has recently started to gain popularity elsewhere in the world. The process is similar to ordinary kitchen composting but it is quicker and has less of a smell if carried out correctly.

Sadly, you need to get hold of a certain 'shop-bought product' to kick off the process. You can buy bokashi from garden centres – just look online or ask in your local shop.

The product is a mix consisting of, among other things, lactic acid bacteria, molasses and wheat bran. You sprinkle the mix directly into your compost bucket (with a lid) in your kitchen. It's important that the environment is oxygen-poor for the process to work. It can't be too wet, either. And the dregs stink! You can, however, heavily dilute this with water (roughly 1/100) and use it as a fantastic liquid fertiliser.

One of the advantages of bokashi is that none of the nutrients disappear in the process, and virtually no greenhouse gases are produced. You can ferment all organic waste, including fish guts, shellfish casings and bones. Another advantage is that the pH level is so low that pests don't like the environment. In three to four weeks, you will have transformed your waste into a beautiful, nutrient-rich soil improver. The microbes in the bokashi mean that the proteins in the food waste are broken down into amino acids – which plants can assimilate almost immediately.

The end product isn't quite humus. For that, you will first have to mix the material into your soil. Once you do this, the bokashi microbes will continue to work, now alongside their new microbe pals in the soil.

His Majesty Ernie Earthworm – king of the soil.
In Sweden, these worms can grow up to 30 cm (1 ft) in
length. In Australia, you can find earthworms which
have grown up to 2 m (7 ft)!

HEROES OF THE EARTH

A good soil is teeming with life, both above and below the surface. Hidden below ground, the soil animals, bacteria and fungi live and work away in secret. These are the true working-class heroes. Worms, insects and micro-organisms are among the best help you could hope for in the garden. For nothing but room and board, they'll work hard almost year-round. Only the cold and ground frost will make them lower the tempo. When that happens, the worms dig deeper into the soil and their body temperatures lower.

A garden's animal life doesn't consist of slugs, mice, lice and other pests alone – even if that's sometimes how it feels. Some of the more welcome guests include butterflies, bees, ladybirds, hedgehogs, birds, squirrels and maybe even the occasional fox or badger. But by far the biggest and best place to mingle is below ground! Down there, worms and microbes go to town on dead plants, leaves and other organic material, transforming it into gold. Well, maybe not quite gold, but almost: humus.

These soil-dwellers dig channels which improve the porosity of the earth, meaning that oxygen, water and nutrients can be more easily transported to the roots of plants, and that any unnecessary water will drain away. Mushrooms and bacteria also help out by breaking down dead organic material. During this decomposition process, when organic material is transformed into carbon dioxide and water, nutrients the plants can later assimilate are released.

WORMS AND INSECTS

Soil-dwelling creatures and their friends (larger insects) pull leaves, dead plants and other goodies they've found down into the earth. They chew them up and process the material. They stir the pot so that the different layers of soil combine, thereby contributing to a soil structure full of pores. And

it is in these pores that other micro-organisms (microbes) live.

Single-cell organisms, roundworms and small ringed worms live in the film of water surrounding the humus particles in the soil, while springtails, mites, pseudoscorpions and fly and midge larva live in the air-filled pores.

Nematodes, tiny little roundworms which help in the decomposition process, are the smallest of the ground's workers. The vast majority of nematodes are good and beneficial, but not all of them. Within commercial organic growing, where chemical spraying of pests is not permitted, nematodes are often used as a kind of mercenary. They are also used within conventional agriculture. Adding nematodes can, for example, help to fight vine weevil (a beetle whose larvae can destroy plant roots). The nematodes then destroy themselves once the enemy has been wiped out.

FUNGI AND BACTERIA

Once the soil-dwelling creatures have done their work, the fungi and bacteria take over, continuing to break down the organic material. Their job is to make the nutrients accessible to the plants again. There are 'good' and 'bad' bacteria and fungi, some which provide benefits and others which cause harm. If

your soil isn't balanced, and the proportion of micro-organisms is too low, the bad can take over and cause problems for your plants. But in a good, balanced soil, they keep one another in check.

Some bacteria strike up an ingenious collaboration with, for example, leguminous plants (see page 199). The nitrogen-fixing bacteria live in special nodules around their roots, where they trap the nitrogen from the air and give it to the plants in exchange for sugars.

UNDERGROUND NETWORKS

An exciting exchange takes place between the roots of certain plants and fungi in the soil. Many different fungi occur naturally in soil, and the name of this mutually beneficial collaboration is mycorrhiza. The fungus receives carbohydrates from the plant, and the plant receives nutrients, water and a greater resistance to disease in return. The mycelium of the fungus also acts as a kind of anchor, helping to strengthen the plant's root system.

Mycorrhiza provides a more effective uptake of nutrients, above all phosphorous, but also nitrogen, sulphur, calcium and the micronutrients. It occurs naturally in the ground around at least 80 per cent of plants, possibly more. And it isn't just one type of fungus, it's hundreds of different kinds. The fungus species found in our gardens is called arbuscular mycorrhiza (AM) and it can be inoculated. Perhaps most interesting for use in greenhouses, where the fungi does not occur naturally.

Mycorrhiza fungi are not a common sight in gardening centres, but you can find them online. Check that the inoculum culture is suitable for those plants you're interested in. There are differences, and if it isn't a good match then the product can be less effective.

SUPPORT YOUR LOCAL SOIL LIFE

Encourage the microlife in your garden by aerating (digging) the soil, watering when dry and adding organic material such as farmyard manure, compost, peat and straw. Balanced annual fertilisation is good, as is varied crop rotation. You should also avoid using chemical preparations that may be harmful to the soil's small heroes. Trying to encourage one species in particular can be difficult, but you can attempt to improve the general living conditions and hope to strike a good balance between the different inhabitants of the soil.

If you have a well-tended and healthy soil, you can expect to find around 2 kg (4½ lb) of micro-organisms and hundreds of worms in just one square metre (yard). A litre (1¾ pints) of soil can contain as many as a billion beneficial fungi and bacteria!

49

WEEDS & INSECTS AS CLUES

One of the things which makes gardens so much fun to observe is how the plants themselves choose where they want to put down roots. Not everything can be controlled – thankfully. Some plants just won't thrive in the spots we choose for them, while others might do a little too well. Weeds, for example. Sometimes, it's a matter of simply capitulating to the power of nature. The alternative is to do something radical about the composition of the soil and its nutrient levels, to change the basic conditions.

Weeds are often those plants we want to control a little more strictly, if for no other reason than that they otherwise steal the show. But by observing which weeds and plants thrive in a particular location, those which really seem to be doing well, we can learn something about the condition of our soil.

If you're really keen, soil tests and analyses are the best method for achieving accurate results. But the indicator plants we'll discuss later can also give you an idea about the nutritional status of the soil, as well as its structure and pH value.

THE SOIL'S INDICATOR ANIMALS

Even the creatures living in the soil can give us hints about the condition and nutrient levels of the soil. Certain insects are particularly at home above, or in the top layer of certain soils.

Woodlice like moisture and are often found in compost or beneath mulch, if you use it (see page 150). Crane flies love lime and can often be found in natural gardens with moderate amounts of humus in the soil. In these gardens, we also find predatory mites, which are useful for biological pest control. Other beneficial creatures are ground beetles (chafer beetles, water scavenger beetles, common sexton beetles and click beetles) which attack invertebrate parasites such as snails. Chafer beetles are found around heavy clay soils, water scavenger beetles around damp soils, common sexton beetles around dry soil and click beetles in sandy soil areas. Millipedes thrive on soil which is lime, potassium and phosphorous poor. And springtails can be a sign that your soil contains a lot of humus, phosphorous and potassium.

WEED OR CULTIVATED PLANT?

The definition of a weed is more a question of taste than a distinct botanical species. Wild or cultivated – everything that grows and blooms has the potential to be beautiful – a bed of dandelions, for example. But the problem with certain plants, weed or not, is that they spread easily and can suffocate their surroundings. As a result, these plants are therefore considered damaging.

Weeds can be split into two categories: the seed-based annuals and biennials, and the root-based perennials. As their names suggest, the seed-based weeds multiply using seeds, and root-based varieties spread using their roots. The latter are slightly trickier to get rid of. The easiest method is to deal with them in early spring: focus on removing the root-based weeds' roots and

nip the seed-based weeds in the bud before they go to seed. A more comfortable approach is to decide not to be such a pedant and to accept a few weeds here and there.

Many weeds, such as ground elder, nettles, dandelions and fat-hen can be both tasty and nutritious additions to salad or other dishes.

PLANT GUIDE

The table below lists which plants will do well, or particularly well, in different soil types. Some like lime-rich soil, others prefer acidic conditions. Some want a lot of nitrogen and others a lot of potassium. If they've made it to the right location, it can be hard to get rid of them, even by force, except by changing the composition of the soil.

NUTRIENT-RICH SOIL
stinging nettle
ground elder
cow parsley
mugwort
dandelion
groundsel
field pennycress
fat-hen

LIME-RICH (CHALKY) SOIL
charlock
veronica
cabbage thistle
Breckland thyme
bloody cranesbill
common poppy
common chicory
field bindweed

NITROGEN-RICH SOIL
stinging nettle
black nightshade
good King Henry

POTASSIUM-RICH SOIL
fat-hen
strawberry clover
white nettle
herb Robert
chickweed

POTASSIUM-POOR SOIL
black medick
brown knapweed
red clover
yarrow

LOW PH
corn marigold
pale persicaria
buttercup
long-headed poppy
sand rock cress
chamomile
field pennycress
lady's bedstraw

HIGH PH
creeping bellflower
crow garlic
charlock
common poppy

HUMUS-POOR SOIL
cornflower
corn marigold
common knotgrass

HIGH HUMUS CONTENT
annual nettle
fat-hen
wild garlic
pale persicaria

COMPACTED, BADLY DRAINED SOIL
coltsfoot
long-headed poppy
field horsetail
creeping buttercup
greater plantain
thistle

LIGHT, SANDY SOIL
common stork's bill
hare's foot clover
bugloss
rosebay willowherb
thrift
water forget-me-not
corn marigold

DAMP, WATERLOGGED SOIL
buttercup
corn mint
tufted hair grass
chickweed
lesser celandine
false chamomile

Source: odla.nu

TERRA PRETA

Biochar isn't some magical fertiliser that will cast a green spell on your garden and give instant results, but it is a very good soil improver. It can give your soil a boost – and retain that effect for thousands of years! Biochar is made of ordinary charcoal or equivalent biological matter, charred straw, for example. It can be used to improve arable soil and trap greenhouse gases. Another benefit is that it seems to keep the snails at bay!

Archaeologists have discovered large areas of mineral-rich, extremely fertile soil in the Amazon, in environments where the ground is otherwise incredibly nutrient-poor. They believe this is because the indigenous population living there worked and cultivated the soil over a thousand years ago. The fertile black soil could also be one explanation for the flourishing civilisations in those areas. *Terra preta* is Portuguese for black earth, and the name has become synonymous with those soil types containing high levels of charcoal. 'Biochar' is the name given to the product.

The layers of soil in the Amazon, often over a metre (3¼ ft) in depth and growing by 1 cm (⅓ in) every year, contain high levels of charcoal. Scientists have taken an interest in these charcoal-rich soils and carried out a number of different tests and cultivation experiments. The results have been remarkably good. Not only were harvests markedly increased, but *terra preta*'s ability to trap carbon dioxide is also amazing.

Carbon dioxide emissions are an important factor when we talk about the greenhouse effect and climate issues. Biochar breaks down incredibly slowly in soil, and during that time it keeps carbon dioxide trapped beneath ground, which is much better than it being released into the atmosphere. Countless reports and articles have been written about *terra preta*. It's something we're probably going to hear a lot more about in the future, both as a way of reducing carbon dioxide emissions and as a means of increasing the yield our harvests. Probably even for hobby gardeners.

A FRIEND OF STRUCTURE

Just like humus, charcoal helps to improve the structure of the soil, loosening it up. The difference is that charcoal breaks down extremely – super-extremely – slowly, meaning that carbon dioxide is taken out of the natural cycle, rather than being given off.

Biochar also increases the soil's ability to hold water and nutrients. This means that any surplus nutrients do not leach out into our waterways, contributing to over-fertilisation and algal blooms. Instead, the nutrients are stored until needed by the plants. And in addition to that, the microlife of the soil also benefits from the looser soil the biochar creates. You will see the biggest effect if you have a humus-poor soil (i.e. sandy soil), but even clay soils can be improved with biochar.

MAKE YOUR OWN OR BUY READY MADE

Nowadays, you can buy biochar everywhere, both with and without added nutrients. The easiest way to make a small amount of your own is to buy ordinary, good-quality barbecue coals and to add the nutrients yourself. If you decide to do this, buy ordinary barbecue coals (FSC and SIS marked) rather than briquettes, which are firmly compressed and contain binding ingredients.

You can steep the charcoal in diluted urine, nettle feed or some other kind of organic liquid fertiliser (see page 126). It's important to add fertiliser before you dig the charcoal into your soil, because otherwise you will create a nutrient drain when the charcoal absorbs the nutrients already present in the soil. You should also crush the charcoal into smaller pieces – around 1 cm (½ in) in size is enough.

THE RIGHT DOSE

You will need roughly 1 kg (2¼ lb) of biochar for every square metre (yard) of soil. That's the equivalent to roughly 5–6 litres (9–10½ pints) of charcoal, but even a smaller amount can have an impact. The biggest difference will be seen in nutrient-poor soils with low humus content. In better soils, you won't see such a marked difference to begin with.

BIOCHAR FOR NERDS

Wood, or some other organic matter, is subjected to extreme heat (at least 500°C/930°F) with minimal or no oxygen added. This process is called pyrolysis. As the organic matter heats, charcoal, tar and gases like methane, hydrogen and carbon monoxide are produced. The chemical process in a charcoal pile buried underground is exactly the same. You can recreate a simplified version of this at home, using a barrel or jar, if you really want to. It isn't difficult, but it does take time. A quick search online will show you how.

The good storage properties of charcoal depend on its tiny structure. It's like a sponge with a huge surface area, sucking up both water and nutrients to be dealt out at the right levels later on.

JET BLACK TIPS

Biochar can even help to retain moisture and nutrients in your pot plants.

Prepare a base of biochar to layer beneath your compost. It will help prevent nutrient leakage.

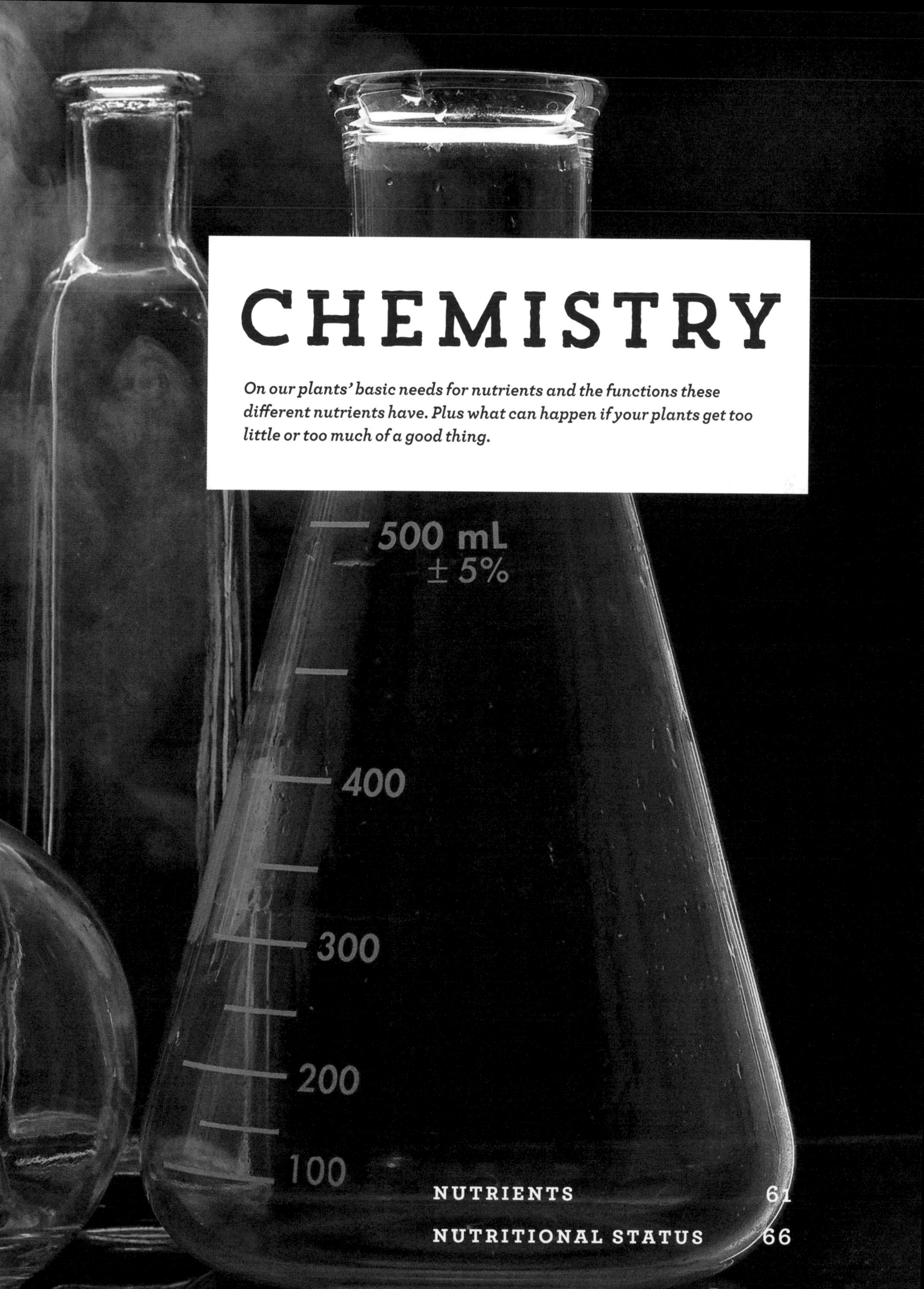

CHEMISTRY

On our plants' basic needs for nutrients and the functions these different nutrients have. Plus what can happen if your plants get too little or too much of a good thing.

500 mL
± 5%

400

300

200

100

Nitrogen

7

N

14.007

A FOOD CIRCLE FOR PLANTS

Plants' table manners differ from ours. Often for the better. They're more discrete at meal times, rarely slurp or gobble, don't spill things and never interrupt others. Sadly, nor do they tell us when they're hungry or want seconds of something. Or not as clearly, anyway.

Light, air, warmth and water are the basic conditions our plants need to live and grow. But those aren't quite enough. A long, healthy life needs nutrients too. Just like humans and animals, plants need different nutrients, some more important than others.

That said, a plant's food circle looks somewhat different to a human's. Our three most important nutrient groups are fats, proteins and carbohydrates, but the equivalents in the green world are nitrogen (N), phosphorous (P) and potassium (K). These elements, and a handful of others, are known as the macronutrients.

Another group of nutrients, just as important albeit in smaller doses, are the micronutrients. A deficiency of any one of these can have an impact on a plant's overall health. Similarly, an abundance of one can lead to a deficiency of another, because certain nutrients compete to be absorbed by the plant. The slightly more difficult word for this is *antagonism*.

Plants need sixteen different nutrients in total. They take carbon from the air (carbon dioxide is absorbed via photosynthesis) and oxygen and hydrogen from the water. These three elements are the building blocks of all life. The remaining thirteen nutrients are absorbed by the plants from the ground.

A BALANCED AND VARIED DIET

The recipe for your plants' health and wellbeing is good access to nutrients through a well-balanced and varied diet. Different manures and fertiliser products contain nutrients in varying compositions and quantities, and there are even differences between different producers or suppliers.

Several different types of fertiliser can be used simultaneously to great effect. By doing this, you lessen the risk of the soil being leached of any particular nutrient. You can, for example, add a first dose of nutrients in spring (read more about primary and supplementary fertilising on page 143) using farmyard manure, bone meal and compost. Not necessarily at the same time.

Later that spring, you can add a dose of chicken manure and supplement that with fresh grass cuttings and nettle feed during summer. This is just one option of many. The point is to cover yourself – and to vary your plants' diets. But it's also to add the right nutrients at the right time – nitrogen during the growth period of spring/summer, for example, rather than when the plants should be winding down for winter in late summer/autumn.

AT THE MACRO LEVEL – NPK & CO

The most important nutrients are the macronutrients nitrogen (N), phosphorous (P) and potassium (K). NPK might well sound familiar to you. Magnesium (Mg), calcium (Ca) and sulphur are also considered macronutrients. Some even argue that silicon (Si) is part of this group.

What's for dinner?

						Helium 2 **He** 4.003
		Boron 5 **B** 10.811	Carbon 6 **C** 12.011	Nitrogen 7 **N** 14.007	Oxygen 8 **O** 15.999	Fluorine 9 **F** 18.998	Neon 10 **Ne** 20.180

Boron 5 **B** 10.811	Carbon 6 **C** 12.011	Nitrogen 7 **N** 14.007	Oxygen 8 **O** 15.999	Fluorine 9 **F** 18.998	Neon 10 **Ne** 20.180
Aluminium 13 **Al** 26.982	Silicon 14 **Si** 28.086	Phosphorous 15 **P** 30.974	Sulphur 16 **S** 32.066	Chlorine 17 **Cl** 35.453	Argon 18 **Ar** 39.948

Copper 29 **Cu** 63.546	Zinc 30 **Zn** 65.39	Gallium 31 **Ga** 69.732	Germanium 32 **Ge** 72.61	Arsenic 33 **As** 74.922	Selenium 34 **Se** 78.09	Bromine 35 **Br** 79.904	Krypton 36 **Kr** 84.80
Silver 47 **Ag** 107.868	Cadmium 48 **Cd** 112.411	Indium 49 **In** 114.818	Tin 50 **Sn** 118.71	Antimony 51 **Sb** 121.760	Tellurium 52 **Te** 127.6	Iodine 53 **I** 126.904	Xenon 54 **Xe** 131.29
Gold 79 **Au** 196.967	Mercury 80 **Hg** 200.59	Thallium 81 **Tl** 204.383	Lead 82 **Pb** 207.2	Bismuth 83 **Bi** 208.980	Polonium 84 **Po** 208.982	Astatine 85 **At** 209.987	Radon 86 **Rn** 222.018
Roentgenium 111 **Rg** [272]	Copernicium 112 **Cn** [277]	Ununtrium 113 **Uut** okänt	Flerovium 114 **Fi** [289]	Ununpentium 115 **Uup** okänt	Livermorium 116 **Uuh** [298]	Ununseptium 117 **Uus** okänt	Ununoctium 118 **Uuo** okänt

Holmium 67 **Ho** 164.930	Erbium 68 **Er** 167.26	Thulium 69 **Tm** 168.934	Ytterbium 70 **Yb** 173.04	Lutetium 71 **Lu** 174.967
Einsteinium 99 **Es** [254]	Fermium 100 **Fm** 257.095	Mendelevium 101 **Md** 258.1	Nobelium 102 **No** 259.101	Lawrencium 103 **Lr** [262]

All plants need these elements, above all N, P and K (and in greater amounts). On fertiliser packets, you'll sometimes see something like 'NPK 21-4-10'. By that, they mean the percentages of each. In that particular case, the packet would contain 21 per cent nitrogen, 4 per cent phosphorous, and 10 per cent potassium (a common lawn fertiliser mix).

AT THE MICROLEVEL – THE TRACE ELEMENTS

In addition to the nutrients mentioned above, plants also need other elements – albeit in considerably smaller amounts. The umbrella term for this group is usually micronutrients, but sometimes they're called the trace elements. Members of this group include manganese (Mn), iron (Fe), copper (Cu), boron (B), chlorine (Cl), nickel (Ni), molybdenum (Mo) and zinc (Zn). Some consider sodium, silicon and cobalt part of this group, and according to others, even aluminium can be included.

To get an idea of what 'in smaller amounts' means, try imagining that plants need kilograms or pounds of the macronutrients per 100 square metres (yards) of cultivation, but only fractions of a gram of micronutrients for the same area. That said, even if the amount is small, it's still important. A deficiency in any one of these elements can have an effect, cause an imbalance between the other nutrients. Growth might be reduced, or your harvest less bountiful.

If you use natural fertiliser, you don't need to worry too much about these elements, they usually form part of it. Even compost can introduce balanced and proportionate amounts of micronutrients.

AIDE-MEMOIRE
Note down what you add to your soil, plus the amounts. In a year, you'll probably have forgotten what you dug in. But if you know what you gave the soil in the past, you can more easily work out which nutrients might have been used up, and which are still present in the soil.

N – NITROGEN

The most important nutrient for plants is nitrogen. Lots of it is needed, it's used up quickly and it leaches away easily if it's in abundance. Sadly, this means that just pouring on the nitrogen is no good. Over-fertilisation doesn't give good results, neither for your plants nor the environment. In fact, too little nitrogen is better than too much – though, of course, just enough is best.

Nitrogen differs from the other nutrients in that it is found primarily in the air, rather than the ground. Roughly two thirds of the air around us is made up of nitrogen gas, but plants can't simply snap up the nitrogen from the air; they have to take it in through their roots, just like they do the other nutrients. In good soils, organisms (bacteria and algae) take care of the process of moving nitrogen from the air into the ground. Unspoiled nature generally handles this by itself, but our cultivated areas of plants need additional nitrogen, which they get from fertiliser. Otherwise, growth will be small or non-existent.

Plenty of nitrogen equals good growth. The leaves will be lush and green, and the stalks and branches will grow nicely. A lack of nitrogen will lead to the opposite: pale, weak and feeble plants. The leaves will turn yellow.

Excessive nitrogen will lead to overgrown plants with dark green leaves and leggy stalks or branches. There will be more leaves and fewer flowers, and sometimes the plants will not bloom at all. Too much nitrogen affects the plant's cells, meaning that they fill with liquid. This makes the plant less resistant to frost. An excess of nitrogen may also make the plant more susceptible to disease and pests. It can even affect the taste and longevity of vegetables like potatoes, which turn bitter. The level of nitrates can rise in foods like spinach, lettuce and beetroot – making them less nutritious to eat (the nitrate can form nitrite, which is unhealthy for a number of reasons).

Since nitrogen is a volatile nutrient (when in surplus, it will leach out of the soil and be lost into the air as nitrogen gas), it is a good idea to spread application across the growing season. Demand is greatest in spring and early summer, when the plants are growing most. Top up levels over summer, but reduce the dose during high summer – from midsummer onwards. Timings can vary depending on where you live and what you are growing.

The reason for lowering the dose of nitrogen is that perennial plants need time to wind down ahead of winter. Since nitrogen stimulates growth, providing it too close to autumn is a bad idea. Annuals do not lie dormant during winter, so for those it makes no difference.

P - PHOSPHOROUS

Phosphorous is important for helping plants to grow big and strong. It is found in the soil and in water in the form of salts, phosphates. Among other things, phosphorous affects the root system, meaning that plants bloom nicely and bear lots of fruit. The nutrient also helps plants to assimilate well in the sunshine.

Phosphorous is a more stable element than nitrogen, and it's more uncommon to see a deficiency of it. It does not leach as readily, though sometimes plants cannot absorb it even when it is present in the soil. This may be because the pH level is too high or too low, or because the ground is too cold. When the temperature of the soil falls below 10°C (50°F), phosphorous will no longer be made available for the plants to absorb. Extreme pH levels can also inhibit the release of phosphorous.

A phosphorous deficiency can lead to a weak root system and a poorly developed plant. Older leaves and leaf stems can take on a purplish-red colour – with a grey tinge. Too much phosphorous can also make it hard for plants to take in all of the vital micronutrients they need, such as iron and boron, meaning that growth slows. It can also have a negative effect on the growth of mycorrhiza (see page 49).

Soils with high levels of humus content rarely suffer from phosphorous deficiency.

K - POTASSIUM

Potassium affects plants' metabolism and fluid balance. It enables woody plants to mature as they should, and to prepare for winter dormancy in good time. Potassium encourages fruit-setting and increases a plant's resilience. It can even have an impact on the quality and longevity of the fruit. Access to a healthy level of potassium will also lead to better vegetables.

Potassium promotes the creation of carbohydrates, which affect sugar levels and lead to sweeter fruit and berries. It has a positive impact on the fluid balance in the plant and the heightened sugar level functions along the same lines as antifreeze in a car engine – enabling the plant to better withstand the cold.

A potassium deficiency will lead to shrivelled, yellowish leaves with brown edges. The leaves may also turn dull in colour. An excessive supply of potassium, on the other hand, can cause a magnesium deficiency. Potassium and magnesium are absorbed in the same way, and compete with one another. If there is too much potassium in the soil, the magnesium's route into the plant is blocked, meaning it cannot be absorbed. As a result, both a surplus and a deficiency of potassium will mean that the plant's growth is impaired.

It is more common for sandy soils to be lacking in potassium than clay soils, as with the other nutrients. The large grains of sand do not have the same ability to bind the nutrients as clay particles do.

Mg - MAGNESIUM

Magnesium is important for the creation of chlorophyll, the pigment which makes plants green. The element is also useful in seeding, so that the plant can multiply.

Good access to magnesium makes it easier for plants to absorb phosphorous. If the potassium level of the soil is too high, a magnesium deficiency can occur – and vice versa – because the two elements are in competition with one another.

Magnesium is easily moveable within plants, and can be transported to those parts of the plant which need it most. Younger, growing leaves therefore take a larger proportion of the magnesium, meaning that signs of deficiency appear on older leaves first. Typical symptoms can be blotchy leaves with yellowing between the veins. The leaves will also drop early. Fruit trees can even lose their leaves during summer.

Clay soils tend to be rich in magnesium, while sandy and humus-rich soils are often lacking.

C - CALCIUM

It's easy to confuse calcium and lime. Lime contains a lot of calcium, but they are two different things. Calcium is a nutrient – and an important one. Lime, on the other hand, affects the pH level of the soil, which is equally important given that the acidity of the soil regulates how the nutrients are freed up and made available to the plants.

Calcium is beneficial to a plant's growth and immune defences, contributing to the intake of nutrients and the way the plant matures. As a nutrient, calcium builds up the plant's 'skeleton', meaning that the cell walls become fixed (rather than fluid).

If there is an excess of calcium in the soil, this can lead to important micronutrients such as iron, manganese and boron becoming fixed and therefore inaccessible to the plant. Too little calcium is no good either. This is often the case when the soil is strongly acidic – when this happens, it's a good idea to add lime to raise the pH of the soil and to provide a calcium boost.

Even if the pH of the soil is normal, a calcium deficiency can still occur. This might be visible through the edges of the leaves curling, for example. Tops, buds and young leaves might also wither away. A calcium deficiency can lead to several very common problems – blossom end rot in tomatoes, for example.

S - SULPHUR

For a long time, there has rarely been a lack of sulphur in our soils close to cities. Industrial emissions have meant that levels in the ground are high, and over the years we have almost forgotten that sulphur is also an important nutrient for our plants. But now that industrial emissions have fallen, the need for sulphur has grown. As with a lack of nitrogen, plants will show weak growth and turn pale if there is a sulphur deficiency. One difference is that with a sulphur deficiency, the problem is first visible on young, new leaves, rather than the older ones.

It's important to maintain a good balance of nitrogen and sulphur. If you increase the amount of nitrogen you add, you will also need to increase the amount of sulphur.

Mn, Fe, Cu, B, Cl, Mo and Zn – THE MICRONUTRIENTS

The group known as micronutrients includes, among others, manganese (Mn), iron (Fe), copper (Cu), boron (B), chlorine (Cl), molybdenum (Mo) and zinc (Zn). Just like the macronutrients, these are vital to plants, albeit in tiny amounts. Often, enough of each occurs naturally in the soil.

But if there is a deficiency of some kind, it's usually the pH of the soil that's to blame. A high pH level will lock up the micronutrients too firmly, meaning that they cannot be absorbed by the plant.

A deficiency in any, or several, of these nutrients can have an impact.

The plant's growth may be negatively affected and the harvest reduced. Often, the symptoms of this will appear on a plant's young, new parts.

The symptoms of an iron or manganese deficiency include a yellowing of the leaves between leaf veins. A lack of zinc can also produce this symptom. An abundance of manganese leads to brown patches on the leaves.

A boron deficiency can cause stunted growth and poor, weak roots. Cabbages and swedes can suffer internal rot. A lack of boron can also cause misshapen, lumpy apples with hard, brown spots in the flesh.

If your soil suffers a lack of molybdenum then broccoli and cauliflower leaves may be small and unevenly sized, with brown edges.

NECESSARY GOOD
Essential nutrients are those which are utterly vital for the survival and successful photosynthesis of a plant. The essential elements include the macronutrients (nitrogen, phosphorous, potassium, sulphur, calcium and magnesium) and a few of the micronutrients (boron, chlorine, molybdenum, copper, iron, manganese, nickel and zinc).

Other micronutrients are not quite so vital, but they do still stimulate growth. They are often called 'beneficial micronutrients'. Sodium, silicon, selenium and aluminium are all examples. Cobalt is a borderline case: the nutrient is essential – completely vital – for nitrogen-fixing bacteria.

OVER-FED OR UNDERNOURISHED?

Feel the flesh. Twist and turn the leaves. Check the colour. Is your plant growing as expected? Does it look like it should? Observe, inspect, investigate. Your plants' appearance, general condition and mood can tell you a lot about their health. So – how are Aunt Iris and Aunt Petunia doing?

The signs will probably be there long before any more serious symptoms appear. And the earlier you can interpret them correctly, the easier you can address any deficiencies – adjusting the nutrient balance, for example. It's often enough to do it by eye, but sometimes you might need to use a magnifying glass.

On the next page, we'll list some of the more or less common symptoms of both deficiencies and excesses of different nutrients. Remember that certain signs can be a result of something other than just a nutritional imbalance – disease, pests, a lack of oxygen or too much or too little water, for example. In fact, it's often a combination of several things. Maybe your plant is lacking in several different nutrients? Remember that certain nutrients are antagonistic – meaning they can counteract or block one another. Too much of one can lead to too little of another. Potassium and magnesium have this type of relationship, for example.

You should also question whether you need to check the pH level (see page 33), since this can also affect the uptake of nutrients. Despite all these *ifs*, *buts* and *maybes*, the next page will hopefully give you a certain level of guidance through the symptoms. Think of them as clues to help make a rough diagnosis. Don't go out of your way to look for faults in your garden, though. That's no good for anyone – least of all you. And one more important thing: remember that all nutrients are important. Just adding potassium and living in hope that it will lead to good fruit setting won't be enough.

HEALTH CHECK:
VISIBLE SIGNS OF NUTRIENT DEFICIENCY OR EXCESS

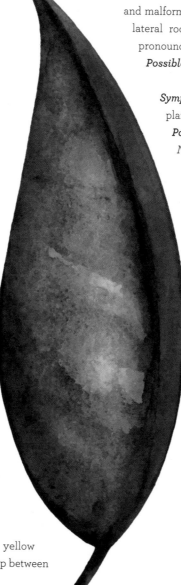

Symptom: Pale or yellow leaves. Plant growing badly. Older leaves turn yellow quickly. The lower leaves turn yellow from the tip towards the stem, then turn brown and dry. The lateral roots are badly developed.
Possible cause: nitrogen deficiency

Symptom: The plant is overgrown and leggy. Dark green and excessively large foliage, sometimes with signs of chlorosis* at the edges. No flowers.
Possible cause: too much nitrogen

Symptom: Weak growth, bad fruit-setting. The foliage is dark green, almost blueish. The lowermost leaves differ in colour (yellow, brown or red). The underside of the leaves has a brownish/purplish colour. Even the leaf veins and stems are brownish purple. Long roots but weak reddish purple lateral roots.
Possible cause: phosphorous deficiency

Symptom: The plant grows badly. Older leaves are greenish-yellow and striped. Frost damage and excessively early maturation.
Possible cause: too much potassium

Symptom: Dry leaf edges, sometimes yellow leaves. Older leaves die. The leaves curl up between

the leaf veins and turn yellowish-brown. Few, and malformed buds. Long primary root but weak lateral roots. Fruit and vegetables have less pronounced taste.
Possible cause: potassium deficiency

Symptom: The leaves are a duller green. The plant grows badly.
Possible cause: too much calcium
NB! Too much calcium can lead to a magnesium or potassium deficiency.

Symptom: Curled up leaves with brown edges. Poor root system. Brown flecks on fruit. Cucumbers can suffer 'blossom-end rot' (visible by the blossom-end of the cucumber) – like in tomatoes. In lettuce, the deficiency results in brown leaf edges.
Possible cause: calcium deficiency

Symptom: The spaces between leaf veins are almost white, the veins are still green. A lack of molybdenum can produce the same symptoms.
Possible cause: iron deficiency

* Chlorosis just means 'lacks normal green colour' in chemistry-speak.

N-NITROGEN

GOOD FOR: Growth

IN EXCESS: Unbalanced growth, dark green and overly lush foliage

DEFICIENCY: Pale or yellow leaves, weak plant with poor growth

NITROGEN-RICH FERTILISER: Farmyard manure, nettle feed, diluted urine, chicken manure, blood meal, fresh grass cuttings

BIG APPETITE: Cauliflowers, cabbages, Brussels sprouts, leeks, garlic, celeriac

MEDIUM APPETITE: Lettuces, spinach, onions, carrots, potatoes, beetroot

SMALL APPETITE: Beans, cucumbers, mange tout, radishes, berry bushes

P-PHOSPHOROUS

GOOD FOR: Root development, flower and fruit growth and seed-setting

IN EXCESS: ---

DEFICIENCY: Weak growth and poor fruit-setting. The underside of the leaves will darken (with a brownish or purplish tinge). Even the stalks can turn brownish purple.

PHOSPHOROUS-RICH FERTILISER: Farmyard manure, algae, bone meal, diluted urine, horn meal, wood ash

BIG APPETITE: Cucumbers, cauliflowers, cabbages, leeks, celeriac, lettuces, onions, beans, Brussels sprouts, carrots, rhubarb

MEDIUM APPETITE: Beetroots

SMALL APPETITE: Mange tout, radishes, swedes

K-POTASSIUM

GOOD FOR: Fruit-setting and resistance to disease.

IN EXCESS: Smaller growth, older leaves turn greenish yellow and striped.

DEFICIENCY: Poor growth and dry leaf edges. Occasionally yellow leaves and misshapen buds.

PHOSPHOROUS-RICH FERTILISER: Farmyard manure, wood ash, rock dust, algae.

BIG APPETITE: Roses, fruit trees, berry bushes, cauliflower, Brussels sprouts, cabbage, leeks, celeriac, spinach, onion, beetroot, carrots.

MEDIUM APPETITE: Beans, cucumber, lettuce.

SMALL APPETITE: Mange tout, radishes.

Leave it be!

PHILOSOPHY

On fertilisers then and now, plus challenges for the future. Attitudes to growing and views on plant nutrition – different fertiliser philosophies if you will.

A CROSSROADS

At a pinch, we could say that there are two ideological approaches when it comes to fertiliser – the biological and the chemical. The biological route calls for the use of natural fertilisers while the chemical prefers synthetic. From the point of view of plant nutrition, there is no difference between the two camps; the phosphorous in natural fertilisers has the same chemical formula as in the synthetic kind. But there are other crucial differences.

Ever since we humans set down roots and began to cultivate the land, we've understood the importance of using fertilisers. For thousands of years, we did it naturally; the nutrients have continually moved through one big cycle between animals, humans and plants.

But as agriculture became more efficient in the nineteenth century and farming moved onto an increasingly large scale, the manure produced by humans and animals was no longer enough. Farmers began to add nutrients in other ways, by growing nitrogen-fixing legumes, for example, or fertilising with phosphorous-rich materials – not least guano from seabirds.

By the twentieth century, agriculture was mechanised to further increase the production of food for a growing population, as well as to free up manpower for the cities. Around this time, farmers began to use synthetic fertiliser in greater quantities, but it wasn't until the mid-1950s that the practice really took off. The focus was on providing enough nutrients to ensure larger harvests rather than on improving the soil in the long term. Minerals were processed into easily absorbed chemical salts in factories, and synthetic fertilisers became easy to use for farmers. It became simpler, quicker and cheaper to fertilise your land. And the plants grew. *So far, so good.*

A TIME OF EXCESS

During the 1970s and 1980s, agriculture was producing such big harvests that there was enough food, and then some. Europe's stores were literally full of grain. In this time of over-overproduction, land was left to one side when cultivation on it became unprofitable, but at the same time alternative agriculture methods were also starting to emerge. Suddenly, there was both space and opportunity for organic farming, which requires larger areas of land to yield the same amount of produce as conventional methods.

Today, there are two main camps within agriculture: the conventional and the organic. Roughly 90 per cent of Swedish fields are farmed using conventional methods, but the excesses of the 1980s are long gone and the stores are empty. In the future, we will have to optimise both our farming and our cultivation methods to make better use of our resources.

ON THE TRAIL OF SYNTHETIC FERTILISER

High-intensity conventional farming and the unbalanced use of NPK fertilisers has led to many soils becoming depleted of important minerals such as iron, copper and manganese. Among other things, this has led to the practice of enhancing animal feed with vitamins and minerals so that the nutritional levels are adequate.

And with synthetic fertilisers come a whole host of undesirable heavy metals as pollution (a certain amount is inevitable in the mining of phosphate rock). During the twentieth century, levels of cadmium in our fields increased by 30 per cent as a result of synthetic fertilisers. Even levels of lead in the earth have risen, by 15 per cent, due to atmospheric deposits.

DIFFERENT FERTILISERS

Natural and synthetic fertilisers are also referred to as organic and inorganic fertilisers. Synthetic fertilisers are produced in factories, using chemical methods, often from industrially treated minerals. Natural fertiliser comes, as you would imagine, from nature. As a result, the nutrients within it come from the plant and animal world.

Another issue with this intense method of farming is over-fertilisation.

The latest generation of synthetic fertilisers are, however, more balanced and contain fewer unwanted heavy metals than before. Farmers have also become better at handling synthetic fertilisers, applying the right doses at the right time – ensuring that the nutrients really are taken up by the plants, rather than leached into the soil.

PLUSES AND MINUSES OF SYNTHETIC AND NATURAL FERTILISERS

The nutrients in synthetic fertilisers dissolve almost immediately in water. This means that the plants' roots can quickly access the nutrients they need. But any excess of the nutrients, anything the plants cannot take up at that moment, will leach from the soil and into our waterways – if the nutrients have been over-dosed, applied at the wrong time of year, or if the soil isn't good, humus-rich soil. The same is also true of natural fertilisers.

The nutrients in synthetic fertilisers are concentrated, which makes them easy to handle. Less is required than when using natural fertilisers. Crops grow well and develop substantial root and leaf masses. If this is later returned to the soil, the ground will also benefit in the long-run, because it gains organic material to convert to humus. Often, however, only the plants' short term needs are satisfied, with no attention given to the build up of humus and beneficial life in the soil, and this is one of the main downsides to synthetic fertilisers.

In fact, one of the principal benefits of natural fertiliser is its complex make up, containing both macro and micronutrients – plus the organic content which helps to build humus and encourage insect and bacterial life in the soil. Another positive effect of natural fertiliser is that it retains and releases nutrients at a more balanced rate. On the other hand, it also takes some time before the nutrients are made available.

ORGANIC FERTILISER

For organic farms, it's important to be aware of the resources available for plant nutrition, including methods such as crop rotation and mulching. Farms with their own animals will, of course, make use of the manure they produce, and if that isn't enough, then they can use animal manure from other organic producers (from dairy cows, for example). There are even a number of fertiliser products which have been approved for organic farming – leftovers from slaughterhouses or yeast production, for example.

Natural fertilisers aren't automatically classified as organic. They are always organic in the sense that they are natural, but they may also come from conventional farming methods. For hobby growers who want to grow organically, it's a case of getting hold of organic fertiliser. Check that it comes with the relevant certification or kitemark. In Sweden, organic products are often marked KRAV (produced in accordance with the regulator KRAV's rules). KRAV is an active member of IFOAM, the International Federation of Organic Agricultrual Movements.

WHICH FERTILISER ROUTE WILL YOU CHOOSE?

There is, of course, a difference between large-scale agriculture and a tiny patch of garden. But getting some kind of perspective on fertiliser, looking at it in a wider context, is still a good idea. Because the same facts and questions apply to whatever you are growing at home.

In other words, that's pretty much the first choice – which way do you want to go? Natural or synthetic fertiliser? It's perfectly possible to use both, of course, and many forms of conventional agriculture do just that. But organic and biodynamic growers don't use the synthetic type.

If you're interested in environmental issues and generally choose organic produce from the supermarket, your choice of fertiliser for your garden will probably be fairly easy. A rational person who wants to make things as simple and easy as possible might choose synthetic fertiliser. Then there are bound to be those who don't choose at all, who don't have any real idea what kind of fertiliser they are using. Maybe they just grab any old bag or bottle from the shelf.

These days, hobby gardeners are probably the only growers who exclusively use synthetic fertiliser. But if you take a look at the shelves in your local garden centre, there's an enormous range available! So despite everything, there must be a market for it.

Hopefully, having read this book, you'll find making your own conscious decision easier. The most important thing is to put back the nutrients we take from the soil when we grow. And that we do that in a smart way.

ALGAL BLOOMS AND DEAD OCEAN BEDS

Large amounts of nitrogen, and above all phosphorous, reach the ocean through our waterways, contributing to algal blooms. Over-fertilisation is one of the most serious environmental problems, and the driving force behind the growth of oxygen-poor zones and dead ocean beds. Roughly 100,000 km² (38,600 square miles) of the Baltic Sea – an area twice as big as Denmark – consists of dead sea floor.

Large algal blooms on the surface are detrimental to the ocean environment. When the algae dies, huge amounts of oxygen are used up. Poisonous hydrogen sulphide is released, which in turn affects all organisms living on the sea bed. Algal blooms are a completely natural phenomenon, but the high nutrient levels and over-fertilisation of the Baltic Sea means that these algae are able to propagate explosively.

Choosing fertiliser is a bit like choosing the food for your table. Completely processed, or natural raw products? Fast food or home made? Organic or not?

DYNAMITE

Who thinks about million-dollar business, world hunger and finite natural resources when they go down to the garden centre for a little fertiliser for the roses back home? Not exactly at the front of your mind, is it? Of course, we're not talking about ordinary chicken manure here, but synthetic fertiliser and its impact on the world. It is, and will become, more controversial, as the world's population increases and our natural resources run dry.

That synthetic fertiliser is a million-dollar industry is far from news. The world needs huge amounts of fertiliser to be able to produce enough food for its growing population. One problem is that synthetic fertiliser is made from a number of finite natural resources like potassium and phosphorous, and that it requires a lot of energy (natural gas, for example) during production.

Today, synthetic fertiliser is relatively cheap – though still too expensive for poor African farmers – and demand is high. But since some of the natural resources used in the production of these fertilisers are finite, this means that commodity prices will inevitably go up in the long run. And when the price of fertiliser goes up, food prices will follow. The rift between those who can afford to eat well, those who can feed themselves reasonably well and those who struggle to survive will probably grow even wider. As the global population approaches ten billion and our phosphorous supplies are used up, many scientists believe we will be facing a global famine. Sorry if that sounds incredibly bleak – things aren't nearly that bad yet, just a little grey and depressing if we don't do something about it.

ENERGY-INTENSIVE PRODUCTION

Synthetic fertilisers are produced through a number of industrial processes. The starting point is often rock or salt deposits, which are broken down and then processed mechanically and chemically. Phosphorous and potassium are mined or taken from salt lakes – the Dead Sea, for example. The nutrients can also be the byproducts of another industrial process. Nitrogen can be fixed from the air through an energy-intensive process (though certain nitrogen production methods – in Norway among other places – do make use of waterpower instead).

A large proportion of the synthetic fertilisers available today make use of energy derived from fossil fuels like oil, natural gas and coal in the production process. For this reason, among others, non-organic nitrogen fertiliser is not permitted within organic farming.

ROCK PHOSPHATE – A NEW GOLDMINE

Phosphorous (P) is an element, and one which is utterly vital (and also irreplaceable) for all life, both for humans and for plants – and consequently also for all agriculture and food production. Phosphorous is stored in the bedrock and the ground, and circulates in a number of different chemical compounds in our food and feed, fertiliser and waste, lakes and seas. It is one of the most important nutrients for plants, and as a result also one of the most vital components of synthetic fertiliser.

Scientists have warned that the world's phosphorous resources are running out, and various calculations have shown that our phosphorous will be depleted some time within the next 30–300 years. This wide-ranging estimate is because it is unclear what kind of development will take place and also which parameters have been used in the various calculation models. But the evidence is clear: sooner or later, our resources will run out.

The remaining workable rock phosphate is unevenly distributed across the world, and this may well prove to be a focal point for geopolitical conflict in the future. Three quarters of the reserves we know of today are located in Morocco and the western Sahara (those parts currently controlled by Morocco). This means that Morocco has the potential to become the new Saudi Arabia, with the oil sheiks being replaced by phosphate magnates. A real treasure trove for the country.

Phosphorous is also found in the rocks and soil in Sweden, as well as in the iron ore currently mined there, but the concentration is low and it's difficult to separate. The availability of phosphorous in the soil also varies across the country. One further problem is that even *if* there is phosphorous in the ground, it can often be so firmly locked up that the plants can't absorb the nutrient.

PHOSPHOROUS RECYCLING

Since supplies of workable phosphorous are limited, we need to develop ways to make our use of phosphorous more efficient and to reuse the existing phosphorous in our various cycles. We need to find smart new solutions and develop better systems – safer methods for recycling the nutrients in our cycles so that undesirable chemicals and heavy metals aren't passed on, for example. Today, sewage sludge from certified treatment works is often used in conventional farming, but this practice is rejected by organic farmers.

Scientists estimate that only twenty per cent of all the phosphorous we mine ends up in our food, the majority simply disappears along the way. In order to create a more sustainable phosphorous cycle, we need to minimise losses and re-use the phosphorous in our waste.

CONTROVERSIAL CHEMISTS

Two Norwegian scientists called Birkeland and Eydes were first to develop a method for fixing nitrogen from the air in the early 1900s. Later, however, it was the Haber-Bosch process – named after its German inventors – which became more prevalent, and which is still used today. The method involves the synthetic production of ammonia from nitrogen and hydrogen, and enables the production of nitrogen fertiliser on a large scale.

One of the inventors, a chemist called Fritz Haber, was awarded the Nobel Prize in Chemistry for this method in 1918, something many consider to be one of the most controversial awards ever made. Synthetic fertiliser has made it possible for many more people to eat well than ever before, but the ethical dilemma stems from the fact that the German was also the inventor of the first chemical weapon, a poison gas used by his country against the French in 1915.

FERTILISER AS A WEAPON

A fertiliser bomb might sound relatively harmless, but the fact is that synthetic fertilisers have been used to produce bombs by the Taliban in Afghanistan, by criminal motorbike gangs, terrorists and other bombers all over the world. The ammonium nitrate in the synthetic fertiliser acts as an explosive. That said, the synthetic fertiliser you'll find in your local garden centre wouldn't be any good for producing a fertiliser bomb – the ammonium nitrate level would be far too low.

Even natural fertiliser has been used as an explosive. In the 1700s, potassium nitrate was extracted from farmyard manure and used in the production of gunpowder.

BIODYNAMIC FARMING

COSMIC POWERS

If the synthetic fertiliser industry represents one extreme, biodynamic farming represents the other. This method of farming has stricter rules than organic farming. It's more extreme and perhaps more controversial, but it's far from new.

There are many similarities between organic and biodynamic farming – both maintain a distance from synthetic fertilisers, chemical pesticides, antibiotics and GMOs (genetically modified organisms). The key difference is that biodynamic farming follows a method based partly on cosmic powers and wonder preparations.

The anthroposophic teaching behind biodynamic farming was introduced by an Austrian named Rudolf Steiner in the 1920s, and it arrived in Sweden in 1935. Its methods and ideas about farming have since slowly but surely spread across the country, and the organic trend, which attempts to replicate nature's own principles, has taken inspiration from the anthroposophists.

Both methods of farming, with a shared attitude towards nature, animals and humans, are based on how we use natural resources like the soil, water and energy in a sustainable way. Biological diversity and the health of our animals also form a part of this.

Another important factor is how we cultivate the ground. Building up the fertility of the soil and being economical with plant nutrition are crucial principles. Chemical pesticides and synthetic fertilisers of inorganic origin are therefore ruled out.

HEALTH FOOD FOR THE SOIL

The idea behind biodynamic farming is to strengthen the organic systems of the earth, and to increase fertility and the ability to provide us with nutritional and healthy food. These ideas also aim to create the necessary conditions for the sustainable development of both humans and the soil. Biodynamic produce can be certified, just like organic products, and they tend to be labelled with a Demeter mark, the largest certification organisation for biodynamic agriculture.

Biodynamic farming involves a comprehensive cyclical approach. Composting and cultivated grassland/green manures (see page 148) are both important methods. The famous biodynamic preparations, life-enhancing mixtures, are meant to affect the earth and the plants, helped along by cosmic powers.

Among the distinctive methods used in biodynamic farming is the swirling water that some of the preparations should be mixed with. The water should be stirred (swirled) alternately clockwise and anticlockwise for an hour.

There is also a special sowing calendar which follows the positions of the stars. Search for the Maria Thun Biodynamic Calendar online if you want to know more about the thinking behind it.

EIGHT WONDER PREPARATIONS

These biodynamic preparations are used to improve the fertility of the earth, increase the resilience of plants and raise the nutritional value of the products grown. Using cosmic powers, the preparations are meant to have a positive impact on both the soil and the plants. According to biodynamic teaching, the preparations should give the plants qualities such as vitality, perceptiveness, power, reason, ripeness and the ability to overwinter.

The first two of the eight preparations are known as field preparations, the remaining six as compost preparations. The field preparations are meant to connect the plant with the soil, and the compost preparations aim to regulate circulation so that the compost becomes more balanced.

The preparations are added in tiny quantities (1–3 grams/$\frac{1}{16}$ ounce), either in swirled water or via farmyard manure. The compost preparations are added to 50 cm (20 in) holes at 2 m (6½ ft) intervals in the dunghill.

The water mix is then sprinkled or sprayed, while the manure mix containing the compost preparation is dug into the soil.

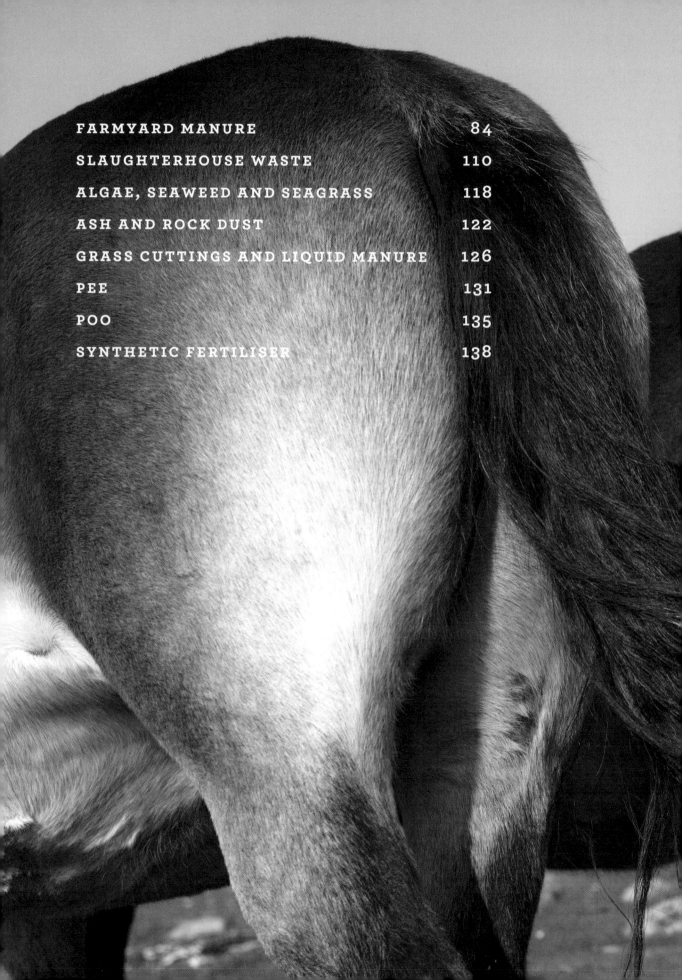

NOURISHMENT

On fertilisers with different origins: from animals, the sea, the toilet and factories, for example. Everything you need to know (plus a little bit more) about nutritional levels, handling and dosage.

BEEP, BEEP, MANURE HEAP

Almost all livestock produces good plant nutrition and soil improvers: 'au naturel' fertiliser, if you will. Cows, horses and hens in particular. But you can also use other animal waste – manure from sheep, goats and pigs, for example. Cat and dog poo, rabbit droppings and waste from other small animals can also be used, but it will sometimes need to be composted first, for hygiene reasons.

When we talk about farmyard manure, we're usually talking about cow or horse dung. Farmyard manure is, however, an umbrella term for everything we muck out from stalls, boxes, pens and cages: dung from cows, horses, sheep, goats, pigs and birds. In other words, it's the urine and excrement from animals, mixed with varying proportions of water and bedding material. By bedding, we mean anything that is used on the floor or ground, such as straw, sawdust or peat.

It's possible to distinguish between fresh, decomposed and composted farmyard manure. To make things even more complicated, we can even distinguish between pure dung and manure mixed with bedding. Manures can also be divided into urines, liquid manures, slurries, semi-solid and solid manures, depending on consistency.

The type we hobby gardeners tend to use most frequently is in solid form, albeit in different mixtures and with different additives. The manure sold in bags from garden centres is always decomposed (i.e. it has been left to lie for a while) rather than fresh. If you pick up manure from a farm or stable near where you live, it might well be fresh.

ALL-ROUND NUTRITION

Farmyard manure is a great fertiliser; a good, organic natural fertiliser with an all-round function. It contains all the important nutrients plants need – nitrogen, phosphorous, potassium and the micronutrients – as well as organic material which helps to build up humus in the soil.

The most important nutrients for plants are nitrogen, phosphorous and potassium. The proportions of these – the distribution of the nutrients, in other words – should be roughly 100 parts nitrogen, 15 phosphorous, and 60 potassium. Looking at a manure heap, that's roughly what you've got in front of you.

The exact level of nutrients in the manure will vary depending on the type of animal, its breed, sex, age and the time of year. How the animals have been raised, how the dung has been handled, and whether it has been mixed with different bedding materials can also affect the nutrient levels.

STABLE TIPS

If you live in the countryside, hopefully you won't be too far from farms that still keep animals. Usually, they'll be more than happy to get rid of some of their dung, maybe for a little bit of money. If you live in a town or city, you could check if any riding schools or stables would let you take some of their horse manure.

Ask about the animals' health first – make sure they aren't on any medication such as antibiotics or deworming medicines. Traces of the medicine can end up in the manure otherwise. This isn't such an

FRESH MANURE – HOT!!!

It is, of course, possible to use fresh (non-decomposed) manure. This type of manure contains a high level of nutrients and humus-building materials, which are always good for the structure of the soil and the creatures living there.

But even if fresh manure is nutritionally rich, your plants may still miss out on the goodies. If the fresh manure is mixed with a lot of bedding (as horse manure often is), then the carbon in this bedding material will break down in the soil. Nitrogen is needed for this decomposition process, meaning that the nitrogen in the soil will be temporarily locked out. As a result, the plants may suffer a nutrient deficiency, rather than the opposite. Once the carbon has been breaking down for some time, the nitrogen will be released as if by magic. This is one of the reasons why it can be a good idea to leave farmyard manure to sit for a while before digging it into the soil. So, if you want to use fresh farmyard manure: make sure it's 'pure' and not mixed with any carbon-rich bedding materials.

Avoid digging in fresh manure in spring, when plants are sensitive to high nutrient levels and more easily affected by disease or pests. Fresh manure is a little too strong for their roots. A bit like a shot of schnapps would be for a child's stomach. The taste of fruit, berries and vegetables can also be affected (and not for the better) by fresh manure. This is especially true of root vegetables.

DECOMPOSED MANURE – MEDIUM!!

If the fresh animal waste is left to rest for a while, the nutrient levels will fall below those of fresh manure, but they also become better in many ways. Any harmful bacteria or weeds will also be killed off as the manure decomposes.

Fresh dung contains bacteria which help in the breakdown process. These continue to work alongside fungi and other beneficial creatures so that the bedding material often present in the dung breaks down. This process produces heat (up to 70°C/150°F), just like in composting. During winter, you'll actually be able to see the dung hill steaming. This heat will gradually drop off, and once the pile has cooled down, the manure is decomposed. The decomposition process will, however, continue, and the nutrient level will drop over time.

It takes a few months, possibly even half a year, depending on the temperature outside, among other things, before the manure is considered 'finished'.

The benefit of decomposed (and even composted) manure as compared to fresh is that you avoid the problems caused by nitrogen deficiency, and the nutrient levels are also more balanced.

COMPOSTED MANURE – MILD!

The clods of waste and bedding found in the manure heap are transformed, after about a year, into a powdery form which is easy to handle. It's sometimes called 'well-decomposed' manure. The nutrient levels are now lower, but the material is definitely still beneficial. Just add a little more of it. Over time, it will be like gold to your soil and plants. You can gradually build up a soil and nutrient level that virtually all plants will be longing for.

Composted manure has practically no scent, and it looks like fine-grained humus.

Shavings from coniferous trees can contain terpenes, but it's a myth that these are damaging to the soil. They just take longer to break down than those from trees.

issue in an ornamental garden as it is in commercial cultivation, but the remains of worming medicines can have an impact on the macrofauna in the soil.

Horse manure from stables that use straw or peat as bedding is better than those that use sawdust. Straw is best and peat is also good, but it is less suitable from an environmental point of view, given that it's a finite natural resource. Sawdust is a carbon-rich material which requires a lot of nitrogen to break down. In the absence of anything else, manure which contains sawdust is, of course, fine; the sawdust will still increase the humus content of the soil. But more crap and less bedding (regardless of the kind) is always preferable. Just not pure crap...

Using locally produced manure is always good from an environmental standpoint, considering the transportation. Maybe you and a few neighbours could club together? Borrow or rent a trailer, and coordinate?

MAKE YOUR OWN HEAP!

If you bring home fresh manure in autumn, it's a good idea to let it lie – at least until spring. As with compost, the decomposition process will benefit from even levels of moisture and oxygen. Once the manure has cooled down and no longer smells so strong, it's ready to be dug into the soil. If you let it lie for longer, a year or so, the decomposition process will continue and the nutrient levels will fall.

Build your heap on a ground layer of some kind, a tarpaulin for example, so that the nutrients don't just leach away. Placing it in shade or half-shade is best. Cover with a fibre cloth or similar, to protect the heap from the elements while also allowing oxygen to enter.

THE TEMPERATURE OF MANURE

In the past, people used to divide manures by 'temperatures'. Some growers still do – the anthroposophists, for example. They rank farmyard manures from different animals on a scale where the 'cold' potassium-rich pig manure represents one extreme. The 'hot' phosphorous and nitrogen-rich chicken manure is the other. In the middle, cow and horse manure, the latter slightly higher in

FAST FOOD OR SLOW FOOD?
Fertilisers can release nutrients at different rates. Some are fast-acting while others work more slowly. Fast-acting ones are quickly depleted, while slow fertilisers can remain in the soil for several years. It's a good idea to use some of each.

Fast-acting fertlisers:
Chicken manure, urine, blood meal and synthetic fertlilisers

Slow-acting fertilisers:
Manure from cows, horses, sheep, goats and pigs, bone meal, rock dust and ash

temperature. The thinking behind this division is to do with sluggishness. Pig manure is slow-acting and has a long-lasting effect. Chicken manure is fast-acting and the nutrients are rapidly used up. Compare the different types in the table on page 90.

Another way to distinguish between manures comes from the time when it was more common to grow using hot beds (see page 157). In this line of thinking, the manures are sorted by the temperature achieved as the manure decomposes. Horse manure is hottest, followed in descending order by dung from cows, pigs, sheep and hens.

THE GARDEN'S CROWN JEWELS

In the past, a large dung hill was a sign that a farm was healthy and rich. It was a status symbol, something which said that this was somewhere with plenty of space, which had plenty of feed for its animals. Lots of feed meant the ability to raise a lot of animals. A large number of animals led to a lot of manure, meaning you could cultivate greater areas of land and reap better harvests.

The equation was tricky for farmers. They couldn't keep more animals than their land could support, and they couldn't cultivate more land than they had the manure for. You can just imagine the consequences of one year's worth of poor harvests...

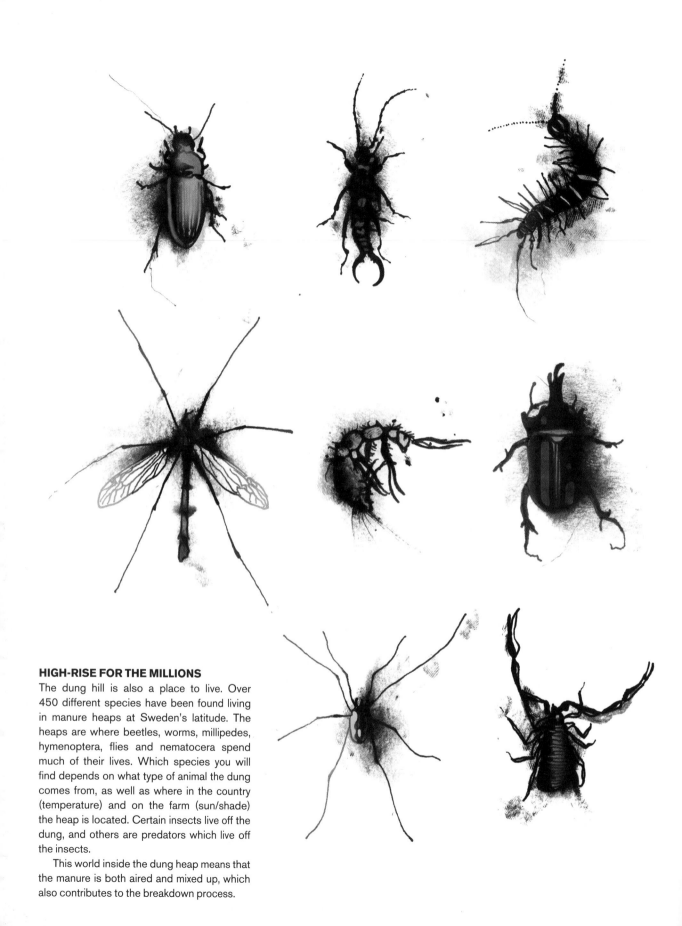

HIGH-RISE FOR THE MILLIONS

The dung hill is also a place to live. Over 450 different species have been found living in manure heaps at Sweden's latitude. The heaps are where beetles, worms, millipedes, hymenoptera, flies and nematocera spend much of their lives. Which species you will find depends on what type of animal the dung comes from, as well as where in the country (temperature) and on the farm (sun/shade) the heap is located. Certain insects live off the dung, and others are predators which live off the insects.

This world inside the dung heap means that the manure is both aired and mixed up, which also contributes to the breakdown process.

NUTRITIONAL CONTENT

The table below shows the content and proportion of the three most important nutrients in farmyard manures. Remember that these figures are rough estimates, because exact levels are affected by a number of different factors including the age of the animal and what it has been eating, as well as the bedding materials, storage and moisture levels.

	NITROGEN (N)	PHOSPHOROUS (P)	POTASSIUM (K)
COW MANURE	0.5%	0.15%	0.5%
HORSE MANURE	0.5%	0.15%	1.0%
CHICKEN MANURE	3.0%	0.8%	1.5%
SHEEP MANURE	0.95%	0.15%	2.0%
PIG MANURE	0.65%	0.25%	0.25%

NUTRIENT RELEASE

The table below shows how the most important nutrients in different kinds of farmyard manure are released over time.

	YEAR 1	YEAR 2	YEAR 3
COW MANURE	45%	35%	20%
HORSE MANURE	60%	25%	15%
CHICKEN MANURE	75%	15%	10%
SHEEP MANURE	65%	20%	15%
PIG MANURE	40%	30%	30%

Above all, what we hobby gardeners can do to minimise the loss of nutrients is to fertilise in moderation and at the right time of year, and to dig the manure into the soil.

ENVIRONMENTAL ISSUES WITH FARMYARD MANURE

Sadly, there will always be a certain loss of nutrients from the farmyard manure along the way, even if we use the manure for growing. This applies to other types of manure, too – not just from the farmyard. Nitrogen, in the form of nitrates, vanishes downwards into the ground through surface runoff and leaching. Some also disappears into the air in the form of ammonia, nitrogen gas, nitrous oxide and other nitric oxides.

Ammonia appears primarily in urine, but it can also be found in solid manure, and it evaporates into the air in stables and cowsheds, from manure heaps and during the spreading of manure. It then falls back to earth as rain, contributing to acidification and over-fertilisation.

Nitrogen gas also evaporates, but it isn't an environmental problem given that the majority of our atmosphere consists of nitrogen anyway. Nitrous oxide, on the other hand, is most beneficial when used in maternity wards. It's a strong gas that we don't want in our atmosphere, because it contributes to the greenhouse effect. The bedding materials from farmyard manure – above all peat – help to bind nitrogen and reduce the loss of nutrients.

Potassium and phosphorous disappear via leaching into the soil. Some phosphorous loss also takes place through surface runoff.

REGULATIONS FOR HANDLING FARMLAND MANURE

In the EU, there is fairly comprehensive legislation on how farmyard manure should be handled and composted in order to be used commercially to avoid the spread of contagion to animals and humans.

Manure must undergo an approved sanitation process before it can be sold on to shops and consumers. The sale or collection of untreated manure direct from a farm to a hobby gardener is not a problem, however, providing the farm/stable and the animals are free from contagion (salmonella, for example).

CAT AND DOG POO, HAMSTER DROPPINGS

Some of our four-legged friends – like cats and dogs – are carnivores, rather than vegetarians. They like to eat birds, mice and any other tidbits they can get their paws on. This means they occasionally eat things which aren't particularly healthy, either for them or for us – bacteria, parasites and viruses, among other things.

Cat poo can spread an infection called toxoplasmosis, which is definitely not something we want in our vegetable patches, or even in our flower beds. So: don't just empty your cat's litter tray straight onto your garden. If you're sure your compost reaches high enough temperatures (at least 50°C/120°F), then animal waste can be composted there. If you're unsure, it's best to bury it elsewhere or just throw it away with the rubbish.

Droppings from small animals like hamsters, guinea pigs, rabbits and birds can also be added to your compost heap if you're sure the animals are healthy. The same principle applies here: any possible parasites and bacteria will be killed off when the temperature in your compost heap reaches more than 50°C/120°F.

PET TOILETS

Cat litter is an environmental problem. It consists of heavy bentonite clay which comes from open-cast mines in countries such as China, and which is then transported half-way around the world to our litter trays. We tend to just throw away the litter with the rest of our rubbish, but it can't be incinerated and just remains where it ends up in our tips. It's better to use locally produced cat litter or pellets (made from wood or cellulose) instead.

If your cat tends to use the same area in the garden as its toilet, then this can be detrimental to your plants. The same applies if your dog has a favourite tree or bush to relieve itself on. The nutrient level can become far too concentrated for your plants!

COW MANURE – MOOO!

Cows are gentle, peaceful and thoughtful creatures. In fact, almost the only time you'll ever see a cow go crazy is when it's put out to pasture in spring, and even that will be in a charming cowlike way. Cows always seem calm and collected, even when they eat.

Lars Krantz, master gardner at Wij Gardens, talks about cows with reverence, about how they eat every blade of grass with care and feeling, as though it was a holy ritual. He says you can practically see the cow focusing on the journey the blade of grass will take through its digestive system. And they enjoy long meals, ones that go on all day out in the fields. Lars talks about how he likes to go down to see the cows in the field whenever he's wound up and needs to get back 'down to earth'. He'll sit down in a glade and breathe in the peace of mind of the cows. In his opinion, the animals seem to have a sense of mindfulness built into their very DNA, and his energy levels improve just by spending a bit of time with them. Something to try, perhaps?

THE COOL COW STOMACH

Considering how carefully cows process their food, it's no wonder that they also chuck out good-quality manure, too. The food they eat passes through their 'four stomachs' in order: the rumen, the reticulum, the omasum and abomasum. The cows' special digestive system means that they spend at least eight hours chewing a day.

It isn't actually true that cows have several stomachs. They actually have just one, exactly like us. But what they do have is a series of bulges towards the bottom of their oesophagus. The largest of these is called the rumen, and it can hold up to 100 litres (22 gallons) in an adult cow. This is where the grass goes first.

The entire digestive process, from the cow swallowing a mouthful of grass to that same grass ending up in the usual intestines, takes roughly four hours – eventually reappearing as a great form of fertiliser. Other examples of cud-chewing animals are sheep, goats, elk, deer and reindeer. Giraffes too, of course. And they fart and release methane gas, the lot of them.

HER ROYAL HIGHNESS, QUEEN MOO COW

Most gardeners agree that the cow is both king and queen of the manure heap. Cow manure is widely praised for providing all-round nutrients to the soil.

One benefit of farmyard manure is that the nutrients remain in the soil for a long time. Roughly half of the nutrients in cow manure are released during the first year, with the remainder being released in smaller doses over years two and three (see table on page 90). This means that you can add a little more manure to a previously un-fertilised soil in year one and then less in the following years. Cow manure is mild and won't burn the plants' roots if you do happen to add too much.

Manure from cows contains all the nutrients – both micro and macro – that our plants need. In it, you'll

BULLIED CUD-CHEWERS

Few have the luxury of their own cow at home. Nowadays, there also aren't many who live next door to a farm full of cows. In fact, there's practically a witch-hunt against cows, those cud-chewing, environmental scoundrels who burp and fart methane gas all day long.

It's true that they fart greenhouse gases, of course. One single cow can fart roughly 500 litres (100 gallons) of methane gas a day. In fact, if environmental issues had been as prominent in the mid-1980s, when Astrid Lindgren took up the cause of animal welfare with *My Cow Wants to Have Fun*, we probably would've been able to read about cow farts there.

find potassium, for example, which encourages fruit setting and root building.

By choosing a long-acting fertiliser like cow manure, plus a faster-acting option like chicken manure, you'll be able to achieve a good overall nutrient balance. And best of all is that the humus content of the soil will also increase and get better and better.

COW IN A BAG

To get hold of cow manure, most of us turn straight to our local garden centre. But cow manure in a bag rarely contains *only* the manure we often imagine it does – pure cow muck, in other words. There are countless manufacturers, and they often change their names or the composition of their products. Commercial manure can contain virtually anything, not uncommonly urine-soaked peat. So-called cow manure is sometimes even mixed with different types of manure, from chickens for example. Not that there is necessarily anything wrong with that – so long as you know what you're getting for your money.

Sometimes, you'll see the words 'natural manure' on the bag. Again, this can contain a huge number of things. Make sure you read the packet carefully. And ask questions! Get answers from the shop or the manufacturer.

Cow manure doesn't decompose as quickly as horse manure, and as a result it needs longer to compost down to a good level of nutrients. Fresh manure from cows is incredibly mucky and difficult to handle, but when you buy it in a bag, it's always in solid form, and more or less composted. Sometimes more concentrated – when it's in pellet or granule form.

It's not easy to know what the exact nutrient level of manure from your own animals is like, or in the manure you've bought from a farmer, but the manufacturers of commercial manure should be able to tell you – and often do. Sadly, manure products present this information in different ways, which can be extremely confusing. Since the nutrient levels are sometimes given by weight and sometimes by volume, it can be hard to understand the numbers. This makes it more difficult to compare types and add the right amount.

USING COW MANURE

Use a maximum of 3 kg/6½ lb (roughly 4–8 litres/7–14 pints) of decomposed cow manure per square metre (yard) during one season.

Split the total amount of manure you add into portions, of which the biggest should be dug in in spring. Further doses can be applied in early summer.

Complement with chicken manure (or another nitrogen-rich manure) later in the season.

Cow manure can be dissolved in water and used as a liquid manure top-up. Stuff the manure into an old pair of tights and leave it to draw in a bucket of water.

Approximate nutritional content of cow manure: nitrogen 0.5%, phosphorous 0.15%, potassium 0.5%

APPLYING FERTILISER AND TOPPING IT UP

The main application of fertiliser takes place once a year, usually in spring. The purpose is to enrich the cultivated soil's nutrient levels so that it can provide the plants with everything they need for the coming season. Farmyard manure and compost are a universal recipe for a good basic mix.

Top ups can then be added several times during summer, supplementing those nutrients which have run out or are needed in greater quantities. You can start to add top ups to support your more nutrient-hungry plants roughly one month after the first application.

Read more about this on page 143.

HORSE MANURE – NEIGHHH!

Horses are of a completely different nature to cows. They're livelier, more sensitive and energetic. As herd animals with an inbuilt fight-or-flight response, speed and action are close at . . . hoof. It's therefore fitting that horse manure is also a little hotter than cow manure, and for that reason it's this type that people tend to use when growing in hot beds (see page 157).

Interest in horses has never been greater in Sweden than it is at present. There are roughly 350,000 horses in the country, most living in or around centres of population. That makes them an underused resource, living so close to so many gardens!

The average horse weighs roughly 500 kg (1,100 lb) and produces 8–10 tonnes of manure a year. Our country's horses, in other words, produce around 3 million tonnes of good, healthy nutrition for our plants annually. Roughly the same amount as one horse gobbles down as feed (their basic diet is grass, hay, silage and concentrated feed with various additives) will come back out as manure, full of both macro and micronutrients for our plants.

The majority of horses live in smallish stables and are used for sport or hobby riding, and those stables will rarely have a need for all the manure they produce. It can actually be a problem for them, and costly for owners to get rid of. Things would be better and cheaper if more people collected manure from stables rather than buying cheap farmyard manure in bags. Plus, finding pure horse manure in an ordinary garden centre is quite uncommon.

DUNG THAT PACKS A PUNCH

A horse's stomach is different to that of a cud-chewing cow's. Grass, hay and concentrated feed are chewed and processed in the horse's digestive system, reappearing out the other end in a drier and coarser form than it would from a cow. The breaking down process hasn't progressed as far as in cow pats, and it's sometimes possible to see food remains in the waste produced by horses.

Horse manure is classed as a warm manure – it decomposes quickly and easily. It's particularly important that horse manure is allowed to fully decompose, because it contains seeds which might otherwise grow in the soil where it is dug in. Once the decomposition process is complete, any grass or weed seeds will have been neutralised. Most seeds will die at temperatures over 60°C/140°F (other than wild oats, which can survive). It's the heat generated when horse manure decomposes which is utilised in hot beds (see page 157).

Horse manure is long-lasting, though slightly faster-acting than cow manure. The nutrients have most effect during the first growth season, but there will be some nutrients left even during the next year. The humus-forming effect is, however, good both in the long and short term.

Neither cow nor horse manure contains a high level of nitrogen, and both can be supplemented with a more nitrogen-rich manure such as that from chickens, particularly if the horse manure is mixed with a lot of bedding material.

WELL-TENDED GEE GEES
Horses are such handsome, valuable animals that most grooms will keep their stalls and boxes extremely clean. This means that some horse manure contains too-high a level of bedding material (wood shavings, straw and peat) – in other words, too much carbon-rich material. Sometimes, they muck them out a little too well, from a gardener's point of view.

Horse manure that is rich in wood shavings is best used as a bedding material for your kitchen compost. In such circumstances, the shavings tend to have a positive effect on the balance between nitrogen and carbon, meaning that eventually, you will have a nutrient-rich compost to use in your garden.

HOW MUCH CRAP DOES A PERSON NEED TO TAKE?

Sorry, but there's no definitive answer to the one question everyone is asking. The whole notion of dosage when it comes to farmyard manure is, sadly, difficult, because the conditions can vary so widely. The amount you need to use depends on what your horse manure is like, if it's decomposed, composted, mixed with peat, etc. It also depends on what you want to grow and what your soil is like: its structure, the humus level and earlier nutrient levels.

This means the guidelines are the same – and they are guidelines rather than an exact figure – as for cow manure. In other words, a maximum of 3 kg (6½ lb) of decomposed horse manure per square metre (yard) of ground during one season. If you mix and blend different types of manure, you will, of course, have to pay attention to the total amount.

USING HORSE MANURE

Use a maximum of 3 kg/6½ lb (roughly 4–8 litres/7–14 pints) per square metre (yard) of ground during one season.

Complement with more nitrogen-rich manure, from hens, for example – particularly if the horse dung is mixed with a lot of bedding material.

Horse manure containing a lot of bedding material is best composted so that you don't suffer a temporary loss of nutrients (see page 86).

Approximate nutritional content of horse manure (from deep straw bedding): nitrogen 0.5%, phosphorous 0.15%, potassium 1.0%

A DONKEY AND THE DUNG HEAP

During antiquity, roughly 2,000 years ago, the donkey was praised for being a good producer of manure. Practical experience of donkey manure is limited here in Sweden, and nutrient analyses are few and far between. If you have access to donkey manure, you should probably handle and use it roughly like you would horse manure.

Lucius Junius Moderatus Columella lived and worked during the reign of Emperor Nero in Rome, at the beginning of the Christian era. He wrote several works about agriculture and farming, by hand and in Latin, of course. In his 'Rei rusticae libri XII' – his Twelve Books on Agriculture – we can read about the advantages of donkeys in a manure context. At the time, and in the area where he lived, the donkey was probably a common animal – something the cow was not.

Columella realised that there were essentially three sources of manure: from birds, from humans and from livestock. He thought bird manure to be best, and he preferred using the waste from dovecotes (!). Next best was the manure produced by humans, ideally mixed with other assorted waste from the farm. In third place, the manure from livestock, and among those animals, the coveted first place was held by the donkey – based on the idea that the donkey ate slowly and therefore digested its food most thoroughly. That meant that the manure it produced was mature, and ready to be spread on the fields.

After donkeys came sheep, according to Columella, then goats and other pack and

HEE-HAW!

draft animals. In last place: pig manure. Columella even wrote that the buried leaves of white lupins created a fantastic source of nutrients (read more about green manure on page 148).

Columella's writing influenced European agriculture right up to the nineteenth century. Much of what we can read applies even today, with fantastically detailed knowledge known as far back as the time around Jesus' birth.

CHICKEN MANURE – CLUCKAAWWK!

Chickens are fast producers of manure. They peck at their food – peck, peck, peck – and virtually the next minute, hot, dry balls of manure come out the other end like a charge of shot – pop, pop, pop. Quick in, quick out.

In other words, chicken manure is of a different calibre to that from cows and horses. It's also more fast-acting. This partly depends on the fact that chickens eat more protein-rich feed. Free range hens will happily peck away at animal matter – worms and insects are delicious to a little hen.

KICK-OFF IN THE GARDEN

Plants can access the nutrients in chicken manure virtually straight away, but they run out almost as quickly. Some of the nutrients, above all phosphorous and potassium, can be buffered in a good soil, but the nitrogen will be used up.

Unlike other farmyard manure, chicken manure contains a lower amount of humus-building materials for the soil. This makes it a good supplementary fertiliser, during top up applications, for example.

Adding less of this fast-acting substance, several times during early summer, is a good idea. You can even add a handful of hen droppings as a kick-off to your more comprehensive application of fertiliser in spring. The high level of nitrogen in chicken manure encourages growth, which means that the foliage of your plants will increase. Chicken manure also contains high levels of phosphorous.

Keep an eye on your plants to make sure you don't overdose them with nitrogen! Doing so will lead to leggy plants with excessively abundant, deep green foliage. Too much nitrogen can also have an impact on the taste of whatever you are growing. It's important to dig the chicken manure into the soil so that the nitrogen doesn't just vanish into the air. Then give it a good watering.

A little chicken manure can give a boost to languishing plants or a sleepy compost.

USING CHICKEN MANURE

Use chicken manure as a supplement to another farmyard manure.

Nitrogen-rich chicken manure is suitable as a top-up manure, perhaps as a fast-acting liquid fertiliser (see page 128).

A few handfuls of chicken droppings per square metre (yard) of ground is usually enough – max. 200 ml (7 fl oz).

Follow the guidelines on the packet if you buy chicken manure from a shop. It might be composted, dried or in granule form. The dried type is more concentrated.

Approximate nutritional content of chicken manure (from broiler hens): nitrogen 3.0%, phosphorous 0.8%, potassium 1.5%

FISH, FOWL OR SOMEWHERE IN BETWEEN?

CHRYSAN – A SHOT OF NUTRIENTS

Look out for NPK fertlisers that have been enhanced with bonemeal and other materials. In Sweden, we have Chrysan: a mixed preparation, not a pure natural product, which has been given a dubious place here in this section on farmyard manures. This mix consists of organic matter like feather meal, bone meal, meat meal, chicken manure and inorganic substances such as suprasalpeter (ammonium and nitrate) and potassium salts. It contains both macro- and micronutrients, but it lacks humus-forming materials.

Just like all organic matter, Chrysan still encourages beneficial life within the soil. The nutrients from the organic components are distributed to the plant over a long period. The urine element provides quick effects, and the feather and mineral meal give long-term benefits. Ulf Nordfjell, the internationally celebrated landscape architect who has won, among other things, prestigious gold medals at the Chelsea Flower Show in London, uses Chrysan to give large perennials and grass a kick start in spring. It's like a shot of Swedish schnapps after a cold plunge.

Products like Chrysan may come in either granule and powder form. They can smell like chicken manure, and can be spread out as it is or mixed with water. The nutrient content is often high compared to chicken manure, so take care not to overdose!

GUANO – CONCENTRATED PHOSPHOROUS

The word *guano* originally comes from a bird of the same name, but it has since become an umbrella term for all droppings from seabirds, particularly those living off the Pacific coast of South America.

In the mid-nineteenth century, bird guano was hard currency for both farmers and gardeners. Guano is tightly packed bird droppings mixed with sand, clay, shells, eggshells and feathers, which have been stored in layers along the coastal strip and rocky islands off Chile and Peru. Sometimes, these layers were several metres (yards) thick.

The indigenous people took care of this effective fertiliser, so much so that those who plundered it were punished by death. Despite this, the Americans and English saw to 20 million tonnes of guano being exported from Chile between 1840 and 1880, becoming rich in the process. The guano was so desirable that fake material circulated around the world. These days, the majority of the guano islands have been completely depleted of their reserves.

Even the waste and remains from fish and bats can be called guano. The word appears in relation to fertilisers made from fish remains, but these products aren't so common today, given that the remains from fish are instead processed to become fish meal (which is used in animal feed).

All the same, bat guano is growing in use as a fertiliser. It's exactly as the name suggests – the droppings from bats. There are a number of manufacturers/distributors. Ask at your local shop or do an online search if you're curious.

Bat guano contains a high level of phosphorous, which encourages fruit setting and bud building. The high level of phosphorous compared to nitrogen and potassium means that the substance should only be used as a supplement to other fertilisers. One positive, compared with chicken manure, is that bat manure has no scent – something which will be highly appreciated in greenhouses, for example. Suitable plants for using bat guano are tomato, cucumber, chilli, squash, aubergine and even strawberries.

Nutritional content of Chrysan (percentage by weight): nitrogen 8.0%, phosphorous 4.0%, potassium 6.0%

Approximate nutritional content of bat guano: nitrogen 2.0%, phosphorous 12.0%, potassium 2.0%

Neither Chrysan nor guano are permitted within organic farming.

SHEEP AND GOAT MANURE – BAAA!

If sheep and lambs say 'baaa', then goats and kids say something like 'mehhh'. They sound quite similar, in any case. Both species produce dry, nutrient-rich manure. Sheep and goat manure is best, just like other farmyard manure, if it is allowed to decompose and compost for some time. Doing so will allow it to become fine and crumbly, which makes it much easier to handle in the garden. If the manure is used fresh, it can contain a large number of seeds from weeds. These will be destroyed if the temperature during decomposition or composting exceeds 60°C (140°F).

Sheep and goats are cud-chewing animals just like cows. Their feed is also digested and processed in their four 'stomachs', meaning that the manure they produce is fine in texture.

NUTRIENT-RICH DEEP STRAW BEDDING

Sheep and goats usually go out to graze, and the pastures obviously benefit from the natural manure they receive in return. Gathering the waste from free-ranging animals in a pasture is extremely labour-intensive, and the nitrogen-rich urine from the animals will also be lost. But during the winter, many sheep and goats are brought indoors and given deep bedding – of peat, wood shavings or straw. This means that the bedding is not completely fresh, but rather layer after layer of something like straw. Over the course of a winter, the lower-layers of this bedding will become nicely urine-soaked. If the sheep are fed with grain, the manure will be more nutrient-rich than the manure of sheep fed on grass would be.

When the time comes to muck out and clean the barn, farmers are left with a huge pile of material that needs to be composted for at least six months.

Turning the heap is a good idea, so that oxygen can reach the bottom – which will also help along the decomposition process. With time, it will transform into a fantastic manure and exemplary soil improver.

A large amount of the nitrogen will be temporarily fixed during the decomposition of the bedding material, so remember that in the beginning, you may need to top up with a nitrogen-rich fertiliser – chicken manure, for example.

Sheep and goat manure is difficult to come by in garden centres. Check whether any nearby farms are selling it, if you're interested.

USING SHEEP AND GOAT MANURE

Manure from deep bedding provides valuable nutrients for your plants.

Mix in sheep manure with your garden compost – or leaf compost. Doing so will give the decomposition process a kickstart.

Manure from sheep and goats is a good soil improver which increases humus levels and encourages beneficial life in the soil.

Approximate nutritional content of sheep and goat manure (from deep bedding): nitrogen 0.95%, phosphorous 0.15%, potassium 2.0%

'It's great being a pig when you get to root about and pig out whenever you like.'

PIG MANURE – OINK OINK!

Little piggy. So sweet and cute. But a fresh pile of pig dung certainly doesn't smell like a bed of roses. Particularly not in a pigsty where the pigs aren't able to go out and root around. From a purely chemical point of view, pig manure does contain a lot of nutrients: balanced levels of nitrogen, phosphorous and potassium.

Pig dung also contains macronutrients like magnesium, sulphur and calcium, as well as the micronutrients copper and manganese.

HARD-TO-GET MANURE

In the past, pig manure was considered potassium-rich and used in potato fields, among other places. Modern measurements have shown that nowadays it doesn't contain nearly as much potassium. One possible explanation is that our pigs' diets have changed. Another is that measurements were made on pig manure from conventional pig farms, rather than the happy, free-range piggies who are given a more comprehensive diet. Whether the nutrients in their manure differs is another matter, but what is clear is that the content of whatever comes out the back end is affected by what goes in the front. Pigs are, by nature, omnivores, just like humans (even if some of us do choose a vegetarian diet). Cows and horses are vegetarians, but pigs will eat virtually anything, given the chance.

As a hobby gardener, it's rare that you'll come across pig manure. You can't buy it in bags from the garden centre, so you'll probably only be able to get hold of some if you have your own pigs at home or live close to a pig farm, and even then, it's likely only to be the organic farms that handle solid manure. If you manage to find one of those, then you should definitely weigh up whether that could be something for your garden.

Don't forget that pig manure needs time to decompose – something which takes time, because it is cold and wet.

The majority of Sweden's pig manure ends up in biogas facilities, where the energy is extracted and the remainder is used as 'natural manure' on the fields.

Approximate nutritional content of pig manure: nitrogen 0.65%, phosphorous 0.25%, potassium 0.25%

THE TASTE OF MANURE?

In her wonderful book *The Gardener's Tracks*, Elisabeth Svalin Gunnarsson writes about how, in Victorian gardens, people attempted to investigate and produce lists of how different types of farmyard manure affected the taste of whatever they were growing. These taste experiences were described in the 1857 edition of the *Illustrated Garden Journal*:

'Pig and privy manure is best for savoy cabbage and gives a pleasant sweet then sharp taste.'

'Leeks saw the strongest development and the mildest taste from privy and horse manure. Cow manure led to a strong, bitter taste; sheep manure made the leeks taste of sheep, and the best taste came from pig manure.'

USING PIG MANURE

Good manure, but difficult to get hold of.

Has a long-lasting fertilising effect, the nutrients are released slowly.

LE JARDIN PARFUMÉ

Mmm... the fragrance of a garden. Honeysuckle, roses and wild thyme. But not all scents in our gardens are quite so lovely: the smell of manure, for example, and, perhaps most of all, pig and chicken manure. Still, if we set our minds to it, we can teach ourselves that natural manure smells ... not bad, at the very least. Or that the smell isn't a good enough reason not to add manure to our gardens, anyway! So pinch your nose and think of how fantastic your flowers will smell later.

A 'fragrance' tends to be something pleasant; an 'odour' is something that probably doesn't smell all that good – but that is, of course, just semantics. There are no definitive answers to what smells good and what smells bad. Each preference is highly individual. Do horses smell good or bad? What about Danish cheeses? Seaweed? Boxwood? Our likes and dislikes are different.

But one thing is crystal clear to all friends of nature: manure should smell. If a fertiliser is scent-free, it's probably synthetically produced. You should be able to smell in the air that work is going on in the garden. Compare it to a kitchen without any smells – it doesn't whet your appetite. A garden without smells, pleasant or not, would be equally flat and soulless.

TEN THOUSAND DIFFERENT FRAGRANCES

There are millions of scent molecules in nature. Flowers and fruits often have particularly strong fragrances, consisting of esters with low molecular weights. Humans can sense around ten thousand different scents, even if we don't have words for them all. It is, however, possible to train your sense of smell, just like you can your sense of taste. That's what all the best perfumers and wine tasters will have done.

WARNING SYSTEMS AND OLFACTORY MEMORY

All living beings can discover and identify chemical substances (fragrances) in their surroundings. For many animals, this sense of smell is important, sometimes utterly crucial, to their survival. The sense of smell is ingeniously designed to direct us to food or protect us from danger. Rotten and rancid smells means danger, just like smoke. A sense of smell also contributes to greater enjoyment. In fact, losing one's sense of smell is a handicap that cuts back one of the pleasures in life.

Our sense of smell also has the ability to bring back memories and feelings, whether we want it to or not. A unique smell can instantly conjure up distinct memories from our childhood, or emotionally loaded events; a special scent can move us through time and space. This reptilian brain behaviour is, of course, also exploited commercially. The smell of freshly baked bread gives us a homely feeling, and the smell of soap makes us believe things are clean and tidy. If we experience a particular smell positively, it takes us straight to our emotional centre.

THE MYSTERIOUS SENSE

Smell has long been the most mysterious of our senses. The American scientists Richard Axel and Linda Buck earned the Nobel Prize in Physiology or Medicine in 2004 for their discovery of 'odourant receptors and the organisation of the olfactory system'. In other words, they argue that smells themselves do not exist outside of our brains, that our receptors sense scent molecules in the air we breathe and set off a pattern of electric nerve impulses in our brain, leading to a sensation of smell. They argue that the smell exists only in our consciousness, that it's created in our minds and that it is our experiences and expectations, good and bad, which affect how we experience these smells.

Since manure doesn't actually smell outside our brains, and we know that it brings so many positives to cultivation, maybe we just have to decide that it actually smells good?

Top notes:
decomposed horse manure
Heart notes:
leather and almond blossom
Base notes:
hay and mature compost

THE WHOLE ANIMAL

Animal products such as blood meal, meat meal, bone meal and horn meal are potent substances ... as fertilisers, of course, nothing else. The thought of using slaughterhouse waste in your flowerbeds or kitchen garden might not sound too appealing, but if you really think about it, it's not much worse than anything else (animal excrement, for example). Natural, organic nourishment from a perfect cycle.

In our resource-conscious and recycling-positive times, using animal remains as fertiliser should be the politically correct thing to do, if they are handled correctly. Naturally, it's up to every individual to decide – vegans will probably have objections. Some also argue that imported slaughterhouse remains can spread salmonella and anthrax.

In any case, animals are not killed for the sake of plant nutrition, and their remains are by-products that would otherwise end up in landfill. Much of an animal can be used as a nutrient-rich fertiliser: meal or chips of bone, blood, horns, meat or hooves, for example. EU regulations on organic farming even accept wool, fur, hair and feathers. The latter do not include much nourishment, but they can still be used as a ground covering (see page 150). There are a number of organic animal products available on the market, even for hobby gardeners. Just ask at your local garden centre.

Manure from slaughterhouse waste doesn't include as much humus-forming organic material as manure, but it does stimulate the beneficial insect and bacterial life in the soil.

BONE AND HORN MEAL

Bone meal is made from the skeletons and bones left over after slaughter. The nutrients in bone meal are long-lasting and particularly rich in phosphorous. The nitrogen is released slowly, which means that the nutrients can even be dug in during autumn – when planting spring bulbs, for example. It also contains micronutrients and calcium. Bone meal is considered particularly good for clematis (it increases resistance to mildew and other fungal diseases), though it also works remarkably well with tomatoes, root vegetables and berry bushes, and is especially good in clay soils.

You can use bone meal during the primary or top-up application of manure. Pretty much any time you like, actually. The risk of overdoing it is small. The nutrients are slowly released over the course of about three years, so adding bone meal roughly every other year is enough.

Dig in around 100 ml (3½ fl oz) per square metre (yard) for established perennials. Add roughly 1 tablespoon per bulb (tulip-size) when planting spring bulbs. Berry bushes can be fertilised immediately after harvest, and fruit trees early in the spring.

Horn meal contains slightly more nitrogen than bone meal. Animal horns (usually from cows) are made of a substance called keratin, which is very high in nitrogen. The proportion of nitrogen does vary between manufacturers and origin of the horns, but it is normally around 8–12 per cent. Check the packaging. One benefit of horn meal is that the nitrogen is released relatively slowly and therefore lasts a long time. It is also good for use on nitrogen-hungry vegetables in greenhouses. As well as in pots.

Remember that dogs might develop a sudden interest in your garden when you use animal remains as fertiliser. Your pooches might decide to try to find the goodies in your soil, and cause a certain amount of mess along the way. Watering after you add any animal remains is a good idea and can help deter your dog from digging.

A mix or combination of bone and blood meal gives both a fast-acting and more long-lasting amount of nourishment which provides high levels of nitrogen, phosphorous and potassium.

Just like blood meal, meat meal is produced using leftovers from slaughter and cutting. This isn't any ordinary hobby gardener product, however. Meat meal contains less nitrogen than blood meal, but it has a higher phosphorous level. Many organic farmers in Sweden use the KRAV marked fertiliser Biofer, which contains meat meal.

USING ANIMAL MEALS

Bone meal is slow-acting and contains high levels of nitrogen and phosphorous.

Dig in roughly 100ml (3½ fl oz) of bone meal for every square metre (yard) of your flowerbeds. Fertilise berry bushes after harvest and fruit trees in spring.

Horn meal is used in the same way as bone meal. Suitable for pots, among other things, where nutrients can quickly become depleted.

Blood meal has a very high level of nitrogen and is fast-acting. Good for topping up fertiliser levels in greenhouses.

BLOOD MEAL AND MEAT MEAL

Blood meal is exactly what it sounds like: dried, pulverised blood from slaughtered animals. It's full of nitrogen, which encourages plant growth. In addition to that, it's also rich in micronutrients. Phosphorous and potassium levels are low, so blood meal shouldn't be applied in autumn. The concentrated and fast-acting nitrogen works well as a top-up for demanding plants such as cauliflower, cabbage, spinach and celeriac. Apply in small doses during early summer. Dig in and water down.

Approximate nutritional content of: Bone meal: nitrogen 7.0–9.0%, phosphorous 8.0–9.0%, potassium 0.3–1.0% Horn meal: nitrogen 9.0%, phosphorous 8.0%, potassium 1.0%, Blood meal: nitrogen 14.0%, phosphorous 0.2%, potassium 1.0%, Meat meal: nitrogen 10.0%, phosphorous 3.0%, potassium 1.0%

BLOOD MEAL STICKS

These sticks are an effective way of keeping roe dear (plus hares and rabbits) at bay – the only thing that really works, if done properly! It's probably the smell of 'death/danger' that the animals instinctively avoid. The effect lasts two to three weeks, depending on the weather, and then you'll need to repeat the process. You can even try adding some kind of weather shield over your blood meal sticks – an upside down pot, for example. Blood meal is available in garden centres and ammonia from DIY shops.

1 litre (1¾ pints) of lukewarm water
200 ml (7 fl oz) of blood meal
2 tbsp of ammonia
a few pieces of oasis (those green
  blocks florists stick flowers into)
thin wooden sticks (kebab
  skewers, for example)

1. Pour the water, the blood meal and the ammonia into a bucket with a lid. Take a deep breath, hold your nose, and mix them together.
2. Dip pieces of the oasis into the mix and then let them soak up as much of the liquid as possible. Put on the lid (it smells like dead rats!) and keep any leftovers for use later.
3. Skewer the pieces of oasis onto the sticks and place these near to any tulips or other plants deer find tasty.

GUEST APPEARANCE:
GÖRAN & MARGARETA HOAS

Gourmet Demands

Cackling and laughter can be heard from outside Lilla Bjers Farm, though less from the chicken coop than from the farm shop. The last customers of the day are disappointed that the strawberries are all gone, but Göran Hoas manages to cheer them up with the promise to reserve a couple of punnets for them the next day. You see, at Lilla Bjers nothing is sold unless it has reached its optimum maturity, not even when there's a line of visitors waiting with wallets in hand.

'We don't pick things before they're ready. That's just how it is,' says Göran. 'Nature has to be allowed to run its course. So much of the taste is in the timing, and I'm not interested in selling anything that's not perfect. The guests'll have to wait for the food, rather than the other way around!'

Lilla Bjers Farm is just south of Visby on the Baltic island of Gotland. Göran and Margareta bought the place from Göran's parents just over fifteen years ago. Before that, Göran worked as a science teacher and the couple ran a handicraft enterprise together: Hoas Hantverk. The business made products from leather, wood and metal, and Margareta also dabbled in calligraphy – something she still does. The plan was to continue with their handicraft business once they bought the farm, growing only enough fruit and vegetables to meet their own needs. But an interest in cultivation soon developed – as did demand.

For the Hoas family, it was clear from the start that they should do their growing without any poisonous sprays or synthetic fertilisers.

'I'm an old biology and chemistry teacher, so with a bit of knowledge of nature, it's hard to get it together in my head any other way. It's like you can't create a balance in a sensible way otherwise. I want to eat good, healthy food, and I can't imagine serving our kids anything else. The fact that they do scoff the odd unhealthy thing is another matter entirely,' Göran laughs. 'You can't let things get boring or stupidly over the top.'

Over time, both their ambition and their efforts in the garden grew. A huge driving force, aside from the joy of gardening itself, was – and remains – a genuine passion for food. The Hoases discovered that the produce from their garden often had a unique taste, and since they already pursued organic methods, it seemed like a natural progression to apply for certification once their business grew and demand increased. In 2001, Lilla Bjers was awarded its KRAV organic certification, and they have continued down that neat path to become world-renowned – first in the local area, then the whole island, country, and now even abroad.

'It's actually pretty crazy when a busload of Americans or Italians pulls up outside,' Margareta laughs. 'That situation is basically the complete opposite of our everyday life on our knees among the plants. We've had a couple of TV productions here, and a load of journalists, authorities and organisations. But all we do is follow our common sense, I think! Obviously it's a lot of work too, but that's not unique to us at all. There's not much glamour in growing

Margareta and Göran Hoas of Lilla Bjers farm on Gotland – sunshine farmers who grow with heart.

'We rotate the crops here in five-year cycles.'

vegetables, so I'm just happy for all the appreciation we get.'

Strict regulations follow the awarding of a KRAV certification. This also applies to the manure they use.

'Almost everything about KRAV is good, absolutely. But sometimes the rules and regulations are more of a hindrance than a help,' says Göran. 'Since we don't have any animals of our own, aside from a couple of hens, we'd like to be able to use pig manure from the neighbouring farms, but it's not allowed. We have to stick to KRAV certified products. It sometimes feels a bit bureaucratic and it goes against our natural cycle approach. These days, we mostly use Biofer, which is an approved KRAV fertiliser made from slaughterhouse remains.'

'Some of our most extreme vegan customers are a bit startled when they find out we use manure made from animal remains,' Göran says with an amused look. 'To me, it feels like a real natural cycle to make use of all the nutrient-rich by-products available. I can't see much of a difference between an animal's crap and what's left over after slaughter. Though I'd also prefer to see all our manure produced locally, so that it doesn't have to be transported here by boat.'

The KRAV-certified Biofer is produced using meat meal from the Danish pork industry, bone meal from beef, pork and poultry production in Sweden, residues from yeast production and organic chicken manure. The whole lot is transported to the Gyllebo Gödning factory in Malmö, where it's heated to 130°C (270°F) and then shaped into pellets. The KRAV organisation wants to see all slaughterhouse remains coming exclusively from organically raised animals, but that isn't always the case today.

'The soil here is made up of old flood defences from when sea levels reached this far inland', Margareta explains. 'It's mostly sandy soil. We use manure from a dairy farm not far from here, plus pellets of Biofer in varying amounts at different times of year, depending on the crop. Since the garlic starts earliest, we give it an autumn treat. The nutrients are stored in the soil and released with the spring warmth. We actually give the garlic an extra spring dose, around the end of March. Then we add fertiliser for the other spring crops, of course, using farmyard manure as a base. The strawberries get Biofer, and we also spray the strawberry patch with iron and manganese during early summer. That way, they can take up nutrients through the pores in their leaves. Those are important micronutrients for strawberries in particular, and they would end up locked in the soil if we just dug in the fertiliser.'

Göran interrupts: 'We rotate the crops here in five-year cycles. First pasture (green manure using fiddleneck, among others), then grains, vegetables and potatoes – in that order. We let the land lie fallow in the fifth year, so the weeds grow. Then it's a case of really getting to work cutting everything back before it goes to seed! All in all, it leaves us with a healthy soil full of good levels of nutrients.'

At Lilla Bjers, roughly 200 different types of grain are grown on 12 hectares (30 acres) of land. During spring, nine types of asparagus – everything from pale green to dark purple – are harvested. They even have 50 hectares (125 acres) of forest and 2 hectares (5 acres) of Christmas trees. Every inch of their land is certified in line with KRAV's regulations and with it, everything the land produces. Even the farm shop and the restaurant have been awarded the KRAV stamp of approval – the very highest level. Everything served in the restaurant, 99 per cent of their raw goods, is organic.

'The Christmas tree sales get going around Advent,' Margareta says. 'It's a nice supplement to the agriculture in that it lengthens the season and brings in some income. We have to live year-round, after all. And obviously we want our customers to be able to buy a KRAV marked Christmas tree!'

117

ALGAE, SEAWEED AND SEAGRASS

NATURE'S DELICACIES

Seaweeds, algae and seagrasses contain plenty of nourishment, even for your garden – they are chock full of valuable micronutrients. Demand for these minerals is tiny, but they are still crucial for the proper development of your plants. Fertiliser from the sea contains practically no macronutrients, meaning it's a good supplement to something like farmyard manure. So get yourself down to the coast and order up a seafood platter!

The nutrients needed by our plants can all be found in a dissolved state in seawater. The plants of the oceans, such as seaweed, algae, seagrass and reeds, trap these nutrients and are therefore a rich resource for growers. Sadly, these sea plants also absorb less healthy substances like the heavy metal cadmium, meaning that these days there is good reason to take care with washed-up seaweed and seagrass from over-fertilised bodies of water. As with the fish which swim there, dangerous substances will pool in these plants.

This washed-up sea vegetation used to be an important source of fertiliser for cultivators. Seaweed (above all bladderwrack), reeds and seagrass were gathered from beaches and used in cultivation on farms. Today, the process of gathering and transporting the plants is considered too time-consuming (as well as that risk of heavy metals being present) and as a result it is no longer especially common. But those who have used seaweed as fertiliser can testify to its fantastic results! You can even grow potatoes using nothing but seaweed.

SEARCHING FOR SEAWEED
Gathering your own seaweed can be an act of sheer charity for your garden. Just check with the landowner before you walk off with it. Most will be happy for you to do it, grateful even – rotten seaweed doesn't exactly smell like roses. And do some reasearch with the local environment agency about the water quality.

Brown algae such as bladderwrack, toothed wrack and rockweed are wonderful raw materials to use as fertiliser. Filamentous red algae tends to be worse, because it often contain more cadmium than the former. Rinse off the sea salt and cut the seaweed into smaller pieces before you use it. Compost or dig the seaweed directly into the soil. Asparagus in particular does especially well when fertilised using seaweed - it is originally a coastal plant, after all.

Adding seaweed to the bottom of a hole when planting something new is also a good idea. Even summer blooms, flowerbeds, bushes and trees like seaweed.

If you want to err on the side of caution, you can avoid using seaweed in your vegetable patch. Cadmium is an element which will not break down (it's sometimes found in batteries, for example). It will, however, be absorbed by your plants, and heavy metals aren't something we really want to be serving up with dinner.

ALGOMIN – THE SWEDISH ALGAE AND SEAWEED SOLUTION

There aren't all that many algae products to choose between in Swedish garden centres. The most common brand we have for hobby gardeners is Algomin, which comes in a number of different algal meal-based varieties.

The base of these products is the same, but they have different additives. Algae are essentially micronutrient fertilisers, so to be able to offer more a comprehensive feed, various macronutrients have been added (nitrogen and phosphorous, for example) to certain products, which do not fulfil the KRAV organisation's criteria. That said, there is a KRAV-marked Algomin product, which comes in a granular or liquid form.

Algomin's products are based on a type of algae which, from a biological point of view, is somewhere between a seaweed and a coral, and is therefore called coralline or calcified seaweed by the manufacturer. The latin name for this seaweed is *Lithothamnium calcareum*. The calcified seaweed grows in the Atlantic, off the coast of France, but it is carried by the current through the English Channel once it dies (a natural death). From there, it is fished up to become a base ingredient in seaweed fertilisers. It is dried out and ground in Saint-Malo on the French coast, and then transported by ferry to Sweden where it is prepared and packed. The product is mixed with material such as brown algae (primarily bladderwrack), which contributes healthy enzymes. These enzymes encourage the insect and bacterial life in the soil and have a positive impact on the development of roots.

Calcified seaweed is a good supplement to both primary and top-up applications of fertiliser, because it is long-lasting and contains many different minerals. Other than providing the nutrients themselves, it also helps to release nutrients into the ground so that the plants can more easily access them. Even the micro life of the soil benefits from algae.

Since seaweed fertilisers contain a high percentage of calcium carbonate, you shouldn't use them on alkaline soils – it will help to raise the pH level. This means that algae and seaweed can be used as an alternative to lime, if you want to alter the alkalinity of your soil. They also contain some sodium (salt), which isn't appreciated by sodium-sensitive plants like tomatoes. Dig in seaweed fertiliser in spring or autumn.

Nutritional content of calcified seaweed: nitrogen 0.6%, phosphorous 0.04%, potassium 0.9% (pH value 8.8)

USING ALGAE, SEAWEED AND SEAGRASS

Dig in seaweed fertiliser during spring or autumn.
Rinse seaweed and seagrass carefully to remove
any salt.

Asparagus loves seaweed!

Nourishment from the sea provides a good nutrient
boost to the soil, but should be considered a
supplementary fertiliser.

IN THE GREY ZONE

Rock and ash may be all that remain after a great devastation. But the fact is that both wood ash and rock dust can provide fantastic nutrients for your plants. The two are 'waste materials' that fall somewhere between soil improvers and nourishment. Both are rich in potassium and raise the pH level of the soil.

The smart (and frugal) gardener will take whatever he or she has at home or nearby, and use it as a fertiliser – throwing away nothing, not even the leftovers of anything they have burnt. It's rare for someone to have access to a lovely pile of rock dust, but take the opportunity to collect drill dust if you get the chance – after drilling for wells or geothermal energy, for example.

Ash and rock dust contain important nutrients, but they can also be used as soil improvers, especially rock dust. The two even have an impact on the pH level of the soil. Large quantities or rock dust or ash will increase the pH level, so take care with any acid-lovers, i.e. plants which prefer a low pH.

Neither ash nor rock dust are true fertilisers, and as a result they need to be supplemented. They contain virtually no nitrogen, but they do offer plenty of potassium, a little phosphorous and calcium, as well as a range of micronutrients. You should think of rock dust and wood ash as a way to round out the nutrients during the main application of fertiliser – or as a way of improving the qualities of your soil.

WOOD ASH AS FERTILISER

Wood ash is particularly good for those plants which need a lot of potassium – vegetables like cabbage, or root vegetables, for example. Potatoes like potassium, but they can become susceptible to common scab if the pH level increases. Fruit trees, particularly stone fruits like plums and cherries, are well suited to wood ash fertiliser, as are berry bushes. Bear in mind that you should take care with plants which like a slightly

more acidic soil (such as raspberries). Peonies and roses will also appreciate a little wood ash. Among other things, the ash helps to create stronger stalks. Many gardeners insist that wood ash can help prevent peony rot or mildew on gooseberry bushes. Potassium is beneficial in fruit setting, and in the plants' maturing ahead of winter.

Some people add ash to their compost and find that it works well. This can, however, lead to an increase in the pH level and cause the nitrogen to turn into ammonia, meaning the plants lose out on some of the important nitrogen they need. Judging the dosage is also easier if the ash isn't mixed in with the compost. If you have a large amount of ash, it's best to return it to where it came from – the forest, in other words.

ASHES TO ASHES

All ashes are not created equal. Mixed ash produced when rubbish and other waste products are burnt isn't any good for the garden, nor is ash from pressure-creosoted timber (that type of thing should be left for landfill at the refuse depot). Painted wood, regardless of the colour, is no good either.

What we're talking about here is wood ash – in other words, ash from deciduous and coniferous trees, for example from stoves or fireplaces. The contents of what you burn reflect the contents of the ash that will be left behind – and consequently what will end up in the soil. When we burn wood/timber, the water and organic carbon compounds disappear. Left behind as ash are the nutrients potassium, phosphorous, calcium, magnesium and iron.

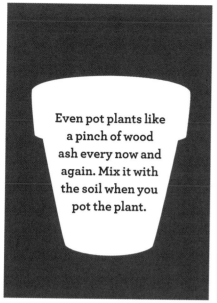

Even pot plants like a pinch of wood ash every now and again. Mix it with the soil when you pot the plant.

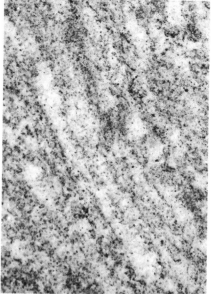

ROCK SOLID TIPS

Mix a little rock dust with nettle feed/liquid fertiliser to minimise the smell.

Rock dust added to compost will speed up the decomposition process (roughly 500 g/1 lb per 10 kg/22 lb of compost).

Rock dust containing a lot of silicon can help protect against fungus and rot.

Avoid using rock dust in clay soils – it will just make them even harder.

Moisture and organic material are important in the release of nutrients in the soil.

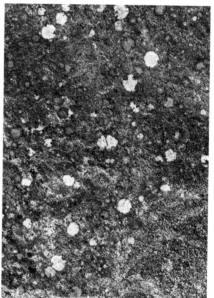

ASHEN TIP

Keep your ash dry. Potassium will leach out with rainwater.

Wood ash is particularly good in light soils, such as sandy soils.

Wood ash is alkaline. Large amounts will increase the pH of the soil. Don't use wood ash as fertiliser for acid-loving plants.

STONE MIX

If you live in an area with mostly granite bedrock, it's best to find rock dust from a different rock type. This is because the minerals from granite in particular should already be present in your soil. A different composition will enrich and widen your soil's mineral make up.

The roots of a tree can also absorb heavy metals from the soil, which then remain in the wood. Lead, cadmium and mercury aren't elements we want to add to the soil unnecessarily. That said, it is difficult to know the exact make up of the wood, so this is one reason to use wood ash sparingly. Heavy metals occur naturally in the soil, but the amount varies depending on the soil type, among other factors.

Not all heavy metals are poisonous or hazardous, but some are. As long as they're left undisturbed in the soil, they won't do any harm. But sadly, the amount of dangerous heavy metals in our natural cycles has increased due to more intensive logging and mining practices, as well as deposits from air pollution.

DOSAGE

Most plants, acid-lovers aside, will benefit from a little wood ash. Despite this, there are several reasons not to overdose your plants, and heavy metals like cadmium are just one. Another reason is that the levels of potassium and magnesium must be balanced for the natural uptake of nutrients to occur. Too much potassium can block the uptake of magnesium. A magnesium deficiency will impact the production of chlorophyll, and can present as light areas on the leaves, between the veins.

Use roughly 100ml (3½ fl oz) of ash per peony or rose. Dig it into the earth during early spring. Roughly the same amount will be enough for a berry bush, slightly more for a fruit tree. In the vegetable patch, you should be a bit more sparing. If you want to raise the pH level for your lawn (to stop moss running riot), sprinkle a thin layer of wood ash onto the last snow, so that it can follow the melt water into the soil. A maximum 1 kg (2¼ lb) of ash per square metre (yard) per year is a good rule of thumb.

ROCK DUST – ROCK SOLID MINERALS

Both wood ash and rock dust are considered inorganic fertilisers. Wood is an organic material which is converted to an inorganic substance by burning. Inorganic fertilisers consist of minerals which have been produced chemically (synthetic fertilisers) or through the processing of natural rock types (rock dust). When we talk more generally about 'mineral fertilisers', this usually means synthetic/commercial fertilisers. In this particular case, we mean pulverised natural rock.

Precisely which minerals and nutrients the rock dust contains depends on the type of rock from which it was made. In addition to the minerals the bedrock contains, the rock dust will also feature minerals from the fractures in the rock. A number of incredibly unhealthy substances come from nature itself: arsenic, uranium and radon are just a few examples. This is why it is important to know where the rock dust comes from and what it contains. Not always an easy task.

HIGH CULTURES AROUND THE FLOOD DELTAS

The world's earliest civilisations appeared along the incredibly fertile land flanking rivers roughly 5,000 years ago. Along the flood delta between the Euphrates and the Tigris, the Sumerian civilisation emerged. In the Nile valley, the Egyptians built their kingdom, and in north-west India, the Harappan (Indus Valley) civilisation grew along the river Indus. And on the Yellow River (Huang He) delta in the north, Chinese civilisation developed.

Wide, long rivers carry crumbled rock deposits (rock dust), minerals and organic material (plant remains) as they make their way from source to mouth. As a result, their sediments become nutrient-rich and when the rivers burst their banks, the flood plains are enriched with this sediment – above all in the delta regions. This means that these areas tend to have the most fertile soil on earth. Some scholars suggest that the biblical paradise, the Garden of Eden, was in precisely such a location – a delta area in southern Iraq.

soil at any time of year. One idea is to add rock dust whenever you prepare a new area or add new plants. You can also 'sprinkle' it onto the soil, around a fruit tree for example, watering afterwards. The best approach is to dig in the dust so that it doesn't form a hard crust on the surface. Use roughly 500g (1 lb) of rock dust per 10 square metres (12 square yards) of cultivated soil, every fifth year or so.

Rock dust is very slow-acting. Its nutrients – potassium, silicon, magnesium and calcium, for example – are released in small doses over a long period of time. This means that the chances of over-dosing are small, and that you can spread rock dust at any time of year – even during autumn if you wanted to. But do bear in mind that large amounts of alkaline rock dust will raise the pH level of your soil.

DIFFERENT FACTIONS

Rock and stone is difficult for micro-organisms to process. The 'chewiness' is as follows, in descending order: rock, stone, gravel, sand and rock dust. The finer the grain the rock dust has, the more accessible the nutrients are to plants. The dust can have a grain size anywhere up to 4 mm (⅛ in).

WHERE, WHEN AND HOW?

It's by no means certain that you'll find rock dust in your local garden centre. There might be products made from volcanic rocks such as basalt or pumice (from lava rock), but to get your hands on a larger amount of rock dust, you'll have to turn to a stone breaker or well-borer. Rock dust is also used in paving and tiling outdoors, so one tip would be to check with paving or flooring companies. We can't guarantee you'll get any answers, but try to find out what type of rock the dust has come from anyway.

Rock dust can be dug in or sprinkled on top of the

USING WOOD ASH AND ROCK DUST AS FERTILISER

Use a maximum of 100 ml (3½ fl oz) of wood ash per peony or rose during spring. Roughly the same amount for a berry bush and a little more for a fruit tree.

Use rock dust as a soil improver with long-lasting nutrients.

Dig around 500g (1 lb) of rock dust into each 10 square metres (12 square yards) of cultivated soil, roughly every fifth year.

Larger amounts of wood ash or rock dust will raise the pH of the soil. Take care with acid-loving plants.

Approximate nutritional content in:
Wood ash: nitrogen 0.0%,
   phosphorous 1.7%, potassium 8.7%
Rock dust (from granite): nitrogen 0.0%,
   phosphorous 0.1%, potassium 2.0-5.0%

GREEN ENERGY

Using grass and weeds as nutrient boosters in your garden is verging on genius. Fresh grass cuttings will provide energy for your plants' growth, and liquid manure from weeds like nettles and horsetail will give a strengthening boost of vital minerals. You can even make liquid manure from farmyard manure and compost.

No matter how carefully or well you add fertiliser to your garden in spring, the nutrient stores will still need refilling sooner or later, particularly for energy-hungry plants like summer blooms and tomatoes. This is also true of light soils like sandy types, which can't buffer nutrients in the same way heavier ones can. As a result, your plants will need top-ups several times during the growth period. Fresh grass cuttings and liquid manure are excellent for this. Try to vary these energy drinks from different sources, but don't over-fertilise.

CLEAN CUT

Fresh grass cuttings are like gold to your plants in early summer. They contain a lot of nitrogen which, among other things, is important for growth. Grass cuttings are fast-acting – the nutrients are released after around a week. Gather up the cuttings when you mow the lawn and scatter a layer onto the soil around any nutrient-hungry plants. You can even do this for pots or in greenhouses. It's better to repeat the process several times than to add a thick layer; 5–10 cm (2–4 in) is enough. Just take care with grass from lawns containing a lot of weeds, and keep an eye out for snails.

GREEN BULL

Weeds like nettles, common comfrey, field horsetail, dandelions and greater plantain are good raw materials to use as a kind of energy drink for your plants, so long as they haven't gone to seed. The nutrient levels can vary, however. With a controlled clump of stinging nettles or variegated Russian comfrey in one corner of your garden, you'll always have access to nutrients for your plants. Both can spread wildly, so make sure to cut them down and use them before they go to seed!

The most common method is to use this nutrient drink to water your plants, but you can also spray it onto them so that they absorb it through the pores in their leaves. Add this fertiliser early or late in the day, so that the goodness doesn't evaporate.

And it's not just weeds you can use to make liquid fertiliser; chicken, cow and horse manure, urine (see page 131) or compost can also be added to water, left to draw and then diluted.

NETTLES – A CURE-ALL

Stinging nettles are one of several species within the nettle family. They tend to be easy to find – sometimes too easy. Nettles often grow in nutrient (and above all nitrogen) rich soil, so if they're growing in your garden, see that as a good sign! Nettles are, of course, weeds, but they can also do good. Not least young nettles, which can be a nutritious addition to your kitchen. Nettles are a broad source of nutrients which contain many of the minerals needed by plants. They provide nitrogen, potassium, iron, calcium and manganese, among other things.

COMFREY – A POTASSIUM BOOST

Comfrey is a sweet plant with pretty little flowers and large, textured leaves. There are around twenty different varieties within the *Symphytum* family.

In Swedish gardens, the most common one is variegated Russian comfrey.

Liquid manure produced using comfrey is above all rich in potassium, but it also contains calcium, phosphorous, magnesium, manganese, iron, selenium and zinc, making it good for tomatoes! You can even mix comfrey with nettles to achieve an extra nitrogen boost.

HORSETAIL – A SILICON BOOST

The spruce-like wild plant horsetail has a peculiar appearance. It contains a lot of silicon, which is thought to be good for preventing fungal diseases, mildew and other ailments. But if your plants are already suffering, simply adding horsetail won't be enough. And never plant horsetail in your garden – it can be almost impossible to get rid of once established!

CHICKEN MANURE – A NITROGEN BOOST

Using just chicken manure and water, you can create a nitrogen-rich liquid which will provide extra energy and be quickly absorbed by your plants. Keep an eye on the colour of the leaves and on their lushness to make sure you don't overdose them. Any nutrients the plants cannot absorb will end up in our seas and lakes, and too much nitrogen can also have a negative impact on the taste of the plants.

COW/HORSE MANURE AND COMPOST – AN OVERALL BOOST

You can dissolve ordinary manure from cows and horses in water, the same way you would chicken manure. Even household compost contains nutrients which can be dissolved. The liquid produced will be very mild, however, but comprehensively nutritious.

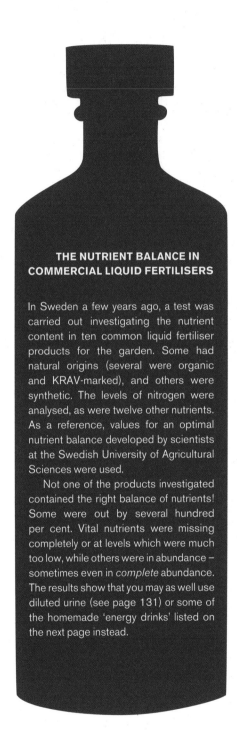

THE NUTRIENT BALANCE IN COMMERCIAL LIQUID FERTILISERS

In Sweden a few years ago, a test was carried out investigating the nutrient content in ten common liquid fertiliser products for the garden. Some had natural origins (several were organic and KRAV-marked), and others were synthetic. The levels of nitrogen were analysed, as were twelve other nutrients. As a reference, values for an optimal nutrient balance developed by scientists at the Swedish University of Agricultural Sciences were used.

Not one of the products investigated contained the right balance of nutrients! Some were out by several hundred per cent. Vital nutrients were missing completely or at levels which were much too low, while others were in abundance – sometimes even in *complete* abundance. The results show that you may as well use diluted urine (see page 131) or some of the homemade 'energy drinks' listed on the next page instead.

HOMEMADE LIQUID FERTILISER

NETTLE FEED

Fill a bucket (ideally with a lid) with nettles and add water. Leave outside for a few days or a week – until it starts to stink. To reduce the odour, you can add a little rock dust to the mix. Dilute with about ten parts water.

Use the mix to water the soil or pour it into a spray can and spritz your plants' leaves. The latter will provide nutrients and help fight the loss of foliage, but it can also leave marks on the leaves.

Alternatively: tie the nettles together in a bouquet and drop into a bucket of water. Once the water has drawn the nutrients from the nettles, you can simply lift the bouquet from the bucket by the string and use it again. The nutrients released will be slightly lower than in the mix above, and can be used with fewer parts water. You can throw the rest into the compost heap. This process works just as well with comfrey.

HORSETAIL BOOST

Extract the nutrients from horsetail by simmering it in water over a low heat for an hour. Then strain it and squeeze out the liquid. Throw the remainder onto the compost heap. Dilute using 5–10 parts water. Mix with some other liquid feed (i.e. nettle or comfrey mix) or spray directly onto the plants. Horsetail can help to counteract fungal infestations.

COMFREY ELIXIR

Cut the big, rough leaves into smaller pieces. Fill a bucket (ideally with lid) with the leaves and add water. Leave it to sit until it starts to stink. Dilute with roughly ten parts water and then use directly on the soil.

CHICKEN MANURE SOUP

Mix a few handfuls of chicken manure with water in a bucket, stir and then leave to draw for twenty-four hours.

Strain the nitrogen-rich nutrient stock into a watering can and use to add a top-up to any plants which look like they could do with a boost – those which are displaying weak growth or are pale and feeble. You can dilute the mix further if you need to – as a rule, the liquid should be the same colour as very weak tea. You can re-use the manure, which will give slightly weaker results, by re-filling the bucket with water.

MANURE AND/OR COMPOST SOUP

Mix a few decilitres of farmyard manure or kitchen compost with water in a bucket or bowl and leave it to stand and draw for a couple of days. You can put the manure into a mesh bag – the kind you might use in the washing machine – if you want the mix to be less mucky and avoid catching in the watering can's filter. An old pair of tights can work well, too. Throw the rest onto the compost heap.

USING LIQUID FERTILISER

Liquid nutrient mixes are best for top-ups – snacks, in other words – rather than the main application of fertiliser.

Water the soil or spray the leaves with your liquid fertiliser

A good alternative if you don't want to use diluted urine (see page 131) on edible plants shortly before harvest.

PEE

LIQUID GOLD

We may as well go ahead and say it: this is probably the best and most useful tip in this entire book. Pee is the uncrowned queen of the fertiliser family. It's just a matter of dropping your pants and letting rip. The best type of fertiliser will always be readily accessible, contain practically everything your plants need from a nutritional point of view, and be free to boot. Supplement this golden liquid with farmyard manure and compost for the sake of building humus, and the whole thing is practically cut and dried.

There isn't actually much difference between urine from achey old men and cute little boys. From a purely chemical standpoint, that is – your plants won't care. Any possible differences are purely in our minds. If handled properly, urine in the garden is nothing to turn your nose up at. It's an excellent raw material for topping up any previous fertiliser during the growth period. It's nitrogen-rich, fast-acting and easy to use. And it's as locally produced as it gets.

Urine is a by-product of our bodies' metabolic processes, a waste product full of the things we don't need, but which plants will gratefully make use of. The average adult urinates about seven times a day, around 1–2 litres (1¼–3½ pints) in any twenty-four hour period. Roughly as much as he or she drinks.

The urine produced by one person over the course of a year is enough to be used as fertiliser on between 100–350 square metres (120–420 square yards) of cultivated soil. The general recommendation is to use 1–2 litres (1¼–3½ pints) per square metre (yard) during the growth period. The actual amount will depend on what you are growing and which type of soil you have, so giving an exact figure is almost impossible. That said, the maximum dosage is 200 ml (7 fl oz) of concentrated urine per square metre (yard) at any one time.

PEE BREAK!

Roughly one month after the main round of fertiliser is applied in spring (farmyard manure and compost, for example), it may be time for a top-up. Once the plants have really started growing properly during early summer, some will need a little boost, above all of nitrogen. This doesn't apply to all plants, only the hungriest types: those which aren't going to overwinter, like vegetables and summer blooms, for example, and pot plants, where nutrients rapidly run out. Bushes, trees and perennial beds can last for a long time on the fertiliser added in spring.

During early summer, and for a while in high summer, growth will be strong and a small snack will go down well, meaning all your plants can live up to expectations and achieve their full potential.

INGREDIENTS

In one litre of urine, you'll find roughly 7.4 grams of nitrogen, 0.6 grams of phosphorous and 1.6 grams of potassium. That's a relatively large amount of nitrogen, and only a small amount of potassium. As a result, urine is particularly good in potassium-rich soils (which clay soils often are). Pee contains roughly 95 per cent water and substances such as urea, chloride, sodium, potassium and creatine. Fresh urine has a neutral pH and does not usually contain contagions. That's because inside the body, urine is sterile. On the way out, and in gathering the liquid, bacteria can be introduced – but this is uncommon, and nothing to worry about if you're using your own urine and keep an eye on the way you produce your liquid fertiliser.

131

A PERSONAL TREASURE TROVE?

The colour of urine can vary depending on how diluted it is. Dark yellow, foul-smelling pee is a sign of too little liquid in the body. Drink more water! The colour should be clear to pale yellow, the smell almost imperceptible. Often, our urine is a deeper shade of yellow and more potent in the mornings, and if your urine is red, you've probably been eating beetroot. If not – seek medical help!

Certain foods can cause our urine to smell different – asparagus, garlic and coffee, for example.

FERTILISER WORKSHOP

The recipe for a urine mix suitable for use in your garden is 1 part urine to 9 parts water. A common rule of thumb is that it should be the colour of weak tea. Very weak tea, we should add, because the colour should barely be visible if you've diluted it with enough water. It should also have hardly any smell at all.

There are those who argue that it's better not to dilute the urine at all, and to simply use it to water the soil after fertiliser has been added. They claim it has less of a smell. But one problem with this approach is that it's difficult to apply the 'right' dose (and we always want to avoid over-fertilisation).

Applying the urine mix using a sprinkler is a method almost everyone agrees is best avoided. It makes the smell more powerful, the nutrient loss greater, and your plants' leaves may become susceptible to sun burn. Plus, we don't want any of the pee to end up on the actual fruit or vegetables we're going to eat!

NOT A VINTAGE

Diluted urine won't benefit from being stored for a long time. This type of nutrient drink should be given to your plants while fresh. That said, you can store urine in a drum with a lid, for example, for a couple of weeks. After that, it will start to smell like 'old pee'. This is because during the breakdown of nitrogen-rich organic material, ammonia is formed. Which, as we all know, doesn't smell particularly good.

MEDICINE, DRUGS AND SALT IN URINE

Certain medicines and chemicals (hormones and narcotics, for example) pass through our bodies, and traces of them can remain in our urine. Most of these substances will quickly break down in the soil, but some, such as hormones (levonorgestrel, found in some contraceptive pills, for example), will not break down quite so quickly, and they can have an effect on both animals and the environment if allowed to leach into the groundwater.

Opinion on whether urine containing these substances should be used as fertiliser is divided. The growth of the plants themselves won't be affected, or not as far as we know. Some argue that ordinary tap water also contains traces of chemical substances

USING DILUTED URINE AS FERTILISER

Diluted urine provides a good shot of nitrogen during top-up fertilisation.

Don't water the actual plants or their leaves, water the soil.

Don't use immediately prior to harvest.

Don't over-fertilise – think 'rather too little than a little too much'.

Use your nose when you add the fertiliser, so your neighbours won't complain about the smell. If it stinks, make sure to water thoroughly.

Add organic material if using nothing but diluted urine as fertiliser.

and that there is no great difference between using tap water and using diluted urine. Others believe that using urine which you know may contain traces of medicine is reprehensible.

Hobby gardeners who use urine as fertiliser usually know where it has come from. If someone in the family is on medication (penicillin, for example), they can just avoid using any of that person's urine during the course of their treatment – if they want to.

Certain plants can be sensitive to salt, both on their leaves and in the soil. The plants can sustain burns from the sun on their leaves. If our diets contain a lot of salt, then these salts (sodium and chloride ions) will also appear in our urine. So, avoid using any urine the day after a salty pig out.

COMPOST FUEL

Garden compost sometimes contains too much carbon-rich material for perfect decomposition to take place – leaves and dry twigs, for example. This means trying to find a good balance between the carbon and nitrogen-rich material, and it's here that urine can step in with its high nitrogen levels. Add a little pee and kickstart the process!

Compost is important if you're using urine as fertiliser. The soil also needs humus-building materials in order to be fertile, and this means that urine and compost complement each other nicely.

UREA/CARBAMIDE
The urine of mammals contains urea, a nitrogenous chemical compound. Urea is formed when our bodies break down amino acids from digested proteins. During this process, ammonia is formed, which is then transformed into urea.

Urea is the first organic substance to have been created synthetically, in 1828. Synthetic (artificial) urea is primarily used as a fertiliser within agriculture and forestry.

LIQUID GOLD

100 ml (3½ fl oz) of pee +
900 ml (1⅗ pints) water =
1 litre (1¾ pints) liquid gold

133

THE OUTHOUSE

Yes, poo is disgusting, and for some reason human excrement is particularly bad – the worst of all. You're not alone if you feel that way; it's part of our culture and our time. But this wouldn't be a book about manure if it didn't touch on the subject! So, you can either leaf forward to the next chapter or challenge yourself. Take a deep breath – we're about to fling the door to the loo wide open.

People do their business pretty much every day, regardless of their gender, age, ethnicity, class, weight, lifestyle, eating habits, religion, culture or values. Everyone does it, all over the world. We've done it since the beginning of time, and we'll probably continue to do it for however long we're still here.

In some corners of the world, human excrement is a source of infection and disease, while in others we just press a button or pull a handle and that little weight vanishes from our minds. But as the global population grows, and with an increasing number of mouths to feed (= increased production of food, greater demand for fertiliser) and a lack of clean water, none of this is sustainable. If we better utilised our waste, we could view it a resource rather than a problem.

The future will probably see the emergence of new technologies which make use of our 'assets' without wasting any fresh water. But don't go out and empty the potty into the vegetable patch just yet!

HUMAN MANURE

Human waste contains, just like animals', the nutrients needed by plants. Most nutrients are found in our urine, which contains high levels of nitrogen, but number twos, our solid waste, contain humus-building materials and nutrients like nitrogen, phosphorous and potassium. In total, each person in the western world flushes away around 5 kg (11 lb) of nitrogen and 600 g (1⅓ lb) of phosphorous every year. We wash it away with around 20 cubic metres (5,200 gallons) of clean water per person – and all from the toilet seat.

Urine is easier to utilise. It doesn't normally contain any bacteria or substances we need to be careful with (as long as it doesn't contain residues of medicines or other chemical substances), and it doesn't have too strong a smell. But when it comes to poo, faeces, more cautious handling is needed.

Excrement can contain contagions (various bacteria, viruses and parasites) and therefore needs to be composted or stored before it can be used as manure on any plants we will eat. The compost needs to reach a temperature of at least 50°C (120°F) for these harmful organisms to be killed off. If the faeces aren't heat composted, then they will need to be stored for at least two years before the manure can be used in our kitchen gardens.

LATRINE COMPOST

Setting up a latrine compost by isolated houses without access to communal sewers, or in areas where removing the sludge is difficult – on islands, for example – can be hugely beneficial. The discharge from faulty private drainage systems (and even from boats and ferries) is one of the villains in the drama surrounding the over-fertilisation of our seas and lakes. Even the quality of our water can be affected when filtration systems, sand filters, stone caissons, septic tanks, etc. don't work as they should. And consequences like closed beaches and contaminated drinking water are not at all uncommon.

The rules vary from place to place, so check what applies where you live. Sometimes, you'll need permission to keep a faecal compost bin, but sometimes simply submitting a notification is enough. It's important that it has a sealed bottom and that the compost is covered with a lid. The composting container must also have air holes. You can either build one yourself or buy one ready made.

SEWAGE SLUDGE FROM TREATMENT WORKS

You've probably never even thought about using sewage as fertiliser in your garden. And nor should you, but it's still interesting to know how it works. Because the truth is that sewage sludge is used within agriculture, on the foods which end up on our plates.

Urine and excrement mix together with sink, bath and toilet water from our households, schools, workplaces, hospitals, industry, etc. in the pipes leading to municipal sewage treatment works. Nutrients like phosphorous mix with environmental poisons like flame retardants, PCBs, medicine residues and heavy metals.

After the water has been cleaned as far as current technology allows and environmental laws demand, all that remains is gunge – sewage sludge. This sludge is good as a humus-building material and contains roughly 2.8 per cent phosphorous and 4.3 per cent nitrogen. It's commonly used as fertiliser on fields within conventional agriculture.

The problem is that it doesn't just provide important nutrients like phosphorous, but also environmental poisons – cadmium, for example, which is extremely harmful to both the environment and human health. Here in Sweden we have the Swedish Society for Nature Conservation and others like them working to outlaw the use of sewage sludge as fertiliser. Research and work towards being able to the phosphorous is ongoing.

DIGESTED SLUDGE BECOMES FUEL

Digested sludge is simply sewage waste which has been treated in a so-called digester. These are used within forestry, among other areas. As the sewage sludge is digested (through a process of fermentation), digested sludge is created as a byproduct. The gas produced is often called biogas, and is used as fuel for engines and the heating of our homes.

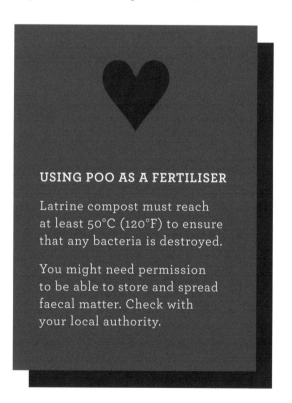

USING POO AS A FERTILISER

Latrine compost must reach at least 50°C (120°F) to ensure that any bacteria is destroyed.

You might need permission to be able to store and spread faecal matter. Check with your local authority.

SERIOUS CRAP

As the population grew in Sweden, the buildings in our cities and towns became more densely packed and faecal matter became a serious problem. A sanitary nuisance, you could say. In fact, rumour has it that you could tell you were approaching a town using nothing but your nose. Right up until the 1870s, waste ran straight out onto the streets, where ditches and gutters directed the runoff to the nearest watercourse – often the same place people used for bathing, washing, and even fetching their drinking water.

Gradually, specialist outhouses began to emerge, containing a variety of technical solutions. These places were hated and loved in equal measure, and they were given many different names: the loo, the outhouse, the bog, the latrine, the privy, etc.

In the countryside, the privy was often among other outhouses, not infrequently close to the manure heap. As a result, human waste was composted down with the dung of animals. In the towns and cities, it was common to see privies outside, often in long rows. Noble residences would have a slightly more private toilet in an enclosed room of some kind, and even the more humble multi-family residences eventually got a shared latrine in their stairwell or attic. They usually had special barrels to collect all the waste, sometimes containers with sand or gravel – not so different from a litter tray for house cats.

NOT ALL CRAP IS THE SAME
Throughout history, we have carried out and managed our natural urges in different ways, from covering the pile with grass or burying it in a pit, to the western world's modern, flushing ceramic toilets.

In high-technology Japan, so-called washlets are commonplace today, not just in Tokyo and the bigger cities, but even in the countryside. Once you've finished your business and flushed away the evidence, all from your heated seat, the toilet can also rinse you off front and back, if you like. Then dry you off with warm air. Like a princess on a WC throne. Utterly different to the toilets in the African countryside.

Our sanitary equipment varies wildly across the four corners of the earth, but regardless of that we produce the same nutrients. Nitrogen, phosphorous, potassium and more.

WC – A MODERN LUXURY PRODUCT
The first flushing toilet, produced in England, was made from cast iron and had a water tank mounted on the wall. During the 1870s, production of ceramic WCs (water closets) began. In Sweden, these became commonplace during the 1920s, when the sewers were adapted to take waste from toilets.

Flushing toilets are a fantastic invention which have brought huge improvements to our health, comfort and lifestyle. All the same, they are also unsustainable in the long run, no matter how efficient the toilets we produce may be. The global population is approaching eight billion people, and clean water is already one of our most scarce resources. Add to that the fact that phosphorous is a finite resource which should return to our natural cycles to provide plants with nutrients – not end up in our oceans and lakes.

QUICK FIX

Starved plants will be as happy as small children at the pick 'n' mix counter when you rustle a bag of synthetic fertiliser. The chemically produced nutrients in the fertiliser take the fast track up from the soil via the plant's root system, and are rapidly dealt out to those parts of the plant which need them. The nutrients in these synthetic fertilisers consist of easily dissolved salts which can be quickly absorbed by the plant. All you need is a little moisture, and the goodies are released.

We often hear that natural and synthetic fertilisers have different origins. Inorganic synthetic fertilisers are chemically produced from minerals in factories, while organic natural fertiliser is made up of animal and plant matter. The natural fertiliser you buy from the garden centre may, of course, have been produced, mixed and packed in a factory, but synthetic fertiliser production is often on more of a large-scale and industrial nature.

FROM THE CHEMISTRY LAB

Inorganic fertiliser, commercial fertiliser, mineral fertiliser, artificial fertiliser, ammonium nitrate – these are all names for roughly the same thing: synthetic fertiliser products. All contain industrially processed minerals, often in the form of salts. In the manufacturer's laboratories, the focus will have been on the chemical elements. NPK fertiliser focuses on nitrogen (N), phosphorous (P) and potassium (K): the essential nutrients needed by plants. The nitrogen is extracted from the air, while the phosphorous and potassium come from natural ground deposits.

Urea is an organic substance (it occurs naturally in the urine of mammals) which can be produced chemically and is used as an ingredient in certain synthetic fertilisers.

A GLORIOUS MIX OF PRODUCTS

The list of inorganic fertiliser products is long, and spans a number of different manufacturers, chemical formulas and compositions – as well as uses. You can buy special formulations for conifers, for example, rhododendrons, Mediterranean plants, lawns and pot plants. Just listing the names of manufacturers and producers of synthetic fertilisers doesn't seem interesting or relevant – not even here, in a book about fertiliser.

If you want to use synthetic fertiliser, check the chemical composition on the packaging in the shop. Remember that if the product is the only fertiliser you plan on using, it should also contain micronutrients. It's also important to add organic material (such as compost) to help build up a humus-rich soil which can handle and store the nutrients well. This applies regardless of whether you're using synthetic or natural fertilisers (if these don't already include humus-building materials like cow manure).

Synthetic fertiliser is sold in all kinds of packaging, in both solid and liquid form: in jars, sacks, bottles, etc. Some products are available in stick form, puck-shaped, as soluble tablets or small pills.

The contents are often concentrated and easily handled – as well as being odour-free. They're practical, to put it bluntly.

One advantage of synthetic fertiliser is that it's easier to know precisely which substances the mix contains, and in what proportions. Recommended dosages are also usually given on the packaging. Things get a bit more approximate when it comes to dosages of farmyard manure, because it can be

Blue fertiliser pellets are like Viagra for your plants: little blue pills which give them temporary potency.

Not all synthetic fertiliser is of the sprinting type, however. There are some products which release the nutrients more slowly. These are known as controlled-release fertilisers and tend to be used on plants in pots or urns as a result of the price – they're very expensive.

difficult to know the exact nutrient content. Synthetic fertiliser often doesn't even need to be dug into the soil like natural fertilisers do, it's enough to simply water them a little, since the chemical nutrients are so easily dissolved.

SPRINTER OR LONG DISTANCE RUNNER?

The nutrients in different fertilisers are released at different speeds. As a general rule, synthetic fertilisers are fast-acting. They simply need to be dissolved by the moisture in the soil. Organic fertiliser, on the other hand, needs to be broken down by the micro-organisms in the soil before the nutrients become available, meaning they have a 'preparation time' during which the raw materials are processed so that they can be served up to the plants in a good, long meal. This can take up to a few weeks.

USING SYNTHETIC FERTILISERS

Follow the dosage recommendations on the packaging.

Many products simply need to be watered in (rather than dug in).

Supplement with organic humus-building material.

Synthetic fertilisers can be used as an emergency remedy for rapid results. The nutrients are often fast-acting.

If you want to garden organically, you shouldn't use synthetic fertilisers.

METHODS

On using fertillisers so that the nutrients are deployed as smartly and effectively as possible. And on cultivation methods which both give and require nutrients.

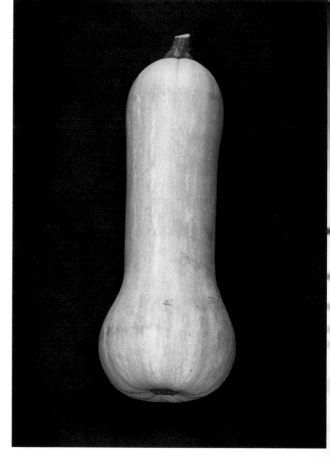

A HEARTY BREAKFAST

. . . and a few snacks here and there. It's important to dish up the fertiliser you use in the right way and at the right time, to fit in with your plants' differing needs and growth periods. Some plants will be happy with nothing but a good feed once a year, but others will also want a couple of snacks, spread out over the season.

We tend to distinguish between the main application of fertiliser and later top-ups. Comprehensive fertilisation should be done every year, usually in spring, to provide the plants with the key nutrients they need for the growth period. Whatever you add should compensate for any nutrients lost through growth, harvest and leaching. The dosage depends on what you are growing and the type of soil you have; the coarser the soil, the more fertiliser you will need, because soils with coarse grains (i.e. sandy soils) have a lower ability to retain nutrients.

Regardless of how much fertiliser you use during this initial application, you may still need to supplement it with a top-up later that spring, or during summer, once the nitrogen (among other things) is quickly used up.

A GOOD SOIL WILL READY ITSELF

A good time to add the main application of fertiliser to the soil is when it becomes ready in spring. The meaning of 'ready' may not be obvious to everyone here, but what we mean is that the soil has dried out a little, that it's workable again. In early spring, soils will often be too cold and wet, and in such conditions, not many nutrients will be released. It's also far from the ideal environment for sowing seeds or planting. So, wait until the soil has dried out a little, until it lets go when you dig a spade into it. It shouldn't stick to the blade and should fall off when you turn the spade. That's when you know the soil is ready.

PRIMARY APPLICATION OF FERTILISER

If you're preparing a new area for planting, it's important to give the soil a good fertiliser base. You reap what you sow, after all. Long-lasting farmyard manure, and perhaps a little fast-acting chicken manure, will provide a good balance of nutrients. This primary application of fertiliser is also a great opportunity to supplement the soil with carbon-rich material, which will help to improve the structure of the soil. Compost is a great choice, because it also contains valuable nutrients – above all kitchen compost.

A new or established vegetable patch or flowerbed can have fertiliser added roughly a week before sowing or planting. That way, there is time for the nutrients in the natural manure to be released, but the fertiliser won't be too strong for the sensitive young plants. A general rule of thumb is that the smaller and younger the plants, seedlings or cuttings, the less fertiliser is needed. But once these plants have really started growing, their needs will be much greater. Think of what a tiny baby eats, and then imagine the same person as a greedy teenager. Roughly like that.

Even established trees and bushes may need a good application of fertiliser, but not as much as a flowerbed full of perennials. Summer blooms and vegetables are the plants which need the most fertiliser, and the same is true of anything with limited access to soil, water and nutrients – pot plants, for example.

The fertiliser should be dug into the soil, not spread on the surface like a blanket or buried too deep. Turn over a shallow layer with a fork, spade, rake, or even just your hands.

At many northern latitudes, ground frost will be prevalent all winter and long into spring. Thick coverings of snow can arrive well into late spring. This means that when the growing season finally arrives, it'll be explosive, and with the short growth season up there, there's no time to waste. In those areas, it can be better to add the main application of fertiliser in late autumn rather than early spring. There won't be any leaching of nutrients as long as the ground is frozen. By adding fertiliser in autumn, the nutrients will be on stand-by until the frost melts and will then be immediately available when needed.

TOP-UP FERTILISER

Roughly one month after the primary application of fertiliser, many plants will need their nutrient reserves topped up. There are many tricks and methods for topping up your fertiliser, mulching with fresh grass cuttings, for example, or watering your plants with diluted urine or some other liquid fertiliser. Certain specialist fertiliser products can also be used.

You can add nutrients to your garden on two or three occasions during the summer. Pot plants and those in greenhouses can be given a top up once a week, or more often if you dilute the fertiliser. There are no rights or wrongs here, and you and your plants will have to come to some kind of agreement on the best solution. Check whether your plants are pale in colour, growing badly or starting to lose leaves. Given a quick snack, they'll rapidly recover and be thriving again within a week.

Above all, it's nitrogen that needs to be topped up most during the growth period. Nitrogen is a volatile substance and the soil cannot store or stock up on the nutrient. Overdosing during the primary application of fertiliser will lead to poor results. In fact, an overdose is never good, either for your plants or the environment. Instead, your plants will benefit from being given small snacks to keep them in a good mood. Don't ignore their needs – it can be vital for the result!

Remember that perennials need time to prepare for winter dormancy. As a result, don't give them nitrogen-rich fertiliser late during the season.

DIG IN YOUR FERTILISER

Digging your fertiliser into the soil rather than leaving it on the surface is good practice. It's down in the soil that it'll do good, not up on top. The risk is that nutrients like nitrogen will simply escape into the air otherwise. It's true that some of the nutrients will follow the water into lower layers of soil, and that even worms will drag down some, but it's still important to make sure that solid fertilisers are mixed with the soil so that the nutrients are accessible to the plants.

FERTILISER ON THE MENU

Farmyard manure is fantastic to use in your primary application of fertiliser – cow or horse manure are most common. You can supplement this with a handful of chicken manure, which will give it an extra kick. Chicken manure is otherwise used mainly for top-ups, because it contains a lot of nitrogen. Even fertilisers from the sea and the slaughterhouse, like calcified seaweed or bone meal, work well as supplements. Fresh grass cuttings, diluted manure, liquid fertilisers (nettle feed, for example) and blood meal all work well as top-ups. Very slow-acting fertilisers like rock dust and wood ash can appear on the menu every now and then, too. Synthetic fertilisers can be used in both primary and secondary applications.

This is easy in a new or empty space. You just turn in the fertiliser with a fork or spade. But if you're adding fertiliser to a flowerbed full of perennials, for example, you'll have to be more careful so that you don't damage the plants' outer roots. Dig in wherever you can, and rake onto more delicate areas.

If you use liquid fertilisers like diluted urine as a top-up, this obviously does not need to be dug in.

FERTILISER IN AUTUMN?

In the past, we were always taught that fertiliser should be dug in during autumn. When the farmers spread manure on their autumn fields, the windows and vents on the cottages in the area would all slam shut. Even hobby gardeners would dig in farmyard manure in autumn. But today, we know that doing so will mean that many of the nutrients disappear from the soil, into the air, and then fall again as rain or appear in meltwater. In other words, that the nutrients end up where they do more harm than good: in our waterways.

These days, many choose not to apply fertiliser at all during autumn; some will add a little slow-acting bone meal when they plant their autumn bulbs. IF you decide to apply fertiliser, phosphorous and potassium are most appropriate – not nitrogen.

Organic material (leaves, straw, garden compost etc.), on the other hand, is definitely beneficial when added at this time of year. It can both help to protect your plants and give worms and other friendly creatures in the soil something to work on. During winter, the material will start to break down, and the worms will drag it down into the ground. By spring, you can simply dig the remainder into your soil, or add it to your compost heap. The soil won't benefit from being left naked in the cold, a covering will do it good – unless you have clay soils and want the frost to break the lumps, of course. Clay soils also have a tendency to hold nutrients better than lighter soils.

That means that adding fertiliser to clay soils in autumn is better than other soil types – if you insist on adding it in autumn.

FERTILISING THE ROOT ZONE

The root systems of trees and bushes often tend to be as big as the crown. The majority of nutrients are taken up through the more delicate roots – not by the trunk or the thickest roots closest to the centre, but in a circle further out. That's where fertiliser will have the greatest impact.

One way to make sure that the nutrients you add are really going to good use is to fertilise the root zone. You can do this by digging holes in a circle following the shape of the outer edge of the crown. Dig holes roughly 30 cm (12 in) deep at 1 metre (yard) intervals and then add a handful of calcified seaweed or bone meal to each. Water well. You can add fertiliser in this way during spring or autumn – or both.

VALUABLE DROPS

Proper watering affects the health and business of your garden. Plants can't chow down on solid food, they have to absorb nutrients dissolved in water. If you're smart in the way you water, you're doing your plants a service and will see better results from any fertiliser you add. With a few easy steps, you can help your plants more easily slurp up those nutrients.

It's rare for summer weather to provide the right amount of rainfall at the right kind of pace for our plants. A rain gauge is a handy tool for keeping track of how much it has actually rained. One millimetre (0.04 in) of rain represents a litre (1¾ pints) of water per square metre (yard), and a general rule of thumb is that roughly 20–30 litres (35–50 pints) of water are needed per square metre (yard) per week (corresponding to 2–3 cm/¾–1¼ in of rain!). Our plants have differing levels of thirst, however, as well as tolerance to drought. On average, evaporation corresponds to around 3 litres (5¼ pints) per square metre (yard) per day.

seeds and plants, vegetable patches, greenhouses, pots and summer blooms, on the other hand, need to be watered properly and regularly. Just adding the occasional splash of water will mean that their roots stay close to the surface, rather than digging deeper. Proper watering will lead to more robust and drought-resistant plants.

The best method is to water the roots, not the leaves. You can use a drip line, dig in hose piping or plastic bottles to make sure the water goes where you want it. Watering cans are also great! If you use a spray nozzle or sprinkler to do your watering, much of it will evaporate or end up where it won't do much good.

THE ART OF WATERING

Morning is the best time of day to water your plants. Evening works too, but it can encourage snails, and night moisture can lead to fungal infestations in greenhouses. After a rain shower is also a good time to water. The ground will be damp, meaning it can more easily take a larger dose. If the ground is very dry, the water will tend to run straight through it. Dig down and see how far the moisture has penetrated. It often won't be as far as you think!

Well-established perennials, lawns, trees and bushes will rarely need watering, other than during prolonged periods of drought. They might look a little tired and withered, but they will survive and perk up once they get a little water. Newly sown

DAMP TIPS

Water during rain or after a quick shower. Make use of the rain water!

Water in the morning. Don't give your plants a quick spritz, water them properly.

Water after adding fertiliser.

Water newly planted plants regularly for the whole of their first year.

Give evergreens an extra drink ahead of winter.

NUTRIENT-RICH RAW FOOD

Usually, the level of nutrients in the soil will decrease as you grow and harvest – unless you add the same amount as you take out. It's a bit like your fridge at home, it'll soon be empty if no one refills it. Green manures are nothing new, they aren't a modern invention. The practice is commonplace within agriculture, above all organic farming. It's a smart way of improving the structure of the soil and restoring nutrients to the ground.

The concept of green manures refers to growing special plants which improve the structure of the soil with their root systems, simultaneously providing nutrients. The plants themselves supply the soil with nitrogen – both for their own and any future growth. They add to, rather than taking away from the nutrient levels of the soil – but only in terms of nitrogen, not the other nutrients.

Often, green manures are grown for these reasons alone, but there are also a number of aesthetic reasons. Many of the plants are also beautiful – crimson clover, for example – and will attract bees and other flying pollinators. Biodiversity provides a good balance between pests and beneficial creatures.

AN AIRBORNE TREASURE – NITROGEN

Leguminous plants such as beans, peas, lupins, sweet peas, alfalfa, vetches and various kinds of clover manage the art of seizing nitrogen from the air through the interaction between their roots and a particular type of bacteria (the *Rhizobium* species). The nitrogen is collected and is available both in the plants' roots and in those parts above ground, which is why it is important to dig the entire plant into the soil once it is cut.

As the plant mass is cut up and dug into the soil, it begins to decompose and the nitrogen is released into the soil. The organic material from the plants is also good for the humus level of the soil. 20–40 per cent of the nitrogen fixed by these plants will be available to the next crop. Some is stored more long-term in the ground, some will return to the air, and some will vanish through leaching (disappearing with rain and meltwater).

THE ROOTS PLUNDER THE BASEMENT

Green manure crops with long roots, such as lupins and ribbed melilot, work their way down to the lower layers of soil and retrieve the nutrients from the basement. When you later dig these plants into the soil, the nutrients they have absorbed will be released into the upper layers of soil. It's so clever – making use of nutrients which would otherwise go unused! An impressive system which also has the benefit that the roots, which die when the plant is cut, leave long channels in the soil. These allow the flow of air, water and nutrients, leading to a loose soil which other plants can more easily establish themselves in.

The roots of the green manure crops also secrete something known as root exudate, which affects the surface of the mineral particles in the soil and makes the nutrients more accessible to the plants.

HOW TO USE GREEN MANURES

You can grow green manure crops between rows, or even between the plants in your garden. Beans in a potato patch are a good and well-known combination. You can even sow green manure crops after an early harvest (of lettuce, for example) or before a late crop, so that the soil isn't left to lie bare. If you choose leguminous plants, there won't be any competition for the nitrogen. But don't forget that even these green manure crops will need to be watered, and that you may need to water more often than usual as a result. It's also important to remember that your plants need more nutrients than nitrogen alone!

If you're preparing a new flowerbed or garden plot, green manures are a great cure for the soil. You may have to wait a year, but in exchange you will ensure that your growing surfaces are in great shape. Choose a mix of seeds which provide nitrogen, loosen up the soil and suffocate weeds. Many green manure crops grow quickly, forming a tight mat. They are great competitors for both annual and perennial weeds, so make sure to sow them closely together if the main aim is to drown out any weeds!

CUT DOWN AND DIG IN

Cut down your green manure crops before they go to seed, unless you want them to self-sow! Some species can be cut down several times over the course of one season (and are perfect for use as mulch). Annuals can be dug into the soil during late autumn.

To minimise the amount of leaching, it's a good idea to leave the perennial green manure crops over winter, not digging them in until early spring – or digging them in as late as possible during autumn. You can also mix in dry leaves, straw or another carbon-rich material to help fix the nitrogen in the soil.

SUPERFOOD PLANTS
There are different types of green manure crops: those which collect nitrogen from the air (leguminous plants, for example), those which loosen up the soil (lupins and ribbed melilot) and those which increase the humus level of the soil by having lots of foliage (i.e. fiddleneck). Which you choose will depend on your aims. Mixing different species can also be a great idea. Ready-mixed packets of seeds are available from most garden centres. Here are a few examples of green manure crops:

CRIMSON CLOVER:
Annual, fast-growing, strong root system, good nitrogen fixer.

COMMON VETCH:
Annual, fast-growing, good nitrogen fixer.

FIDDLENECKS:
Annual, fast-growing, good ground cover, not a nitrogen fixer but good at absorbing available nutrients in soil.

LUPINS:
Annual, good nitrogen fixer, strong root system. Yellow and white lupins suit lighter soils – blue lupins suit heavier clay soils.

REVERSED CLOVER:
Annual, good nitrogen fixer, needs a lot of water.

ALFALFA:
Perennial, slow-growing, good ground cover, deep root system.

SUBTERRANEAN CLOVER:
Annual, good ground cover, good nitrogen fixer, strong root system, tolerates shade.

RIBBED MELILOT:
Biennial, good nitrogen fixer, strong taproot.

TUCK IN

Some cover up with straw, others with grass cuttings. Some use seaweed and there are those who like to use a blanket of wool. A layer of organic material on top of the bare soil will help to retain moisture and increase the humus content of the soil. Mulching is a way of mimicking nature, where virtually no soil is left bare. Left to its own devices, the ground will almost always be covered with plant growth, leaves, or some other kind of decaying organic material.

Nature itself doesn't spend time straightening sheets or making the bed with woollen blankets and fluffy duvets, but it does make sure to tuck in the soil in other ways. With bright blankets of wood anemone, velvet-soft mosses and fragrant herb beds, for example.

A bare soil is more exposed than a covered one. It will blow away, dry out, crack and form a hard shell which water will find it increasingly difficult to penetrate. The nutrients will leach away when the roots fail to absorb them. Creatures and macrofauna living below ground will become fewer in number, because there will be no food, work or shelter for them. It's a vicious circle, and the soil will eventually become depleted.

GROOVY, HEALTHY SOIL

All types of soil – whether sandy or clay or anything in between – will benefit from a layer of mulch. This is true in both summer and winter. When you add a mulch, the humus content will increase, the soil will become looser, and it will find it easier to retain nutrients and hold oxygen and water. The fluffier, more porous structure will provide plants with better conditions for good development. And the fact the temperature will be more steady is also a positive. Plus, a mulch will help to keep any weeds at bay.

In reality, mulch is a form of compost, and sometimes the process is known as surface composting. Just as in ordinary composting, the organic material on the soil surface is transformed to fine humus. The benefit of mulching is that it leads to a lower loss of nutrients and fewer greenhouse gases than ordinary composting, because the same high temperatures are not achieved. The downside is that it can look a bit messy, but it all depends what you choose to cover the soil with. And what you find ugly.

COVER ME!

Cover the bare soil in flowerbeds, between the rows in your vegetable patch (and wherever you've picked anything) and anywhere else without any covering. You can use a range of materials – whatever you have access to. Autumn means leaves, summer grass cuttings, and during harvest time there will be plenty of plant debris. First, cut your material into smaller pieces, maybe by giving it a run over with the lawn mower. Hay, straw, bark, seaweed are just a few of your options. At Mandelmann Gardens in Österlen, they even put sheep's wool on their garden paths.

Add a layer which is thick enough to help retain moisture, but still airy enough. Between 5 and 30 cm (2–12 in) will do. Grass cuttings can clump together and become compacted if the covering is too thick, so it's better to add in layers as the grass breaks down and collapses. Grass cuttings are high in nitrogen and should not be used on overwintering plants too late during the season. The nutrients will become available roughly one week after you add them. The method is equally applicable to outdoors as to greenhouses and pot plants.

NUTRIENT-RICH MULCHES:
LEAVES, STALKS, PLANT WASTE, GRASS CUTTINGS, CLOVERS, HERBS, DRIED WEEDS, SEAWEED

NUTRIENT-POOR MULCHES:
BARK, WOOD CHIPS, STRAW, HAY, LEAVES, WOOL

During the actual decomposition of the natural carbon-rich material, some of the nutrients will be used up as fuel in the process. You can counteract this by using diluted urine as fertiliser, or adding liquid fertiliser made from chicken manure, for example. If your mulch consists solely of carbon-rich material like bark chippings, the nutrients from the soil can even vanish, leading to a nutrient deficiency instead! By adding fresh materials such as grass cuttings, the loss of nitrogen will be lower. The fresher the material, the more nutrients.

A GOOD TIME UNDERGROUND

After a while, if you lift the lid a little, you'll notice an increased level of activity in your garden. There will be more and bigger worms, and the small insects will increase in numbers. Great! The micro-organisms might be more difficult to see, but the results of their work will reveal themselves in the soil. Underground life thrives on moisture, so add a little water if things seem dry. These soil workers will get to work breaking down the mulch and pulling it into the soil. Worm waste is alkaline, which means that overall, the pH level will be more stable.

Sadly, snails and rodents will also enjoy spending time in the damp environment beneath the covers. Some people have real problems with this, others none at all. Where you live, what you're growing and how thick a cover you've used can all have an impact. A thinner or airier layer of mulch often helps. If you're lucky, frogs will find their way to your garden, and snails are party food to them. As they are for hedgehogs and certain hens and ducks.

WEEDS AND WATER

Mulching may not be the answer to a completely maintenance-free garden. The only solution for that is called asphalt, or possibly concrete. But mulching will lighten your workload considerably. The need to loosen, fertilise (depending on what you use as mulch), water and de-weed will all decrease. Mulches provide moisture and reduce evaporation, seed-based weeds will find it more difficult to grow on the covering, and root-based weeds will have trouble breaking through the organic material to get sunlight. Well, perhaps not if your name is Mr Thistle or Mrs Couch Grass. But still, those that do manage to break through the cover are easier to pull out when the soil is looser.

Rake away the covering in spring so that the sun's warming rays can reach the soil. Otherwise, the mulch layer will keep the earth beneath it cool.

GROWING IN SAND AND GRASS CUTTINGS

Acclaimed Swedish gardener Nils Åkerstedt has been growing in sand for over forty years, with fantastic results. His method can be used for all types of plant, in gardens, greenhouses, flowerbeds or pots. All you need is sand, grass cuttings or some other form of greenery, and compost.

CROP ROTATION

A FOUR MOVEMENT SYMPHONY

Like a classical symphony, many methods of crop rotation follow a regular four-part structure. That isn't to say that having four movements is the only way – you can double it, halve it, or choose six- or eight-year rotations, too. But the four-year method is the simplest and most common among hobby gardeners. The point is to rotate and vary the plants in your plot of land, to exploit their different nutritional needs and adapt your rotation to that.

Rotating your plants is one way of avoiding any worries, a bit like a vaccination. It won't provide guaranteed protection against problems, of course, but the resilience and nutrient levels of your soil will increase, and you will enjoy bigger harvests in the long run. Crop rotation isn't exactly a method of fertilising, more a type of housekeeping, a smart way of distributing resources – and one which has other positive effects.

A MEMORABLE METHOD

Crop rotation is far from a new invention. It's a time-tested method that has been used by both farmers and home growers for years. Rotating your crop is as easy as growing in the 'normal' way – without any rotation, in other words. The biggest difficulty is remembering what you grew where the previous year. Write it down! And try to remember where you put that note.

GROW BY EXCHANGE

Rotation isn't a method to use everywhere, across the entire garden. It's primarily for use in your vegetable patch (though it also works well in window boxes), where you grow annuals that can be moved around every year. Perennials don't need to be moved, thankfully. Berry bushes, rhubarb, currants and asparagus can also stay where they are, being fertilised like normal, in the same spot.

The purpose of rotation is to maintain the vitality and nutrient levels of your soil. The method also reduces the risk of certain soil-related plant diseases and pests (fungi, bacteria and pests can overwinter in the soil) which can occur during normal gardening. These unwelcome freeloaders will find it harder to take hold if the type of plant changes every year. And by rotating the location of different plant types, you can also avoid the soil becoming depleted of the same nutrients year after year.

Different plants have different nutritional needs. Some have big appetites, some are more discriminating, and some even enhance and fix nutrients in the soil – something the rotation method utilises in a fantastic way. Another benefit of rotating your plants is that the root systems of certain species will loosen up the soil, meaning it can better hold water and oxygen, and ensuring that nutrients can be more readily released.

If you don't have the time, energy or desire to rotate your plants in line with the four-year model set out here, at least consider swapping the spot used for growing potatoes and other vegetables.

RECIPROCAL ACTION

The different plant families tend to be grouped as follows:

Nutrient givers: nitrogen-fixing plants such as peas, beans and other leguminous varieties. A number of green manure crops also belong to this category (see page 149).

Large nutritional needs: plants with big appetites such as cabbages, leeks, garlic, pumpkins and squashes.

Moderate nutritional needs: plants with average appetites such as onions, root vegetables, lettuce, dill and parsley.

Small nutritional needs: plants with small appetites such as potatoes and Jerusalem artichokes.

SEVERAL PIECES OF CAKE

If you're setting up a new growing area, it might be a good idea to think in stages (growing boxes, beds, etc.) from the very start. It will make things easier if you want to rotate your crops.

Remember that the soil depth should also be suitable for everything you want to grow – carrots, for example – so that they don't end up in the shallow lettuce box after a while! All the crops are going to rotate round, round, round, after all.

Year One
During year one, you should grow leguminous or green manure plants which will enrich the soil with the help of nitrogen-fixing bacteria. They don't need any extra fertiliser when you plant them, but you can boost their growth by giving them a little starter kick (a handful of chicken manure, liquid fertiliser or grass cuttings, for example) if the soil is particularly nutrient-poor. And compost is always good! Once the peas and beans have been harvested, dig the plant remains into the soil. This will benefit the structure of the soil and add a further nutrient boost.

Year Two
Now is the time for a real dose of fertiliser – we'd suggest farmyard manure – and for planting the most demanding and hungry of your crops. You can top up nutrient levels with liquid fertiliser or add grass cuttings between the rows during the growing season.

GROWING IN TURN
It's common to divide your growing space into several areas (we'll say four for simplicity's sake), meaning you can grow all of the different plants in the same year. Then you just rotate the crops between these areas, possibly going clockwise.

Year Four
The last year is when you grow those plants with low nutritional needs. A quick starter dose in spring is usually enough, we would suggest chicken manure. Good crops to grow during this stage are potatoes and artichokes. Growing beans between the rows is also a good idea, and broad beans are particularly suitable. They will fix nitrogen from the air and seem to have a 'generally favourable influence' on their bedmates. After this year is over, it's just a matter of starting over from square one – with your leguminous plants.

Year Three
Now that you're into the third year, it's time for those plants with lower nutritional needs, like root vegetables, onions and leafy plants. Dig in a little fertiliser well before sowing/planting, but only a little. Farmyard manure is good. Both onions and root vegetables can develop an unpleasant taste from growing in freshly or over-fertilised soil.

CRYSTAL PALACES

Having a greenhouse is a symbol of happiness to many growers, the ultimate level of garden joy, the crowning glory and true focal point of the garden. Maybe it's just the thought of cosy coffee breaks beneath the grapevines. Or perhaps it's the lengthened growing season that's most appealing? Either way, growing in greenhouses requires a lot of nutrients, not least nitrogen.

A greenhouse means that you can sow seeds earlier in spring and plant out your shoots as soon as the temperature rises slightly, giving you a great head start on the season. Whatever you grow during summer will have time to mature before the first frosts arrive, and you can continue to harvest longer into autumn. Then, when the winter chill descends, you can overwinter your most difficult and delicate plants.

But written in huge letters on the flip side of the greenhouse coin are the words: MORE OF EVERYTHING. Growing in greenhouses means more maintenance, more water, more fertiliser, more of pretty much everything. But doing so also gives more in return!

The greenhouse environment means different living conditions than if your plants were growing outdoors. Indoors, it's even more important to offer good soil and maintain a healthy balance of nutrients. Many common problems, fungus and pest infections, for example, come from the soil itself. Good ventilation and a healthy temperature are two more key conditions.

A CRASH COURSE IN GREENHOUSE GROWING

Greenhouses tend to come in two main varieties: heated and unheated. The most common in hobby gardening is the unheated kind. A heated greenhouse needs insulation with double glazing and a heat source. Even simple greenhouses can be insulated, fully or partly, using bubblewrap or heated with a portable fan heater, for example, to keep the space frost-free or a little warmer. What's best for you will depend on how you want to use your greenhouse.

You can choose between growing in soil beds or pots, or a mix of the two. The advantage of soil beds is that the roots of your plants will grow deeper and the soil will hold both water and nutrients better. The limited volume of pots means that that type of growing is more demanding, but since the soil in greenhouses needs to be changed often, ideally every year – because of disease and pests (which will affect almost all greenhouses sooner or later) – growing in pots is perhaps a little more convenient.

Other important factors for healthy plants and impressive harvests are good ventilation, good watering systems, enough space and plenty of nutrients. If the greenhouse becomes scalding hot in high summer, you may need to dampen the sun's rays with a lime-based whitewash on the glass. Make sure you deal with pests in time, too.

Don't use chemical pesticides in the greenhouse if you're growing edible plants. They aren't especially appetising. You'll achieve better nutrient levels and create a happier environment by encouraging the pests' natural enemies, their biological competitors,

than you will using chemical solutions that kill the whole lot – good and bad. If your local garden centre doesn't stock (or can't order in) nematodes, you can find beneficial living organisms online. Just search 'biological control'.

Some of the plants which are particularly suited to growing in greenhouses are cucumbers, tomatoes, chillies, peppers, basil, grapes and melons. Those plants and vegetables which do well and mature on time outdoors will grow better there. Carrots, onions, berries and strawberries will all thrive best when left in the garden. Not that growing a box of potatoes in the greenhouse in time for a midsummer feast will do any harm, of course. But otherwise, root vegetables are best left outdoors.

A NUTRIENT-HUNGRY GROWING ENVIRONMENT

Regardless of whether you do your growing in a heated or unheated greenhouse, in soil beds or in pots, the soil will need to be well-fertilised in spring. Farmyard manure and compost are always good, but you can also supplement these with bone meal, horn meal, algae or chicken manure.

Afterwards, it's usually easiest to add top ups of liquid fertiliser, with the dosage tailored to whatever you're growing. Nettle feed, fresh manure or urine which has been thinned out with water until the colour is like a nice refreshing lager are all great sources of nutrients with high nitrogen content. Grass cuttings will also provide plenty of nitrogen. Of course, you can also buy ready-mixed bottles of plant feed from your local garden centre.

There are special watering systems for greenhouses which you can combine with liquid fertiliser to ensure equal application. You can even buy sticks, disks, granules, etc., all containing long-lasting nutrients, which you simply push down into the soil.

Many of the plants we tend to grow in greenhouses have large appetites. This condensed method of growing, where everything grows more quickly than it would outdoors, means more nutrients are needed.

Keep an eye on the general condition of your plants and check the colour of their leaves. If they begin to turn pale green, they may be lacking nitrogen. If the foliage is dark green and luxuriant, the nitrogen dose may be too high. This will lead to lots of leaves but fewer flowers and fruit. Over-fertilisation can lead to a more muted, or worse taste in whatever you are growing, so neither too little nor too much is any good.

MINI GREENHOUSE – COLD FRAMES

Using a cold frame is an alternative to an expensive, space-consuming greenhouse. These were more common in the past, and allowed people to start growing in early spring, even late winter, reaping earlier and bigger harvests from a small area of land.

A cold frame may consist of a wooden, concrete or stone frame, with a lid made from some kind of see-through material – often glass or plastic. It could also be a type of grow tunnel, where plastic or fibrous material is stretched over a series of hoops. The principle is similar to greenhouse growing, as the bed becomes a kind of forcing-house where the glass or plastic lets in warmth and light from the sun while also preventing moisture from evaporating.

Cold frames can also serve as additional space outside your greenhouse, or in your garden itself. You can sow or grow seedlings which will later be planted outside, or harvested directly. Fresh potatoes ahead of midsummer, for example!

It's also possible to use cold frames as a method for increasing the hardiness of your plants (gradually acclimatising them to outdoor temperatures before they are planted out in the cold for good), or for the over-wintering of sensitive plants in the soil (rosemary is one example) – so long as the frame is given a warming cover on the coldest of nights.

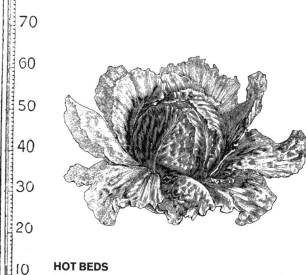

COLD FRAME

Fill the cold frame with soil and good quality fertiliser – decomposed farmyard manure, for example, ideally mixed with compost. It's a good idea to change the soil relatively frequently, perhaps every other year, in order to keep it light and healthy – just like you would in an ordinary greenhouse. You can then add the old earth to your compost heap, where it'll be given a new lease of life.

Once you've applied a good dose of fertiliser, that may well be enough for the season. It depends on what you are growing, and for how long. If you continue using the frame to grow over the summer, you will need to top up fertiliser levels – using diluted urine, nettle feed or some other liquid fertiliser, for example.

The temperature of the soil needs to be at least 12°C (54°F) for sowing. Use a thermometer. Once you have sowed or planted, you will need to keep an eye on the air temperature, the ventilation and watering.

HOT BEDS

What distinguishes a hot bed from a cold frame is the addition of warmth – more than the sun would provide to a cold frame. This heat can come from electric heating elements in the ground or similar, but the classic method is to line the soil bed with decomposing fertiliser. Horse dung with a little straw is best. Since cow manure decomposes more slowly, it won't provide the same level of warmth.

In other words, you make use of the warmth given off once the decomposition process has begun. Anyone who has spent cold winters wearing rubber boots in a stable will know the best place to warm their feet: in the manure heap, of course. At its warmest, the temperature will reach 50–60°C (120–140°F), which is far too hot for growing (but perfect for frozen tootsies). After a few weeks, the temperature will fall to a more suitable 20–30°C (70–90°F) and by then, the nutrient levels from the horse manure will also be better for sowing.

By using a hot bed, you can have fresh lettuce in the dead of winter! Cucumbers, tomatoes, melons and squash are all varieties which tend to thrive a little later during the season.

PLANTS

*On different plants' needs and cravings. Even if their
basic need for nourishment is the same, their wishes
might vary, and that can be the crucial difference!*

MAGIC CARPETS

The lawn is the pride and joy of many home owners, the jewel of their plot of land. Others view lawns with more of a bad conscience, perhaps as an unachievable dream. But one of the secrets hiding beneath that thick, green 'deep-pile carpet' is fertiliser. Lawns have a real sweet tooth. Meadows, on the other hand, those species-rich floral carpets, have the exact opposite needs. The poorer and more miserable the nutrient levels, the more beautiful they become.

For some reason, tending to grass is often seen as a manly activity, a bit like barbecuing. But in fact, nothing about it requires enormous muscles. It's true that a good deal of work goes into the perfect golfing green, but meadows require only the smallest amount of effort once they're established – and only then.

BREAKFAST–LUNCH–DINNER

When the grass starts to grow in spring, it wants a good dose of nutrients – something like chicken manure or calcified seaweed, which is a great all-round grass fertiliser. Calcified seaweed also contains calcium, which raises the pH level, meaning that moss will find it hard to establish itself. For 100 square metres (120 square yards), 2–3 kg (4½–6½ lb) will be enough if you use a specialist lawn feed or organic fertiliser. And remember: always read the packaging if you buy ready-made fertiliser!

Take care that the fertiliser doesn't cause burns in the strong spring sunshine. To avoid this, a good tip is to add the fertiliser while it's raining. The rain water will help to rapidly transport the nutrients to the roots. Spread a thin, even layer across the surface of your lawn.

The first spring dose will act like a vitamin booster shot for your lawn. The grass needs nutrients to develop strong roots, to out-compete any moss, stop weeds from establishing themselves, and to build up

a resistance to the summer's wear and tear and dry period. Your lawn will appreciate one or two smaller applications of fertiliser later that summer. Grass experts often talk about 'breakfast–lunch–dinner' when it comes to lawns. A golfing green will need a lot of nitrogen during summer.

You can also add fertiliser during autumn, though this isn't always necessary. Avoid using nitrogen-rich fertiliser if you do, even during late summer. The phosphorous and potassium found in substances such as wood ash are, however, both good in helping the lawn to survive winter. You can add a thin dusting of the ash – something like the icing sugar on a sweet bun – at any time of year.

AVOID CHEMICALS
Nature lovers try not to use moss and weed killers or chemical lawn feeds. These preparations aren't good for the microfauna and, instead, spread chemicals and poisons across your garden. That's where children are meant to run barefoot, where animals exercise their soft paws! You can get rid of moss using fertiliser, and dig up any dandelions by hand. A bit more work, better results – from all points of view.

1

LAWN BOOST

Leave some of the cut grass behind when you mow the lawn during summer – this will enable the lawn to develop its own natural cycle. The grass cuttings will function as nitrogen-rich green fertiliser. Just don't leave a thick layer or clumps here and there, as this can lead to yellow patches.

You can also top dress your lawn in autumn by allowing some of the leaves which fall to remain on the grass and then going over them with the lawn mower. Many modern lawn mowers have a function called 'mulcher' or 'mulching'. Make use of it! These leaf clippings are delicious to the worms and insects in the soil, and they will drag them below ground. You won't get many nutrients from carbon-rich material like leaves, but the structure of the soil will be improved.

2

LAWN BOOST

Mix one third compost (a leaf compost, for example), one third well-decomposed farmyard manure and one third sand with a few optional handfuls of chicken manure. This will act as a top dressing that will both fertilise your lawn and improve the structure of the soil. Spread it as evenly as you can, raking or brushing it into the lawn. You can buy ready-made top dressing in bags or sacks, but making it yourself will always be cheaper.

The best time to top dress is early spring when the grass starts to grow. Remember that adding a top dressing in spring should be done instead of a spring application of fertiliser – making sure your lawn doesn't die of an overdose! It's enough to top dress your lawn every third year. You can do it in autumn, too, but without any fertiliser.

'On midsummer night
you pick clover
and timothy,
devil's nettle
and cotton sedge,
shy forget-me-nots,
bluebells and violets'

Swedish tradition

FAIR, FRUGAL FLOWER MEADOW

The meadow is the polar opposite of the lawn. A blooming meadow shouldn't be cut – and it definitely shouldn't be given fertiliser. Nor should it be limed or even watered. The poorer the soil, the better. Perfect, you might be thinking, just my cup of tea; you can see yourself lying back among the meadow flowers, listening to the buzz of bees, can't you?

An established meadow requires minimum maintenance but . . . there's always a but. Starting a new, traditional meadow back home in your garden isn't something you can do in a hurry. A diverse flower meadow, somewhere that winter food for animals has grown for generations, takes time to create. It's a place where the soil hasn't been worked or fertilised for a long, long time. But, with that said, it is absolutely possibly to create something similar to our dream summer meadow. In the long run, the effort needed will be very minimal.

A SLIMMING REGIME FOR MEADOW PLANTING

If the soil is too rich and full of nutrients, establishing a meadow will be difficult. One method is to dig away most of the topsoil (the upper layer), down to the subsoil (the greyish, unworked mineral layer). Mix the topsoil with the subsoil or add poor, sand-mixed soil. Afterwards, you can either sow or roll out some pregrown meadow turf. Search online if you're interested in this kind of meadow-roll. You can buy them with different meadow flowers.

It's also possible to take nutrients from the soil by growing potatoes there for a year. If the soil you sow in is too nutrient-rich, grasses will take over, meaning that the herbs and flowers are drowned out. Not recommended.

MEADOW MOWING

The established meadow should be cut back in late summer once the majority of flowers and herbs have finished blooming and gone to seed.

Meadows should ideally be cut with a scythe rather than a strimmer or brush cutter, so that the stems are cut straight rather than broken. You can find smaller tools or traditional scythes in shops. To begin with, using a scythe can feel tricky, but you'll quickly pick it up. Cutting at 6–8 cm (2½–3¼in) is good.

Once the meadow has been cut, leave the hay to lie for a few days, setting seed. You can help this process along by rummaging about in it. It's important to then take away all the cuttings (put them into your compost bin) so that they don't decompose and fertilise the soil. Fertiliser benefits grass (and weeds!) which will result in your meadow flowers eventually disappearing. The most important thing is to ensure low levels of nitrogen and phosphorous.

MEADOW HAPPINESS

Being able to pick huge bunches of meadow flowers at home in your own garden is a genuine joy – cowslip, saxifrage, cats foot and violas. And seeing butterflies, honey bees and bumble bees happily buzzing around. Maybe you could establish a meadow in one part of your plot of land or garden? Meadows don't have to be so big, after all.

FRAMEWORK

Trees, bushes and hedgerows are the very skeleton of a garden. They can be modest and mundane or unusual and exotic. Regardless of which, they're the backbone which carries everything else, which create a sense of space and protect us from peeping eyes and winds. They hide, emphasise and give structure.

There's no clear cut line distinguishing a tree from a bush. Certain species can grow as both bushes and trees, depending on the variety and where they're growing. Some bushes can grow very tall, others can be shaped to grow like trees. But what all trees do have in common is that they are ligneous (woody) and have harder trunks – though even bushes can have lignified trunks. 'Ligneous' means that they have a coarser and harder structure of cellulose and lignin.

The differences between trees and bushes play less of a roll when it comes to fertiliser. Here, it's more a case of addressing the particular plant's needs and age.

FERTILISER ADVICE

Large, mature trees and bushes will rarely need fertiliser. Those going through a pronounced growth period – the newly planted, for example – will need more nourishment, just like those which are blooming or fruit-setting. Plants which are subjected to intense shearing or cutting, such as hedgerows, may also need more nutrients to be able to continue growing.

Deciduous and evergreen trees and bushes have slightly different growing cycles – growth phases when they need their nutrients. As a result, they can be given fertiliser at different times of year. Deciduous species will generally need their main meal in mid-spring, followed by a smaller snack in early summer. Organic fertilisers like farmyard manure need to be processed by the macrofauna of the soil for the nutrients to be accessible by the plants, and since this takes a few weeks, it's a good idea to apply fertiliser before the growth period gets underway. Read more about how to fertilise evergreens on page 170.

A very general recommendation for the amount of fertiliser: count on using around 5 litres (9 pints) of composted farmyard manure and a small handful of bone meal per large tree, and half of that for a large bush. Compost is always beneficial and it's difficult to overdose on that (kitchen compost is, however, more nutrient-rich than general garden compost). If you're planning to add fertiliser on more than one occasion during the season, you should split the total amount into two smaller portions. Covering the ground beneath trees and bushes with grass cuttings will add a shot of nitrogen to the soil and can help to drag down the remaining fertiliser. If digging in the fertiliser is difficult for some reason, then fertilising the root zone can be a good alternative (see page 145).

BEHIND THE HEDGEROWS

A newly planted hedge will need supplementary nutrients during its first few years, ideally split up into a number of applications. Add fertiliser in spring, before any new leaves appear, around midsummer and possibly again in early autumn (though not using nitrogen fertiliser). Check whether the type of hedge you have has any particular needs. A developing hedge can be given an all-round fertiliser in spring, farmyard manure for example, and this should be dug into the soil. Count on using 100–200 ml (3½–6¾ fl oz) per running metre (yard) of hedge. A trimmed hedge will benefit from an additional dose around midsummer.

Once the hedge has grown to the right height and only needs to be trimmed, its need for nutrients will no longer be as great. Rake in some leaves beneath the hedge during autumn; this will protect and increase the humus level of the soil.

PLANTING TREES AND BUSHES

The best time to plant trees and bushes is spring or autumn, when the ground is damp. You can also plant container-grown plants during summer, it's just a case of being extra careful with the watering. Dig a good hole, at least twice as wide and deep as the pot the plant is growing in. The majority will want to end up at the same height as they are in the pot. Planting at the wrong height is a common mistake that many people make. Just double check what your plant likes.

Mix the existing soil with compost, composted bark and long-lasting fertiliser (such as farmyard manure or bone meal). Wait a few weeks to fertilise berry bushes after replanting.

MULTICULTURAL GARDEN

In the Visby Botanic Garden, or 'Botan', as it's known locally, there are a number of unusual plants, not least trees and bushes. Some are real rarities. From its sheltered location behind the city walls and the curtain of trees shielding it from the sea, the garden has a microclimate which seems more Mediterranean than Scandinavian. As a result, giant redwood, dawn redwood, Lebanese cedar, empress trees and various handkerchief trees thrive on the island in the Baltic. Even mulberries, magnolia and figs feel at home in the gardens.

Lasse Pettersson, head gardener at Botan, argues that trees and bushes have roughly the same basic needs when it comes to fertiliser, even the more exotic species, but that certain varieties may need a special diet. At Botan, they therefore attempt to satisfy each individual plant's particular wishes.

In addition to the hardy and less hardy trees and bushes, you can also distinguish between deciduous and evergreens, as well as between those which avoid lime and those which don't. That alone will give plenty of clues about a plant's demands for soil type and fertiliser.

The gardeners at Botan use natural fertilisers, primarily cow manure, as their main source of nutrients, and they occasionally add different micronutrients to certain plants. Roses, for example, can sometimes have trouble absorbing iron and manganese during spring, and the gardeners give them a little extra to counteract that. In summer, top-up fertiliser is added to the more nutrient-hungry plants, and in late summer those which find over-wintering tough are given a boost of phosphorous and potassium.

FERTILISER – SHORT AND SWEET

Count on using around 5 litres (9 pints) of farmyard manure and a small handful of bone meal per large tree, half that for a large bush.

Use 100–200ml (3½–6¾ fl oz) of farmyard manure per running metre (yard) of hedge.

Compost is always good!

Supplement with bone meal, calcified seaweed and wood ash, for example.

Portion out the application of fertiliser in suitable doses, on several occasions.

SWEET AND SOUR

Evergreens like yew and rhododendron are in their element during winter, when everything else is flowerless, leafless and bare. They can be proud solitary beings or a neutral backdrop. Coniferous plants aren't always acid-loving, but their needles do lower the pH of the soil as they break down. Neither conifers nor acid-lovers are particularly greedy when it comes to nourishment.

Like all other plants, both conifers and acid-lovers do, of course, need nourishment – macro and micronutrients, in other words. But their appetites are slightly smaller, and they can have special demands of their environment, such as the acidity level of the soil.

ACID-LOVING PLANTS

Acid-loving plants need a lower pH level (usually between 5 and 6) in the soil to be able to absorb nutrients from it. Some are very sensitive to the acidity level, but the majority are pretty tolerant and can cope in slightly more alkaline soils.

It isn't always the case that an entire plant group within a particular genus is made up of acid-lovers – just take magnolias. There are certain magnolias which want nothing more than an acidic soil, and others which will only thrive at a higher pH. Lilies are another example. Just check what's what when planting something new.

A high pH level in the soil will block an acid-loving plant's ability to absorb iron and manganese, which will lead to signs of deficiency such as yellow mottled leaves. The plants will turn pale. This can be remedied by mixing the soil with natural peat (unfertilised and unlimed) or with an acidifying substance – aluminium or iron sulphate, for example, which are sometimes used in agriculture (though tricky to find in smaller amounts).

Typical acid-loving plants are rhododendrons and azaleas, hydrangea, heather and Japanese maples. This list could, of course, be much longer, and contain everything from perennials, climbing plants, grasses and ferns, to deciduous and evergreen bushes and trees, and berry bushes like northern high bush blueberries.

FERTILISER FOR ACID-LOVERS

Beware of fertilising acid-loving plants with lime, because this will raise the pH of the soil. Avoid limed peat, bone meal, horn meal and calcified seaweed. Even ordinary cow manure contains calcium, but the amount is so small that it won't have much of an impact on the pH of the soil. If you applied fertiliser at planting, using half a bag of cow manure per square metre (yard), for example, then the nutrients will last at least one year. After that, you can dig in 5–10 litres (9–18 pints) of cow manure and composted bark every other spring.

Special fertilisers for acid-loving plants are available, but that might seem unnecessary and expensive. Any fertilisers containing ammonium nitrate or ammonium sulphate (which contain nitrogen and sulphur) will make the soil more acidic.

A great calcium source for plants such as rhododendrons is gypsum – calcium sulphate. It won't raise the pH level, but it provides the nutrient calcium.

BEDS FOR RHODODENDRONS AND AZALEAS

Rhododendrons and azaleas do best if planted in a location shielded from the wind. Azaleas like more sun than rhododendrons, often gaining their beautiful autumn colours as a result. The soil should be well-drained, light and humus-rich. Both plants have fine, shallow roots which are susceptible to drying out and, as a result, watering is particularly important.

Dig a good sized hole, at least 50 cm (20 in) deep and ideally twice as wide, and mix the existing soil with equal parts composted cow manure, composted bark and natural peat, or alternatively with ready-mixed rhododendron compost from a bag – half existing soil, half new, as above. Moisten the peat well before adding it to the mix. The bed can also be raised. If it sinks down, fill with rhododendron compost or some other organic material, composted bark for example. Rake in leaves beneath the bush during autumn, or use leaf compost.

NOTHING BUT NEEDLES

The conifers are a large woody plant group consisting of a number of families and roughly 650 varieties. All have needles rather than leaves, and the majority also have cones. Conifers aren't always prickly, some can actually be extremely smooth and soft – larch, for example, which drops its needles in late autumn but retains its sweet little cones for a long time afterwards.

HUNGRY FOR NEEDLES

Coniferous plants aren't all that hard to please once they are properly established. The Douglas fir prefers an acidic soil, but the majority of conifers are pretty tolerant when it comes to pH level. The soil should be on the lighter side, and ideally humus-rich. Heavy clay soils are full of nutrients, but they are also compact and difficult to grow in. Root systems will be smaller than normal, which can be devastating to a large tree. Like someone who is six feet tall having size two shoes. Unsteady, to say the least.

Improve the existing soil with composted bark, peat and compost before planting. Moisten the peat before you add it. Wait a few weeks before applying any fertiliser. After 2–3 weeks you can dig in a bucket (about 10 litres/18 pints) of cow manure for a smaller plant and a couple of these for a larger one.

Going forward, you can add roughly the same amount of cow manure and compost in late spring so that the conifer will have all the nutrients it needs for growth during early summer. If you're feeling particularly ambitious, you can add fertiliser during both spring and late summer, when conifers have their growth periods. Split the total amount of fertiliser into two portions (so as not to double it).

You can buy special fertilisers for conifers from garden centres. That said, using ordinary cow manure or some other type of fertiliser with organic origins will give equally good results. You'll also help to increase the humus content of the soil, which conifers like. Covering the soil beneath the tree or shrub with leaves is also a good idea. This will increase the humus content, reduce evaporation and stop weeds which use seeds to multiply from growing.

Yellow needles can be a sign of drought. Brown needles can be a sign of a magnesium (which is needed for chlorophyll production) deficiency. You can buy ready made magnesium mixes to spray onto the plant or add to the soil.

Conifers can be planted in both spring and autumn. The advantage of doing so in spring is that the plant will have time to take root and develop a more stable base ahead of winter. At the same time, planting in autumn requires less careful watering.

FERTILISER – SHORT AND SWEET

ACID-LOVING PLANTS: use cow manure as a base fertiliser and add composted bark during spring, roughly every other year. Take care with lime-rich fertilisers.

CONIFERS: fertilise with 5–10 litres (9–18 pints) of cow manure and compost roughly every other year.

The Christmas tree isn't the only one that drops its needles. All conifers lose their older needles in autumn. These will provide good ground cover, maintain moisture levels in the soil and eventually return to the plant as nutrients.

Dear bulbs, corms and tubers:
crocus, scilla, hyacinth,
daffodil,tulip, fritillary,
allium, and others.

A warm welcome to the
garden warming party!

This year, we've a phosphorous
and potassium buffet with
bone meal canapés.

Free bar with cooling meltwater
and gentle rainwater cocktails.

SPRING FEELING

Suddenly, they appear one sunny winter's day. Stubborn and defiant against the cold: winter aconite and snowdrops. So longed for, so very welcome! And not long after that, the first petals on the most energetic crocuses will emerge from the soil. Six months later, and autumn and Bieberstein's crocuses will bring the season to a close with a pretty but slightly sad farewell to summer.

There's nothing as rewarding as planting spring bulbs. The vast majority, along with any tubers you plant, will come up nicely as planned the next spring. Depending on the species you choose, where you plant them and what condition your soil is in, things may differ in coming years.

Generally, it's important not to do too much cleaning. The bulb or tuber itself is an ingenious source of food for the flower, but it will need topping up. Let stalks and tops wither away at their own speed, so that the nutrients can return to the bulb/tuber. That way, photosynthesis can do its job, generating new energy for the bulb. You can snip off the flower (unless you want it to re-sow itself, of course) – ideally before the seed head forms, saving nutrients in the bulb. If you add a little fertiliser, bone meal, for example, the bulb will be even more willing to provide you with flowers.

SOIL AND NUTRIENTS

The majority of bulb and tuber species like a well-drained soil rich in humus and nutrients. Some prefer sandy or gritty soil. Bulbs will rot in soil which is too damp, and heavy clay soils aren't ideal for either bulbs or tubers. The pH level should be roughly neutral, somewhere between 6.5 and 7.5.

When planting new bulbs, it's a good idea to apply bone meal. This is because it is a slow-release fertiliser. The same applies whether you're planting your spring bulbs in autumn or vice versa. Newly planted bulbs will also need watering. Bulbs and tubers don't require as much water later, but if you're experiencing a period of drought they'll always be grateful for a quick splash.

Opinions differ on when you should add fertiliser. Some argue that it's best to do after flowering and others claim that autumn is best, since that's when new roots are forming. Some even argue that fertiliser isn't necessary at all. With that said, the majority of those growing bulbs prefer to apply fertiliser in spring, sometimes giving a quick top up during autumn.

In spring, blood meal is a great product which will deter hares and deer while also providing nutrients to your bulbs (it does contain high levels of nitrogen, however, so make sure to add only a small dose). One downside is that the smell of blood – something that any uninvited freeloaders will detest – will vanish with the spring showers and need to be topped up. An alternative is to use bone meal. One or two tablespoons for a tulip-sized bulb. Take care to dig in the fertiliser well during early spring, before the first leaves appear. Add another dose during autumn if you like, to build up nutrient reserves ahead of winter.

Above all, bulbs need phosphorous and potassium. Nitrogen isn't of such great importance. Too much nitrogen can lead to dense foliage but no flowers. Phosphorous is needed for building new roots and bulbs, for flowering and fruit setting. Potassium is important for the transportation of nutrients and water, as well as for forming leaves. Both nutrients are found in fertilisers like wood ash or bone meal.

WHERE'D THE FLOWERS GO?

Sometimes, bulbs won't flower after a few years. This isn't always a sign of a nutrient deficiency. Over-enthusiastic tidying, specially bred hybrid varieties, a lack of sun, too much water and overcrowding can all be causes. If you want to be sure of flowers every year, then choose traditional varieties, don't go overboard when tidying up the garden, add fertiliser annually and spread out the bulbs if things are too cramped. The simplest method is to dig them up after they flower, tops and all, and split the parent and baby bulbs before replanting them.

SLIGHTLY WITHERED BUT HAPPY

Some think that withered leaves are untidy and ugly, others find a bit of decay beautiful. Bulbs will start to wither in different ways. Those which fade quickly are allium, dog's tooth violet, crocus, winter aconite and scilla, for example. Daffodils, tulips, autumn crocus and the majority of lilies have a more drawn-out process. Allow the leaves to remain until they're very yellow and dry – only then should you remove them. This will take around eight weeks. Especially important if you want bulbs in your lawn: don't cut them back with the lawnmower too early.

BELOVED SUMMER TUBERS

Dahlias like a sunny position in humus-rich and well-drained soil. Fertilise using farmyard manure in spring, a few weeks before you plant the tubers. Top-up a few times during summer, though not after August. Cut down the stalks and leaves when you dig up the easily damaged tubers in late autumn and store them somewhere dark, dry and cool.

FERTILISER – SHORT AND SWEET

1–2 tablespoons of bone meal per bulb (tulip-sized). Less for smaller bulbs.

Garden centre bulb mix will also work well.

Don't remove the leaves until they have withered back. Do snip off the seed head after flowering.

GREAT BULB TIPS

Hide your bulbs' withering leaves by planting them alongside late-blooming perennials such as day lilies, common lady's mantle, hosta, sage, catnip or decorative grasses, etc.

If you can't stand having withered leaves in your beds, you can use bulb baskets when planting, which you then simply dig up and place out of sight.

Plant the varieties deer and hare consider delicacies (i.e. crocuses and tulips) alongside deterrent bulbs (i.e. allium and fritillaries).

Plant snowdrops in spring. The dry bulbs you often see in garden centres in autumn often won't be up to scratch, and they also won't have time to take root ahead of winter. Snowdrops can be split after they flower in spring. Carefully divide the clumps right after they wither and replant straight away in a different spot. Don't forget the bone meal and water!

THE REGULARS

Having a few more long-lasting relationships can be soothing. It means you have time to polish the relationship, fix any small mistakes, account for any deficiencies, swap out one thing and supplement with something else. Mull over ideas and enjoy the results. Take good care of your perennials and look forward to a wonderful reunion in spring.

Perennials provide a stable base for the garden. The majority are faithful and will loyally come back every year – if given a little attention. Some like to play a bit more hard-to-get and will throw in the towel if they don't feel right.

Simply put, perennials are plants which (hopefully) survive winter and come back every year. They wither away in autumn (in fact, some perennials are evergreen and keep their leaves) and then start over with new shoots, leaves and flowers every year. Many of the flowering plants we tend to grow in our flower beds are perennials, but even grasses and ferns are included in this group, as are certain herbs and spices.

TILL DEATH DO US PART

No living thing is eternal, not even perennials. Their life span differs from species to species. To extend and increase their lifespans, many will benefit from being divided every third or fourth year. A general rule of thumb is that autumn blooms should be divided in spring, and spring blooms in autumn. By splitting them in this way, old plants can be given a new lease of life and can better fill a perennial bed.

There are certain perennials, peonies for example, which want to live their lives in peace, and won't appreciate being sliced in two. So check the recommendations for every single plant before you get the knife out.

FERTILISER – À LA CARTE

In one single flower bed, there will often be a number of different individuals. The majority of plants have similar needs when it comes to essential nutrients, but some may also have special demands. Roses are one such case, a picky and greedy friend which wants one or more extra portions. Certain herbs and spices have opposite needs, they prefer things dry and sparse. In such cases, compost or fertiliser can do more harm than good.

Generally, though, perennials have moderate demands for nourishment. Larger plants will want more nutrients than smaller ones, and if the soil is good then using one or possibly two types of fertiliser in combination will be enough: one slow-release and one fast-acting. Expensive shop-bought fertilisers are quite unnecessary.

Farmyard manure and kitchen compost are both long-lasting and contain a good overall balance of macro and micronutrients which will satisfy the majority of plants' needs. The nutrients are released at a steady rate, meaning the plants can absorb them as they need them, and the organic material also helps to build up the humus content of the soil. Perfect for the primary application of fertiliser in spring!

Dig in the nutrients superficially, so that they reach the plants' roots and won't evaporate into the atmosphere. If the fertiliser is left on the surface, the nitrogen can evaporate into the air as a gas, in ammonia form. Just be careful with the roots when you dig in the fertiliser – some may be fairly close to the surface.

Later, in early summer, you can top up the first dose of fertiliser with a fast-acting, nitrogen-rich

During summer, you can clear away any withered leaves and flowers to make things look a bit neater, but in autumn it's best to leave your perennials alone. In the past, people were advised to cut back their flowers once summer was over, but this meant that stalks and leaves acted almost like drainpipes and directed the autumn rain straight to their roots, which can be devastating. Stalks can also act as snow traps, which will help to provide an extra layer of protection against the winter chill. So: wait until early spring to neaten up your flower beds. Plus, there's little more beautiful than a frost-bitten flower bed under a winter sun.

Withered plants will bring both nutrients and humus to your soil. Rake any autumn leaves into your flower beds, they'll do good there. Particularly sensitive plants can be covered in pine needles or similar.

fertiliser – such as chicken manure. This should your plants more stable, helping to firm up their stalks and prevent them from flopping so easily. Mix the chicken manure with water, and you can simply water it in. Diluted urine and grass cuttings are also a great choice. Some prefer to add a little bone meal, which is extra long-lasting, later in autumn, at the same time as they divide certain perennials and plant new bulbs, or at the same time as the primary application in spring. Calcified seaweed contains many micronutrients as well as a good amount of calcium.

Try to vary the fertiliser you use, and don't apply the same dose of the same fertiliser every year. Keep an eye on your plants from day to day and see how they're doing. If they're looking pale and weak, they might need an extra nitrogen boost.

SEASON FINALE
Towards the end of summer, you shouldn't add any more top ups (this is slightly dependent on where you live, but as a general rule: not after midsummer). Perennials need time to go into dormancy ahead of winter, so that they can survive the cold and damp. Often, it's these damp conditions which cause the greatest problems – raised beds are particularly good for this reason.

ROSES, PEONIES AND CLEMATIS

PRIMA DONNAS

Delights like roses, peonies and clematis offer beauty, entertainment and joy in our gardens. Some of them have slightly higher nutritional needs than other plants. In a relatively short period of time, they need to charm and seduce the world around them with their scents and splendid blooms. That isn't to say that all of these garden artists are demanding divas. Many of them are much more shy.

As always, it's a case of carefully choosing the variety whenever you buy a new plant: the right type, in the right place, in the right soil. It's always easier to use the actual conditions you have as a starting point, rather than trying to change them; working *with* nature, rather than *against* it.

What roses, peonies and clematis have in common is that they want nutrient-rich, well-drained soils containing clay and a lot of humus. In other words, a rich and balanced diet is what's in order. The pH of the soil isn't of huge importance, but a relatively neutral level is still best – somewhere between 6 and 7. More important is to tend to your plants with care and attention, and to add fertiliser in the same way. Coddle your prima donnas. Stroke them, sing to them, pamper them.

There are a confusing number of tips on how to best take care of and fertilise these beauties. Below, we'll go through a handful, though these are far from the only truths.

ROSES

Roses are often split into three main groups: shrub, climbing and standard roses. The first two groups contain the wild varieties. Specially bred roses tend to need more nutrients than the wilder varieties, and larger bushes often require more than small. Remontant (repeat flowering) roses will need nutrients for a longer period – in other words, more nutrients overall, split into a number of portions. Climbing roses will also need a little more nourishment, but one large dose during spring will be enough for those which flower once, and two doses for repeat flowering varieties, split between spring and midsummer. Wild roses have a smaller appetite and will do fine without much fertiliser.

Giving exact dosages or measurements is impossible, because the amount your plants will need depends on the soil, location, variety and type of fertiliser (as well as the quality of the latter) you want to use. View the following as general advice and adapt it in line with your common sense and feeling.

DIET

Give your roses fertiliser twice a year, during early spring and again around midsummer. Add a little compost or well-composted cow or horse manure in spring, and supplement this with chicken manure. Around midsummer, once the main flowering period is over, you can repeat the process. Carefully dig the fertiliser into the soil and then water.

It's important not to add fertiliser too late during the summer, particularly not if the fertiliser you are using is nitrogen-rich. The roses need time to put on the brakes and lignify any growth ahead of winter, otherwise they will be susceptible to frost damage.

Many rose growers like to use Chrysan (see page 102) on repeat flowering varieties. They apply farmyard manure in spring, a small dose of Chrysan around midsummer, and perhaps one more a few weeks later. A pinch of wood ash will provide a potassium and calcium boost, among other things. Diluted urine can offer a good dose of nitrogen and potassium, as well as a range of trace elements.

If you are planting roses from scratch, the simplest thing to do is buy ready-prepared rose compost in a bag. The composition of this will also work well on both peonies and clematis. Mix this pre-prepared soil with the existing soil in your garden – roughly half and half. You can even add a little bone meal if you like. If you follow this process during spring, you won't need to add any more fertiliser for the remainder of the first year. If planting in autumn, add a dose of fertiliser next spring.

ROSE-WEARY SOIL

Once roses have been growing in the same spot for some time, the soil can become 'rose-weary' (often known as rose sickness). You will notice that your roses no longer seem to be thriving: growth to their roots and shoots will be poor and they'll look generally out of sorts. It's thought that a particular kind of nematode (a type of roundworm), the root-knot nematode, is to blame. The nematode destroys the plant's cells and causes sores on their roots, meaning that bacteria and fungi can run riot.

If you suspect your roses are suffering from this, the simplest solution is to replace the soil with new, fresh soil. Throw away the affected plants. A less drastic approach is to try to minimise the symptoms by planting marigolds around the roses. It's thought that marigolds secrete a substance which the nematodes dislike. Whether the aesthetic combination is a success or not is a different matter.

Try to build up your soil's resilience and prevent the problem by adding organic material and general nourishment. Farmyard manure is good – alternate between different types. Supplement this with top-up fertiliser such as grass cuttings during summer.

PEONIES

Just like roses, there are many different varieties of peony – all with slightly different requirements when it comes to the nutrients in your garden. As a rule, though, peonies are tolerant and long-lasting.

The wild, herbaceous peonies will generally survive in poorer soils. Common peony, fennel-leaved peony, *Paeonia anomala* subsp. *veitchii*, Wittmann's peony and Mollie-the-witch all belong to this wild group. They prefer well-drained soil, ideally in half shade. *Paeonia suffruticosa* are exotic beauties from China. They like well-drained soil and tend to be low maintenance once established.

Cultivated beauties such as *Paeonia × festiva*, hybrids and the Chinese peony will require more nutrients. They like deep, nutrient-rich soils. These can also be lime-rich and contain clay.

PEONY TREATS

Wild, herbaceous peonies can be fertilised with bone meal once flowering has finished, often around midsummer. Don't add the fertiliser too close to the root crown. *Paeonia suffruticosa* will also appreciate a little well-decomposed garden compost at any point during the season. Avoid nitrogen fertilisers during autumn.

When the tender buds of the cultivated peonies emerge from the soil in early spring, they are as delicate as newborn babies. As a result, farmyard manure can be a little too strong for them – particularly fresh manure, which can also contain fungus spores. Peonies can develop grey mould if their buds come into contact with farmyard manure. It's safer to use bone meal or calcified seaweed. If the peony receives too much fertiliser, it will be tall and leggy. The right amount of fertiliser means a well-balanced plant. Too much of the good stuff can also lead to increased foliage and decreased flowering. Scatter some wood ash around the plant a few times a year – roughly 100 ml (3½ fl oz), no more. Wood ash will also raise the pH level slightly.

Using fresh grass cuttings around peonies is good as a snack during summer. A few centimetres of cuttings in a ring around the peony will provide a good level of fertilisation and help to retain moisture. Re-apply a few times during summer. Just keep an eye out for snails.

CLEMATIS

These garden acrobats throw and wind themselves up towards the light. The clematis family consists of a few hundred pure varieties, and the hybrids number in the thousands – both large and small-flowered. And what's more, every year, new varieties appear! You can find types for all locations, but east or west facing spots tend to be best.

It is said that clematis should be planted 'head in the sun and feet in the shade', and read tips about planting low perennials in front of them to cast shadow on the lower parts of their stems. This is to retain the moisture in the soil, which the shadow of another plant can help with. Just remember that anything you plant alongside them will also drink water and use up nutrients.

SOIL AND NUTRIENTS

Clematis are often tolerant plants once they are established. They can cope in the majority of soils, even lime-poor ones, so long as they aren't too wet – or dry. That said, they do best in well-drained, humus and nutrient rich soils which retain moisture well. The pH level isn't so important. As a rule, a large-flowered clematis will require more nutrients and more water than its small-flowered counterparts.

Apply farmyard manure and compost in early spring. Large-flowered clematis will appreciate a top up during summer, enabling them to bloom bountifully and for an extended period. You can also add a little bone meal in autumn. Clematis with small flowers don't require as much fertiliser, so it isn't the end of the world if you forget for a year or so. Just don't over-fertilise or add too much fertiliser too late in the summer. An excess of nitrogen will lead to dense foliage and fewer flowers.

THE PANGS OF LOVE

When planting a new clematis, you should dig a hole which is at least 40 cm (16 in) deep and equally wide. Stand the plant in a bucket of water for a while, until the soil around it is saturated. Add farmyard manure and a little bone meal to the bottom of the hole (and, as always: protect the roots and stems from direct contact with the manure). Water and fill the hole around it with soil. Specialist rose soil out of a bag is good. Mix that with the existing soil. Alternatively, you can use one third clay soil, one third gravel or coarse sand, and one third peat.

Just as with roses, the plant should be placed deep in the hole, ideally with the main body of roots ten centimetres beneath the surface of the soil. This will enable it to develop a good root system. Cover with soil and water again. Then comes the most heart-rending moment: cut back the plant so that only 20-30 cm (8-12 in) are left. It's painful, but it'll be worth it in the long run. Next spring, you should top the new shoots above the first pair of leaves a few times, so that the clematis can better branch out.

FERTILISER – SHORT AND SWEET

Wild varieties generally survive with less fertiliser than cultivated types.

ROSES:
Fertilise in spring and top up during summer. Roses often prefer to have their nutrients split into several portions, particularly repeat flowering species. Use farmyard manure, compost and chicken manure, for example.

PEONIES:
Fertilise with bone meal, calcified seaweed or chicken manure during spring, or after flowering. A little wood ash every now and then will also do them good. As will a covering of grass cuttings during summer.

CLEMATIS:
Large-flowered clematis will need more nutrients than small-flowered varieties. Fertilise with farmyard manure and compost in spring. Top up large-flowered varieties in early summer. Supplement with a scoop of bone meal in autumn.

PICK AND MIX

Wild strawberry ice cream, strawberry jam, raspberry sorbet, apple sauce, plum compote, blueberry pie, gooseberry juice, redcurrant jelly . . . Just reading those words is enough to make your mouth water. There isn't much that can beat homemade – and from your own harvest! If anything, berries should be picked sweet, sun-warmed, straight from the bush or tree. Not that there's anything wrong with candied raspberries, but the best treats don't grow in the sweet shop.

It's easy to get into a spin during harvest. It's the time of year when everything should be put to use: flowers, seeds, leaves, fruit and berries. Invite people over for a Harvest Festival and get them to help out if there's more than you can manage yourself. Make jams, juices, dried fruit and sauce – throw anything you don't use into the freezer.

But this chapter is about the road leading to that point, about growing fruit and berries, and above all about fertilising them. Because the way you do it will have an impact on how good your harvest is, as well as how your jams and juices will taste.

APPLES AND PEACHES AND PLUMS, OH MY!

Choose reliable and resilient varieties for lower-maintenance growing if you are planting new berry bushes or fruit trees. Varieties that are resistant or have a high level of resilience to certain diseases are often available. It's impossible to protect against every problem that might affect your plants, but by choosing well, you will be making things easier and more fun for yourself going forward.

Another good idea is to choose different types of fruit tree – this will help with pollination. You can also buy so-called 'family trees' where several different cultivars are grafted onto one single tree. Good for small gardens! Just be extra careful with

the watering of your newly planted trees and bushes during the first year. And protect their trunks from wild animals such as hares, roe deer and mice, as well as any berries and fruit from thieving birds.

A PLACE IN THE SUN AND A GOOD SOIL

Virtually all berry bushes and fruit trees prefer a sunny location. Northern high bush blueberries, blackcurrants and raspberries can tolerate a little more shade. Blueberries like to grow in a more acidic soil (a pH of between 4 and 5), and raspberries also prefer a lower pH.

It's always good to keep the ground beneath bushes and trees clear, particularly during the first few years after planting, stopping any grass or weeds from growing there. Anything that does take root beneath them will steal both nutrients and water. Instead, cover the soil with some kind of material like straw or composted bark. Fresh grass cuttings can provide too much nitrogen, so use only sparingly.

As with all forms of growing, a good soil which can retain both oxygen and water is vital. It should be porous and humus-rich. Heavy clays are no good for fruit orchards. Soil can be improved using compost and farmyard manure (cow and horse) during spring.

BERRIES DON'T GROW ON TREES,
DO THEY?
Both currants and gooseberries
can be grown in pots like
small trees, even on a porch
or balcony. Good if you don't
have much space.

FERTILISER – POTASSIUM AND PHOSPHOROUS

Plants which bloom and produce fruit need phosphorous for good fruit setting, and potassium, which affects sugar levels (crucial for a good taste and better longevity). Nitrogen is also needed for growth, and this is particularly important for newly planted bushes or trees. But adding too much of the good stuff – nitrogen, in other words – can mean that the foliage increases to the detriment of fruit setting. Slow-release fertiliser with high levels of potassium and phosphorous is therefore perfect for fruit and berries.

Farmyard manure and compost are always good, but they aren't needed in large quantities. Bone meal and horn meal are great sources of both potassium and phosphorous. Wood ash is also good for berry bushes.

Micronutrients such as iron, manganese and boron, for example, are all more or less important for plants to be able to stay healthy and yield good fruit and berries. Normally, the small quantities needed by plants are found in the soil. Hobby gardeners will rarely need to apply these separately. Even farmyard manure contains these elements.

FRUIT TREES AND BERRY BUSHES

Big old fruit trees don't need much extra nourishment, but they will still be grateful for a little bone meal and compost in spring (assuming that the earth around their trunks is free from other plant growth, so that you're not just fertilising grass, for example). This will increase the humus content of the soil and provide nutrition which will be released slowly.

If you notice that your old fruit tree has suddenly stopped growing, you should add more fertiliser – it may be suffering from a nutrient deficiency. Read more about how to fertilise the root area inside the crown of the tree on page 145. Calcified seaweed and bone meal are both good for this. You can even add a circle liquid fertiliser around the root zone. Leave cow manure to soak in water in a bucket or bowl and then water down. Diluted urine and liquid chicken manure both contain high levels of nitrogen, making them less suitable for this task. The best method is to 'pre-water' the tree with plain water so that the liquid fertiliser can more easily reach deeper and closer to the tree's roots. Spreading fertiliser on the surface of the grass won't have much benefit for your tree and will actually encourage grass and weeds. The best time to apply fertiliser is before the buds open.

If planting a new fruit tree, you can improve the soil using compost, composted bark or peat and a couple of buckets of composted farmyard manure. Keep the area closest to the trunk, roughly 1 metre (yard) in diameter, free from grass and weeds for the first five years. You may want to add a layer of grass cuttings (but not too much) so that the tree can gain access to the nitrogen it needs for growth and for better holding fruit. Don't forget to add a stake for support and a barrier to protect the tree against animals.

Berry bushes don't need all that much nourishment, but they will benefit from the soil being humus-rich and able to retain moisture. Compost is excellent for this. Too much fertiliser can lead to smaller harvests and make the bushes more susceptible to disease. Add fertiliser during spring and early summer, rather than later during the year. Be very sparing with nitrogen-rich fertilisers.

FERTILISER – SHORT AND SWEET

Fruit and berries primarily need phosphorous and potassium. You'll find these in farmyard manure as well as in bone meal and horn meal.

Wood ash will also provide a good boost.

Be sparing with nitrogen-rich fertiliser.

Picked at Home

APPLES

Apple trees like humus-rich soil which isn't too damp. Thin out the unripe fruit (the apples-to-be) during spring. Do this a few weeks before the end of the blooming period. Apply compost, farmyard manure and a little bone meal in spring (if the ground is free from other growth).

Remember that nutrients are best absorbed by the finer roots further out, not by the thicker, inner roots closer to the stem. Fertilising the root zone can be done for all fruit trees (see page 145).

PEARS

Pear trees like soil rich in humus and nutrients. Thin out the unripe fruit during spring so that the remainder has the chance to grow and mature. Add compost, farmyard manure and bone meal if the ground beneath the tree is bare. A few litres of wood ash will also give a potassium boost. This applies to all fruit trees.

PLUMS

Plum trees grow best in deep, warm and nutrient-rich soil. Thin out the unripe fruit in spring. Apply fertiliser and improve the soil using compost, farmyard manure and bone meal during spring.

CHERRIES

Cherry trees like warm soil and a sunny location. Birds also find cherries delicious, so pick the fruit quickly once the berries ripen, or else protect them using a net or a scarecrow. Add fertiliser in the same way as for plums. Watch out for basal shoots (suckers).

RASPBERRIES

Raspberries like light, ideally slightly acidic soil, and will grow in sun or slight shade. In autumn, after harvest, cut back all canes which bore fruit. Those which didn't can be saved for next summer. Thin out to roughly ten canes per metre. In spring, you should cut back any long canes to around 170 cm (5½ ft) and tie them up – dig poles into the ground and string lines between them. Autumn-fruiting raspberries will provide berries on that year's canes and can be cut back after harvest in autumn.

Apply 2–3 litres (3½–5¼ pints) of farmyard manure per running metre in spring. Compost will always be beneficial too. A little wood ash and bone meal from time to time will top off their diet – just be sparing with the dose so that the pH level doesn't increase.

BLACKBERRIES

Blackberries have roughly the same requirements in terms of soil and fertiliser as raspberries, but they do prefer a slightly more lime-rich and well-drained soil.

Apply fertiliser in spring, as for raspberries. Train or tie up the plants against a sunny and warm wall. Blackberries produce fruit on the previous year's canes and should be cut back like raspberries.

CURRANTS

Currants prefer a humus-rich soil and sun or light shade. Cut back any damaged stems and carefully thin out the oldest during autumn, after harvest, so that the plant can get some air and the berries some sun. Blackcurrant bushes can be thinned out more aggressively than white and redcurrants (which will produce the most berries on older stems). Apply fertiliser sparingly – 2 litres (3½ pints) of farmyard manure every other year, for example. Add compost and wood ash every year.

GOOSEBERRIES

Gooseberries thrive in humus-rich, moisture-retaining soil, and will grow best in direct sunlight. Thin out carefully, taking away any older, damaged or low-lying shoots. Be sparing with the fertiliser. Compost and wood ash will be enough. Avoid nitrogen-rich fertiliser (it increases the risk of mildew).

STRAWBERRIES

Strawberries like humus and nutrient-rich soils and prefer to grow in sun or light shade. When planting new plants: add compost and fertilise with 2–3 litres (3½–5¼ pints) of farmyard manure and a handful of bone meal per square metre (yard) before you add the plants. The plants shouldn't be harvested during the first year. In years two and three, you can add fertiliser in autumn, after harvest, using the same amounts as above. After year four, the soil will need to rest. Buy new plants or grow new ones from the runners, and plant elsewhere.

SEA BUCKTHORN

Sea buckthorn will look after its nourishment itself, at least when it comes to nitrogen. Just like leguminous plants, sea buckthorn can fix nitrogen from the air. It's a beautiful grey-green shrub with extremely vitamin-rich (A and C) berries. Sea buckthorn prefers light, sandy soils and a sunny location, and is easy to grow and maintain. Both male and female plants are needed for fertilisation. Varieties named after the lovers 'Romeo' and 'Juliet' as well as 'Svenne' and 'Lotta' are the most common.

VEGETABLES

GROWN HERE

The garden's pantry might be the most fun part of all. Growing your own health and happiness in a garden, greenhouse or pot on your balcony. This is where you can really let loose with a variety of unusual species or different tastes – experiment, explore and learn. One year's misfortune is nothing but experience, and it might even lead to next year's success. As locally grown and fresh as it gets.

Growing your own vegetables is sheer pleasure and enjoyment. And possibly also the occasional drop of blood, a little sweat and maybe even some tears. Just like life itself, in other words. So if you've got space to grow – *just grow*! And if you're in the process of creating a new area in your garden – breaking new ground – remember how important proper watering is. A watering system will give you freedom and stop you feeling tied down by whatever you later grow. We don't always have friendly neighbours to step up and take over, after all.

Below, we'll give you some general advice for your vegetable patch. Read more on pages 199–227.

FERTILISER AND TIMING

It's common to add fertiliser to a vegetable patch only once a year, during spring, as the soil becomes ready after winter. In other words, when the soil becomes workable, when it 'runs off' rather than sticks to the spade. It's a difficult concept for the uninitiated, but clear as day for those in the know. Once you've felt a soil which is workable and one which isn't, you'll know exactly what we mean.

The time point for when the soil will be ready depends on the climate and the weather, and the timing for adding top up fertiliser to your vegetable patch isn't precise either. Try to consider your plants' nutritional needs, how quickly they grow and their possible maturation dates – in other words, the amount of time that the plants which will overwinter need before they go into dormancy. The nutrients

from the primary application of fertiliser will last roughly a month and then drop off.

PRIMARY APPLICATION OF FERTILISER – RULES OF THUMB FOR DOSAGE

The amount of fertiliser you should use depends on the type of soil you have, what you want to grow, and what kind of fertiliser you are using. One advantage of synthetic fertilisers is that you know the exact content, and the manufacturer can give precise advice on dosage. The nutrient content of natural fertilisers is more variable, so using them will always be more approximate and based on experience. To properly fertilise your vegetable patch, you can count on using the following rough amounts per square metre of cultivated soil:

- 3 kg (6½ lb) of composted farmyard manure (roughly 4–8 litres/7–14 pints depending on moisture content, or a similar number of good spadefuls)
- 2 kg (4½ lb) of compost (roughly 3–5 litres/5–9 pints)
- Possibly also a small amount of mineral-rich fertiliser like rock dust, calcified seaweed or bone meal.

Adjust the amount of fertiliser to your particular soil and what you plan to grow, and pay attention to the types of fertiliser you have used in the past. Remember that natural fertilisers tend to be long-lasting. Bone

meal can slowly release nutrients for three years, for example, and even farmyard manure will continue to provide nutrients over a number of years (see table on page 90). This means that you also need to bear any previous doses in mind. One last tip: variety is the spice of life. If you've used cow manure in the past, maybe you could try something else this year? Horse manure? More minerals? Perhaps a little algae and rock dust?

TOPPING UP

Generally, nitrogen is the most important nutrient when it comes to topping up fertiliser levels. The soil can't retain large amounts of nitrogen, and plants have a great need for the nutrient during growth periods. As a result, it's difficult to satisfy their needs completely during the primary application of fertiliser. Roughly one month after you first apply fertiliser, the more nutrient-hungry of your plants will need a top up. Different plants' needs do vary, but you can read more about this over the next few pages.

Topping up can be done with liquid fertilisers (see page 126) or perhaps using grass cuttings as mulch. Usually, these 'snacks' will need to be repeated. The dosage will depend on dilution, the condition of the soil and the type of plant. And, as always – don't add nitrogen too late in the growing season.

MIX YOUR OWN WONDER SOIL

You can mix the best planting soil all by yourself. The older generation of head gardeners always used to do so, sometimes following this wonder recipe – a well-nourished blend of all the goodies a plant can dream of.

5 litres (9 pints) of garden compost
5 litres (9 pints) of farmyard manure
2 litres (3½ pints) of garden soil
4 litres (7 pints) of composted peat
4 litres (7 pints) of sand
100 ml (3½ fl oz) of rock dust (or wood ash)
100 ml (3½ fl oz) of algae (or calcified seaweed)
200 ml (6¾ fl oz) of bone meal
200 ml (6¾ fl oz) of horn meal
200 ml (6¾ fl oz) of blood meal

Mix carefully and leave the soil to rest, ideally for a few months. We suggest mixing the soil during autumn, ahead of spring planting. Mix together and leave to lie (airy but covered, so that the nutrients don't leach away).

RIVALS OR COUPLES?

Certain plants will get on well together in your vegetable patch, others won't. This is to do, among other things, with pests and nutrient uptake. Some plants seem to counteract any harmful attacks on their neighbours, essentially collaborating with one another. Peas like growing close to carrots, cucumbers and mint, for example, but they don't seem to like growing alongside onions and potatoes.

A good source if you want to delve deeper into this subject is a book called *The Mix and Match Guide to Companion Planting* by Josie Jeffery.

LEGUMINOUS PLANTS – SUPER PEAS AND COOL BEANS

Wax beans, broad beans, green beans (haricots verts), runner beans, string beans. Mange tout (of which sugar snap is one variety), shelling peas and marrowfat peas (the ordinary 'green pea'). Peas and beans are leguminous plants belonging to the Leguminosae family. There are many wonderful varieties, some of which grow extremely high as well as lower bush varieties. These plants are easy and quick to grow and give plentiful harvests. Peas prefer cooler weather and tend to be ready for harvest in early summer. The more you pick, the more pods there will be. And they fertilise themselves!

Beans need more heat than peas, and they produce later harvests, often in mid-summer. Both are thirsty plants, however, and require large amounts of water. If you add a mulch to the ground, this will help retain moisture in the soil. Grow outdoors or in roomy pots or buckets. The soil doesn't need to be especially nutrient-rich but it should ideally be porous so that the roots can grow and spread out.

If you want to raise the plants yourself, it's a good idea to soak the seeds for a few hours before you sow them. It's important not to sow them before the soil has had a chance to warm up to 12–13°C (54–5°F), otherwise they might just wither away. Large seeds like these should be in several centimetres of soil to be able to grow. One option for an earlier harvest is to sow indoors or in a greenhouse, and plant them outside later.

INGENIOUSLY SELF-SUFFICIENT

Peas and beans are, like all plants in the leguminous family, nitrogen-fixing. This means that while they don't require much in the way of fertiliser, a little nitrogen can still encourage growth. The plants take nitrogen from the air using special ground bacteria by their roots, providing themselves with the nutrients they need in the process. They are also decent enough to leave a little nitrogen behind for any subsequent plants. This is why peas and beans should always be a part of any crop rotation plan (see page 152).

If your soil is nutrient-poor, you can dig in a little farmyard manure prior to sowing to help the plants get going. Like all plants, peas and beans also require potassium, phosphorous and other nutrients, not just nitrogen. Compost and a little wood ash are therefore good materials to dig into the soil as you prepare it ahead of sowing. Digging in plant remains in autumn, once the harvest is over, will also be beneficial. Doing so will provide an extra nutrient boost to the next year's plants.

If it's your first time growing beans or peas in a particular spot, you can check that the bacteria necessary for nitrogen fixing to function properly are present in the soil. Note that there are different types of bacteria culture for peas and beans. Look out for small knots on your leguminous plants' roots. If you find those and they are pink inside, everything is OK.

If you suspect your soil lacks the necessary bacteria (if your beans/peas are growing badly) and want to be on the safe side, ask your local garden centre if they can order in any products for inoculating your plants. Alternatively, you can dig up some soil from another spot where things seem to be fine and mix it into your own soil.

FERTILISER – SHORT AND SWEET

Apply a small amount of farmyard manure and some compost if the soil is nutrient-poor. A tiny amount of nitrogen will encourage growth.

Peas and beans need a lot of water. Mulching is therefore beneficial.

Dig plant remains into the soil after harvest.

CABBAGES AND ONIONS – STAPLES FROM THE VEGETABLE PATCH

Naturally, there are stars who shine among the unspectacular everyday essentials. Savoy and pointed cabbage are now served as delicacies in countless star restaurants, sometimes as the main ingredient. But common onion and ordinary cabbage are viewed more as wallflowers at a disco, necessary for the others to shine. They form a base, like almost all root vegetables, for the majority of dishes across the world. Hardly spectacular, but things would be so boring without them!

The problem is that not all onions and cabbages are the easiest of things to grow. Cabbages and leeks in particular have high nutritional demands and they are especially susceptible to pests. Choose simpler varieties like kale instead of white cabbage, or broccoli instead of cauliflower, at least, if you're not an experienced gardener. It's so easy to lose interest after a suffering a setback, particularly at the start of your growing career.

Many varieties are so beautiful in both shape and colour that their appearance alone is reason enough to grow them. Alongside some summer blooms, perhaps? Cavolo nero and English marigolds or golden marigolds? Take a look at Simon Irvine's fantastic work in the gardens of Läckö Castle if you're ever in the Lidköping area. So inspirational!

CABBAGE HEAD – NOT AS CRAZY AS IT MIGHT SOUND

Brassica could be the name of a cool jazz band or a great brass band. But in this book, *Brassica oleracea* refers to cabbage plants, which are just as good. Generally, growing cabbages calls for soil with a high pH, which can help to reduce the risk of clubroot (a real drag). Masses of fertiliser, too.

It's also important not to grow cabbages in the same location year after year – instead, you should rotate them and give the soil at least four years' break in between. In any crop rotation plan (read more on page 152), cabbage should be grown after leguminous plants. Peas and beans will *provide* nutrients, and cabbage will take them away. In other words: cabbages after leguminous plants. Leeks also like a lot of nutrition, but not quite as much as cabbages. That said, cabbages and leeks will grow very well alongside one another.

FERTILISER ADVICE FOR CABBAGES

There are many different types of cabbage: white cabbage, red cabbage, cavolo nero, kale, pointed cabbage, savoy cabbage, Brussels sprouts, broccoli, cauliflower. Oriental varieties like pak choi and mizuna are also types of cabbage, *Brassica rapa*. All are very good for you and full of vitamins, minerals and antioxidants. For that to be the case, they need nutrient-rich, well-drained soil – ideally containing some clay. All like to have a high pH level (over 7), steady moisture and plenty of nutrients.

Apply a good amount of farmyard manure and add bone meal, rock dust and/or calcified seaweed, which will provide minerals and increase the pH level. Cabbage is originally a coastal plant, just like asparagus, and as a result, both seaweed and algae are great as fertilisers.

Those varieties of cabbage which grow slowly – white cabbage, for example – will need a fertiliser top up during summer, using something like blood meal. If you cover the ground with organic material, this will help to retain moisture. Certain varieties such as cauliflower can turn limp and tasteless if given too much nitrogen, so avoid using diluted urine, chicken manure or fresh grass cuttings.

The cabbage family is big and diverse – read up on each variety, because growing advice can vary between types. Another tip when it comes to fertiliser is to powder the leaves with wood ash or lime to make them less attractive to cabbage fly and cabbage white moths. Wood ash on the soil will also prevent flea beetles.

ONIONS – THE NAVEL OF THE KITCHEN

Just like cabbage, the onion has made the leap from wild to cultivated plant, and has been an important base vegetable in Scandinavia since the Middle Ages – as a food, flavouring and medicine. The common onion belongs to the *Allium* genus. Chives, garlic, yellow and red onions, shallots, pickling onions, leeks, salad onions and Chinese chives are all related to one another.

Ordinary cooking onions aren't particularly difficult to grow, it's drying and storing the onions once harvested which are the most common source of problems. As well as weeds taking over. Onions have shallow roots, so take care when de-weeding, and make sure the spot you have picked out is completely free of weeds before planting! You can either sow seeds or plant onion sets, the latter being more common. That said, many believe that seed-sown onions are better and healthier than those grown from sets. If you choose to use seeds, sow these indoors before planting out later. Onions are usually planted in late spring.

Avoid growing onions too close to peas or beans, as they aren't good bedfellows. Otherwise, onions will grow well alongside many other plants, cabbage being one of them. Rotate the spot chosen for growing so that at least four years pass between uses. Leeks, chives and salad onions can be grown in the same spot for longer.

FEEL-GOOD FACTORS FOR ONIONS

Onions will thrive in sunny, warm, airy locations, in humus-rich and light soil, ideally containing sand. They can cope with slight drought and don't need too much in the way of nourishment (leeks and salad onions excluded).

Over-fertilisation won't lead to good results, and as a result preparing the soil as early as autumn can be a good idea. Dig in a mix of compost and farmyard manure. In spring, before you plant your onions, you can add a little calcified seaweed or rock dust. Onions need potassium above all else, and too much nitrogen will lead to thicker necks, smaller onions and shorter longevity. You can sprinkle wood ash or rock dust onto the ground in summer, or spritz the leaves with nettle feed a few times over the season – this will provide nutrients and can help to keep onion flies at bay.

Leeks and salad onions require more nutrients than any other edible onions – above all potassium and nitrogen. This means they need more fertiliser during spring and top ups during summer, using something like blood meal. Green manures such as grass cuttings will also provide nutrients. The pH of the soil can be a little higher, so calcium-rich fertilisers like bone meal and calcified seaweed are both good additions.

Mix compost into the soil when you plant garlic in the autumn, and cover the soil with straw or leaves. During spring, you can then dig in bone meal and calcified seaweed. Water if it gets very dry.

FERTILISER – SHORT AND SWEET

CABBAGE:
Fertilise using farmyard manure, compost, bone meal and/or calcified seaweed in spring.

Top up the more nutrient-hungry plants with liquid fertiliser.

Powder the leaves with wood ash.

ONIONS:
Fertilise as early as autumn using farmyard manure and compost.

Add calcified seaweed and/or rock dust in spring.

Powder the soil with wood ash/rock dust.

Spray nettle feed onto the leaves.

Top up using liquid fertiliser during early summer.

Leeks and salad onions need extra nitrogen – fresh grass cuttings are good.

FERTILISER SEASONING
The taste of lettuce depends on how the plants have been fertilised. Too much nitrogen can increase levels of nitrates and result in a bitter taste. The leaves may look delicious, lush and green, but they will taste awful. Too little nitrogen will produce underdeveloped, pale or light green leaves.

Both too much and too little fertiliser can also lead to the plant blooming (bolting), which also affects the taste.

LEAVES, BUDS AND STALKS – MIXED SALAD

The vegetable patch isn't just a place for growing food. It can easily be the most beautiful part of the garden, where colours, heights and shapes vary from year to year. New themes, new combinations, new tastes: practically good enough to devour with your eyes.

Many vegetables would look equally at home in the flowerbeds as they would in a vegetable patch. The artichoke is a cocky rock star in the majority of contexts. Easily grown chard can have huge textured leaves and thick, powerful stems in a number of colours: white, red, yellow or multicoloured. What more could you want? To eat them up, of course. Cut them down and toss them into a mixed salad.

LEAFY PLANTS – CLEAN SHEETS

Anyone can grow leaf vegetables, even someone living in a tiny inner-city studio flat. They will grow in pots or outdoors, and certain varieties can even be grown indoors during winter. In fact, there are a number of plants which are truly worth growing: 'ordinary' lettuce – *Lactuca sativa*, various species from the cichorium genus – *Cichorium* (frisée, endive, escarole, radicchio, etc.), and the Oriental leaf vegetables (of which the majority belong to the cabbage family). Then there is chard, spinach, goosefoot, nasturtium, purslane, rocket and many more.

Lettuce can grow as a head, where you harvest the all of the leaves in one go, or loose leaf, meaning you can pick off the leaves as you need them all summer long. Sometimes, these are called 'cut and come again' plants. Oak leaf lettuce, purslane and chard are all examples of this.

Some species will do best when sown indoors, but the majority can be sowed directly outdoors or in pots. Some plants can even be sown in stages, and can continue to be harvested until the verge of autumn – spinach for example.

Leaf vegetables can be grown as catch crops between rows of other plants in your vegetable patch. Just remember that these catch crops will also need nutrients and that you may need to top up fertiliser levels. Read up on every variety you want to grow!

COMMON DENOMINATOR

The majority of leaf vegetables are grown in roughly the same way. They like to be in sun or half-shade, in a humus-rich and well-drained soil, just like many other vegetables. On the whole, leaf vegetables have average needs in terms of nutrients, they have neither a big nor a small appetite when it comes to fertiliser. That said, they are sensitive and will react to the wrong dosage of both fertiliser and water. They want steady moisture, which means that mulches are suitable. Use grass or some other fresh cuttings, which will provide both nutrients (primarily nitrogen) and also help to reduce evaporation.

For the primary application of fertiliser in spring, compost and farmyard manure are good (yes – we know it's starting to get repetitive, but it's still as relevant here). To get an idea of how much fertiliser you should use, think about how quickly the plants will grow before harvest. If there's only a month between sowing and harvest and you've applied a good amount of fertiliser, the nutrients present will be enough. If you then sow again, or if you're growing 'cut and come again' plants, you can bank on needing to supplement these plants with fertiliser – topping up, in other words. This is even applicable to more slow-growing leafy vegetables.

The most important nutrient, and the one which will be used up most quickly, is nitrogen. This suggests that mulching with grass cuttings or using liquid fertiliser is appropriate. Diluted urine or liquid chicken manure are perhaps best avoided on leafy vegetables. It can be difficult to apply without getting any on the leaves.

GLOBE ARTICHOKES

So pretty – and so tasty! Globe artichokes aren't the easiest things to grow, but once the impressive-looking thistles start to emerge, all the effort will be worth it. The tasty flowers should be cut back when the buds start to open and the tips start to turn down. If you don't cut them down to eat, you'll get to enjoy a pretty little thistle bloom instead.

Globe artichokes like warmth and for their roots to be in deep humus and nutrient-rich soil. Give them a good dose of fertiliser with farmyard manure and compost in spring, followed by several top ups over the course of summer. Applying grass cuttings as mulch is a great alternative. If you choose a perennial, the plant should be covered up during winter.

ASPARAGUS

Asparagus is both fun and beautiful to have in your vegetable patch. A furrow or two of asparagus will grow into elegant metre-high rows. It takes a little time from planting to harvest (you can cautiously harvest after three years), but then it is fairly unassuming and easy to grow. And just like rhubarb, it's a perennial plant.

Asparagus has both male and female plants. The female plants produce pretty seeds, but the male plants will give more shoots.

The green shoots are what you harvest when they poke up from the soil during spring. By covering these shoots with soil, or ideally with sand, you can 'bleach' the asparagus, meaning you will later be able to harvest white asparagus. Different varieties are available for purchase, but the majority can be grown to produce both white and green asparagus.

Originally, asparagus was a coastal plant. As a result, it likes to grow in deep, light and sandy soils, in a sunny location. The soil should be nutrient-rich. Use compost, farmyard manure and calcified seaweed to fertilise. If adding new plants, you can fertilise the soil as early as the autumn before (though if doing so, wait to add the calcified until spring).

Cover the ground with grass cuttings or some other organic material. The very best is seaweed and seagrass, if you have access to them. Just remember the risk of cadmium (read more about this on page 118). That amount of fertiliser should be enough, but if you notice that the asparagus isn't growing well, you can add liquid fertiliser during summer – ideally nettle feed.

RHUBARB

A summer flavour to crave. To ensure your rhubarb is really tasty, you need to both fertilise and water it, above all when planting and during the following year. It likes to grow in a moisture-retaining, humus-rich soil, and should be well-fertilised with farmyard manure in spring. Mulching with grass cuttings is also good.

FERTILISER – SHORT AND SWEET

Apply farmyard manure and compost in spring.

Mulching – with grass cuttings, for example – is good.

The coastal plant asparagus is particularly keen on seaweed.

Add top up fertiliser during early summer (avoid diluted urine on leafy vegetables).

Cutting back the beautiful blooms (they can grow up to 2 m/6½ ft tall!) if the rhubarb is left to flower is truly painful, so if you don't plan to harvest any more, perhaps you can leave it to flower? Otherwise, cut back the stalks early.

The method of growing is all that
distinguishes green from white
asparagus. The plant is the same.

ROOT VEGETABLES AND POTATOES – HIDDEN BENEATH THE SOIL

What would Swedish home cooking be without root vegetables? Like an Italian country kitchen without pasta. Completely inconceivable, in other words. Root vegetables have been important base ingredients for hundreds of years, though more recently, they have been banished to the back of the earth cellar as different diets and advice have come and gone. But it's a real shame to send these delicacies to the corner. *Nobody puts Baby in the corner!*

Potatoes and root vegetables grow underground – obviously. They also grow above ground, but it's the sub-soil part we're really interested in, not the leaves. This means you should be careful about using too much nitrogen fertiliser, because it will lead to increased foliage and smaller roots. Over-fertilisation with nitrogen can also have an impact on taste. Phosphorous and potassium are most important for the roots. In fact, root vegetables aren't particularly nutrient-hungry, but they do still need to be fertilised, albeit in smaller amounts.

DEEP-SOIL DIVING

Since root vegetables' roots develop downwards in the soil, you need a deep, loose soil. Yes, radishes can survive in shallow soil, but carrots and black salsify need deep soil for their long, fine roots to grow well. If the soil is too dense or compacted, the roots will have limited room for manoeuvre.

Gravel and stones can lead to 'misshapen' roots and tubers. That might well add to their charm, but it's still good to know. Root vegetables' roots are sensitive, so this is also applicable when you de-weed.

Earth up the soil as the root vegetables grow. This will produce better tubers and roots. Many types of potato and root vegetable can be harvested either as tender summer vegetables or as more robust autumn and winter vegetables.

POTATOES – RESPECTABLE TUBERS

The differences between the various types of potato can be *enormous*. There are considerably more varieties than just 'floury' or 'waxy', which will sometimes be your only options at the supermarket. The range has become slightly better in recent years, but the most tasty potatoes are, of course, still those you grow yourself – whether that's in a bucket on your balcony, in a grow bag, or outside in your vegetable patch. We Swedes eat, on average, 80 kg (175 lb) of potatoes per person per year. Only 2 per cent of commercially grown potatoes are organic. Yet another reason to grow your own.

Potatoes like to be positioned in a sunny location. The soil can be sandy but should also be humus-rich and moisture-retaining. Add plenty of fertiliser – farmyard manure and wood ash (which will provide extra potassium). In the past, it was common to use pig manure on potatoes, but it isn't always the easiest thing to get hold of.

Potatoes don't like to grow in lime-rich soils – as a result, you should avoid using calcium-rich fertilisers such as bone meal, rock dust or calcified seaweed. Too much lime can cause scab. Some growers lime their soil only after the potato crop has been harvested.

Potatoes are usually grown as the last step in a crop rotation plan (see page 152). It's important to change their location every year, ensuring that they aren't grown in the same patch of soil any more frequently than every fourth year. The risk of harmful nematodes, viruses and other things we want to avoid will be present otherwise. Potatoes which are harvested early run a smaller risk of being affected than later varieties.

JERUSALEM ARTICHOKES

The Jerusalem artichoke belongs to the same wider family as the sunflower, and can grow almost as tall. Not all varieties bloom, so choose 'Bianca' if you want 2 m (6½ ft) high plants with golden flowers in early autumn as well as delicious tubers beneath the surface!

Jerusalem artichokes are perennials and can easily become a weed. Take care to dig up every single tuber after harvest. Save a few to re-use for seed. It's best to swap the location every year, as with potatoes, otherwise the tasty little tubers will grow smaller with each year.

Jerusalem artichokes like to grow in sun, with humus-rich, light and deep soil. Fertilise using farmyard manure and compost in spring, and cover with grass cuttings or some other organic material (straw, for example).

These little treats grow best with steady levels of moisture. Topping up the fertiliser won't be necessary. If the artichokes are growing in a particularly windy area, you'll need to tie them up, but otherwise their stalks are rigid enough.

CARROTS

Carrots don't have to be elongated and orange with broad shoulders and narrow waists. They can be round, snub-nosed, purple, white or yellow. There are even different varieties for summer and autumn harvests. The plants are biennial. If you don't harvest them in the first year, they'll bloom with pretty lace-like white flowers the next.

Carrots like to be able to stretch out their roots and will grow best in a loose, humus-rich soil which should ideally be deep and mixed with sand. A good application of fertiliser – compost and farmyard manure – before sowing in spring will usually be enough. Phosphorous and potassium-rich fertilisers such as wood ash and rock dust can be added. Just take care not to add too much nitrogen,

because this can affect the taste of the carrots and cause them to split.

The sweet smell of carrots can attract pests such as carrot flies, aphids and carrot psyllid. A good trick is to confuse these pests with other strong smells – from onions, golden marigolds or English marigolds, for example. You can also try sprinkling wood ash or lime onto the leaves. Swap the growing location at least every other year to prevent pests from overwintering and becoming even more abundant.

If a carrot has a small green collar by the base of its leaves, it has grown in too-shallow a soil. You can still eat it, but if potatoes are green, they should be thrown onto the compost heap. The green colour means they have also been subjected to light and developed a poisonous

If a carrot has a small green collar by the base of its leaves, it has grown in too-shallow a soil. You can still eat it, but if potatoes are green, they should be thrown onto the compost heap. The green colour means they have also been subjected to light and developed a poisonous substance called solanine. It can cause illness and isn't healthy at all.

substance called solanine. It can cause illness and isn't healthy at all.

RADISHES

Radishes are easy to grow, a perfect cover crop to sow between other plants in your vegetable patch. Or wherever you like, actually. They'll even grow well in pots. Their roots aren't overly deep, and they also grow quickly.

Sow in stages once the ground readies itself in spring, continuing until late summer. Choose a sunny or half-shaded location, and make sure the ground is loose and humus-rich. Their demand for nutrients isn't large, a small application of farmyard manure and compost will last for a while. If you sow in several stages over summer, adding top up fertiliser can be a good idea. The most important thing to remember is to water and ideally cover the soil.

Wood ash and rock dust are good for powdering or sprinkling between the leaves to help ward off flea-beetles and cabbage flies.

BEETROOT (BEET)

Beetroot is easy to grow, a great root vegetable which has really gained in popularity during the recent veggie trend. It comes in red, orange, candy-striped, yellow and white varieties. The taste differs slightly, but the same advice applies to all: lots of potassium and not much nitrogen.

Beetroot likes to grow in a sunny location, in nutrient-rich soil. Use farmyard manure and compost as fertiliser. You can also sprinkle a little wood ash to raise the potassium levels slightly.

Water if the ground becomes dry. Too much nitrogen can increase nitrate levels, which isn't especially healthy. Young beetroot leaves are tasty and can be used in the same way as chard.

PARSNIP

Parsnips tend to prefer heavier soils, ideally with a lot of clay. That said, it can't be so dense that the roots aren't able to grow. Parsnips are biennial and will produce pretty yellow flowers in the second year if you don't harvest them. Grow in sun or half-shade, and fertilise using compost and farmyard manure.

Take care when watering, otherwise the parsnips can split. Top up with liquid fertiliser during summer, when growth is taking place. Wait until the first frost to harvest – doing so will lead to a better taste.

PARSLEY ROOT

A tasty plant which doesn't need to be grown in large amounts. Nip off a little – just a little – and use as seasoning. Parsley root likes the same kind of conditions as carrots, but needs top up fertiliser during the height of its growth phase in late summer. Apply liquid fertiliser then. Harvest during late autumn. Unlike many other root vegetables, the biggest and thickest roots taste best.

TURNIPS

Turnips, with their gentle, wonderful taste, have made a welcome comeback in recent years. Plant sparsely in sunlight. Most important for the soil is that it is well-draining *and* moisture-retaining. Add fertiliser in the same way you would for parsnips. Turnips can be mulched to reduce evaporation.

HORSERADISH

Horseradish is another good seasoning you won't need masses of. It's easy to grow – almost too easy, in fact, it's very happy to spread. Grow in a buried bucket or pot to limit its spread.

Horseradish likes to grow in deep, humus-rich soil. This will produce the best tasting vegetables. Sun and shade are less important. Apply fertiliser – manure and compost – when planting. Can be harvested in either autumn or spring. The horseradish can then be frozen in appropriately sized pieces.

BLACK SALSIFY

This is a delicacy, sometimes known as serpent's root or the black oyster plant. Its roots need a deep, humus and nutrient-rich soil to grow in. They are fragile and slightly tricky to harvest.

Fertilise using farmyard manure and compost in spring. Add a top up of something like bone meal, calcified seaweed and/or wood ash during summer.

Luqaz Ottosson, head chef at Gårdskrogen, Lilla Bjers
– sensual master of the tastes of the earth.

The terroir of the place

Soil tastes . . . well, like nothing else. It also tastes of different salts and minerals, and comes in different consistencies. There are differences between soils, just ask any three-year-old. You might find out that worms taste of lemon, too. With age, we learn not to put everything into our mouths, but when growing crops, daring to taste the soil is actually an advantage – it allows you to *feel* the difference. You don't need to chew or swallow, and it's probably not the best idea to taste newly fertilised soil because of the risk of bacteria.

That said, this isn't the type of taste experience served up in the restaurant at Lilla Bjers. There, the 'taste of earth' has a completely different meaning to gravelly lettuce or dirty potatoes. And someone who has physically learnt to understand the relationship between soil, growing and taste is Luqaz Ottosson, the chef there.

'We're convinced it's the soil on the farm which makes our produce taste so good. We've tried growing different varieties, different kinds of potatoes, strawberries and asparagus, and it's crystal clear that some suit our soil better than others. The same variety can taste completely different grown on a farm not far from here, so I think part of the explanation has to be in the chemistry of the soil, the composition of minerals and things like that. It's about finding *the perfect match* between soil and crop. And then seasoning it with plenty of love and a pinch of salt, of course.'

In a wine context, you'll often hear about the *terroir* of the grapes and the vineyard. It's a French word which comes from the Latin *territorium*. A very loose translation would be 'the taste of the soil' – in other words, the characteristic scents and tastes of the place where something was grown. In the reference book *Dictionnaire Hachette du vin*, you can read that the word means 'all the characteristic, natural factors which define a wine-growing climate: the bedrock, the soil, topography, slope and exposure to the sun'. Continuing the loose translation – this time into the language used on the island of Gotland, the term *terroir* could equally be used to describe Lilla Bjers' products. They all have a unique taste, a distinctive character. At least if you believe Luqaz's tastebuds.

Since the restaurant opened in 2012, both it and those in charge have been awarded a number of wonderful prizes and awards, among them Sustainable Restaurant of the Year, Rising Star of the Year, and Sustainable Gastronomy of the Year. Luqaz was named Organic Chef of the Year in 2014, something another of the restaurant's chefs, Fabian Olli Johansson, was awarded the year before. Lilla Bjers' restaurant has the highest level of KRAV certification, meaning that over 90 per cent of products are organic. But Luqaz won't be happy until he reaches 99 per cent!

'Well, why not? My kitchen's in the middle of a vegetable patch, not forgetting all the other fantastic things the island has to offer. Not many people are lucky enough to live in Sweden's best pantry, so of course I'm going to make the most of it. I usually do a round of the allotment when I get in to work, to see what's ready for harvesting. After that, I'll set the menu. The availability of the best raw produce is what steers things, not the other way around. I work closely with the Hoas family who own and run the farm. We learn from each other and we're about as engaged in the field as we are in the stews we make.'

TOMATOES, CHILLIES AND CUCUMBERS – HOT FAVOURITES

Tomatoes and chillies are among many gardeners' absolute favourites. There are even a number of groups and associations for the biggest enthusiasts. Cucumbers, squashes and pumpkins have their fans too. But what all these plants have in common is that they are worth the effort – they'll reward you with a great harvest if everything goes to plan. That means warmth, water and care. And plenty of fertiliser.

TOMATOES – LOVE APPLES

When the first tomatoes rolled ashore in Sweden in the 1600s, they were known as love apples. Cute, no? Of course, they don't belong in the Swedish climate, but they're happy to grow in greenhouses, outdoors, in grow bags or in a pot on a balcony or in a sunny courtyard.

Growing tomatoes is relatively easy, and being able to harvest your own ripe, sun-warmed fruit is the greatest of feelings – as far from the tasteless, nutrient-poor tomatoes available from supermarkets in winter as you can get.

Tomatoes belong to the potato family, *Solanaceae*. Chillies, peppers and aubergines are also members. We tend to distinguish between vine (indeterminate) tomatoes, which need to be tied in, and bush (determinate) tomatoes. The former need to be pinched out, the latter don't. This involves removing the small shoots which appear where the leaf stem joins the main stem as soon as you notice them. Doing so ensures that the plant puts its energy into growing taller and setting fruit.

Within these two umbrella groups there are many different varieties, several thousand or so, all differing in colour, shape and taste. One-colour, streaked and spotted. Choose one or several varieties suitable for our short summer. If the summer is a cool one, you might not otherwise be able to harvest until late autumn (providing the frost doesn't get there first).

YOUR OWN TOMATO PLANTS

Choose a variety which will suit your chosen spot: pot, greenhouse or outdoors. You should count on the plant needing roughly 10 weeks before it will be ready to plant out. Use nutrient-poor sowing compost and make sure to keep it damp. Sow 2–4 seeds in a small sowing pot. Once the seeds have germinated, they will need more light. Move them closer to a window. When they have two pairs of leaves, they will need to be replanted (pricked out) in more nutrient-rich potting compost and given even more light. Move them to a south-facing window or use special plant lighting.

When the tomato plant is roughly 20 cm (8 in) tall, it's time to replant it in an even larger – ideally deep – container full of fine potting soil. If the plant will remain in a pot, it needs at least 10 litres (18 pints) of soil. Plant so that the soil level is just beneath the first leaf pair. The root system will develop from the stem and make the plant more stable. Use the same nutrients you would for normal pot plants.

Before the plant is moved outside permanently, it needs time to acclimatise. Take it out during the day and bring it back in at night for roughly one week. The temperature should be no lower than around 10°C (50°F) at night when you plant it outside for good. Night life can be hard on a young plant. Burning sun is also something you should pay attention to at first. But later, the tomatoes can hardly get enough of it. Just make sure you water meticulously!

If you manage to grow more tomato plants than you need, maybe you could give a few away? That'll usually be appreciated.

TOMATOES IN GREENHOUSES

Greenhouses mean that you can grow and harvest earlier during the season. If you don't have access to a heated greenhouse, it's best to sow and allow the plants to stay indoors for the first 5–6 weeks. This will depend

DRIED TOMATOES
500 g (18 oz) cherry tomatoes

Heat the oven to 100–125°C (215–50°F). Rinse and halve the tomatoes. Line a baking tray with parchment and place the tomatoes cut side up. Put the tray into the oven, and dry the tomatoes for 3-4 hours. Open the oven door a fraction every now and then.

on where you live, of course. The seeds need a temperature of around 25°C (77°F) to grow, but things can be a little cooler after that – somewhere around 18°C (64°F).

If you sow indoors, take care with the sun when you move the plants out into the greenhouse. Use a sheet or shade cloth to help protect your plants for the first week. You can grow tomatoes in either pots or beds in your greenhouse. If you choose beds, it's important to improve or change the soil each year. Farmyard manure, compost and bone meal will form a good base. Tomatoes have high demands when it comes to nutrients. Topping up the initial application of fertiliser at a later date is vital (see below). You can even grow plants directly in a bag of good commercially available compost mix. Poke a couple of drainage holes into the side of the bag and draw a cross where you have placed the plants. That said, even bags like this will need a top up of fertiliser after a few weeks.

FERTILISER ADVICE

Tomatoes like to grow in good soil – in *especially* good soil, actually. By that, we mean it should be deep, loose, moisture-retaining and nutrient-rich. That said, there are those who grow the plants in peat-mixed sand using grass cuttings as their only source of fertiliser – and who get great results from doing so. If you decide to grow your plants outdoors, you can improve your existing soil by adding a lot of compost and decomposed farmyard manure. Bone meal is good for

fruit setting because it contains potassium and phosphorous, so mix in some of that when you first apply fertiliser. Calcified seaweed and a pinch of wood ash are also good things to add during the first application of fertiliser. When growing tomatoes, you'll benefit from making use of the entire fertiliser range. Ask ten different tomato growers and you'll get ten different opinions! Anything which works and doesn't have a negative impact on the environment is fine.

A few weeks after moving the plants outside, you should start to top up the fertiliser levels at least once a week. Remember not to add too much nitrogen (symptoms can be large, dark green leaves), because this will lead to fewer tomatoes and poorer-tasting fruit.

All tomatoes, regardless of where they are growing, will benefit from a mulch, but remember to leave the area around the root crown clear. Fresh grass cuttings two or three times during the summer will provide the nitrogen the plant needs for growth. If you use a nutrient-poor mulch like straw, you should top up using something like diluted urine. Even nettle or comfrey feed will work well (apply to both the soil and the leaves). Liquid organic fertilisers work too.

Tomatoes are thirsty plants and need watering virtually every day. If the plant dries out, the fruit can split. Using drip irrigation or self-watering systems will mean you can go away for a few days without worrying about your plants drooping.

CHILLIES – CHILL OUT

Chillies have become the darling of many gardeners – they might even boast more enthusiasts than tomatoes. Join a chilli society if you get the bug – swapping experiences and seeds is always fun. Because there truly are many different kinds of chilli: roughly thirty known varieties, and within these tens of thousands of different subspecies.

The chilli has its roots in South America and belongs to the same family as tomatoes and potatoes: *Solanaceae*. Peppers are a close relative, and are grown in a similar way to chillies (though they like even more sun and warmth).

The *Capsicum* genus includes *Capsicum annuum*, *Capsicum baccatum*, habanero, jalapeño and peperoncino. The most common, and the one most chilli growers recommend for beginners, is *Capsicum annuum*.

Chillies grow as a small green bush, roughly 50 cm (20 in) in height, and have sweet little flowers. They

GREEN TOMATOES
If your tomatoes don't have time to ripen before autumn, you can bring them indoors to mature. Green tomatoes can also be pickled or cooked in olive oil. Squeeze in a little lemon and a pinch of salt.

219

grow best in pots in our climate, in a spot shielded from the wind or in a greenhouse. Peppers grow best in greenhouses. Both chillies and peppers may need some kind of supporting stick.

GROWING CHILLIES

Chillies aren't quite as demanding as tomatoes when it comes to nutrients. Neither chillies nor peppers need to be pinched out, but they will grow new flowers if the fruit is picked after the chillies ripen. This makes them extra fun to have in your summer kitchen. The more you pick them, the more fruit they'll grow.

If you want to sow your own chilli plants, it's best to do it early, in mid- to late-winter. That said, it's also important to make sure your plants get enough sunlight in the winter darkness. You can raise chillies in the same way as tomatoes. Replant in bigger and bigger pots as the plant grows, because this will create a healthy system of roots. And plant deep, so that the roots grow from the stem. The last pot before planting out should hold at least 5 litres (9 pints) of soil, ideally double this.

Use a good soil, as for tomatoes. Either buy ready-mixed, well-fertilised soil or improve the soil you already have with farmyard manure and a little calcified seaweed.

A few weeks after planting, your chilli plant will need topping up with organic liquid fertiliser such as a chicken manure solution, diluted urine or Biobact. Chillies also like nettle feed. Some chilli growers even use bat guano with good results (and no smell). A number of different products are available, such as Chilli Focus, which is specially produced for chillies and peppers. The plants will be happy with natural 'standard fertiliser', however.

Mulch the pots with straw or grass cuttings. This will help to retain moisture and the organic material will also provide nutrients. Make sure you water enough, too: chillies are as thirsty as tomatoes. Pinch off some of the first fruit soon after blooming and it will reward you with more later on.

You can attempt to overwinter your pots indoors as house plants. If you're lucky, you'll get an early harvest the next year.

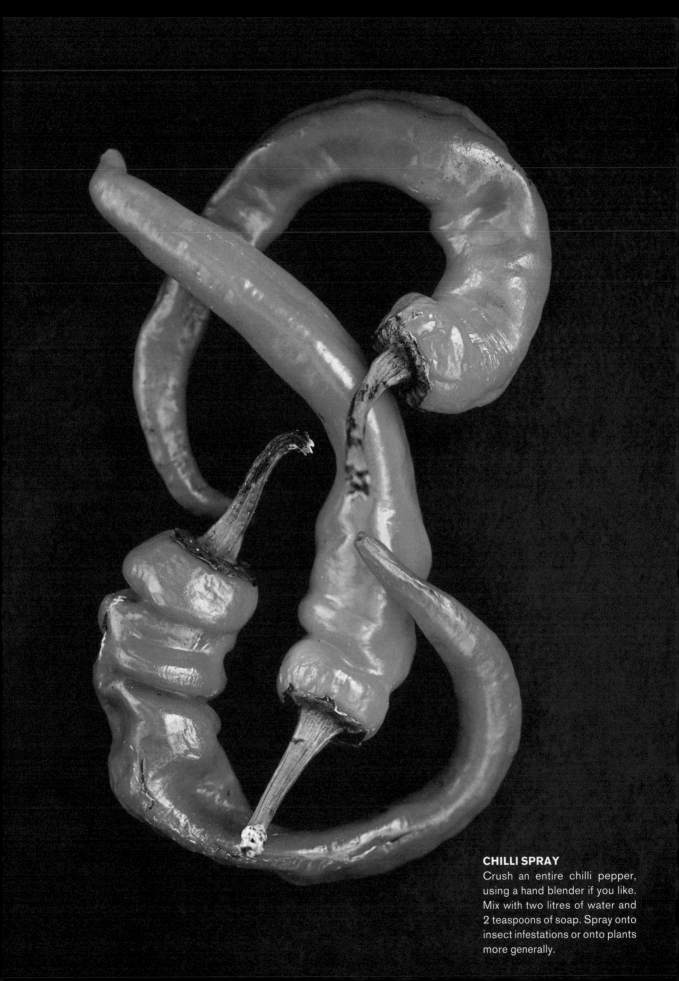

CHILLI SPRAY
Crush an entire chilli pepper, using a hand blender if you like. Mix with two litres of water and 2 teaspoons of soap. Spray onto insect infestations or onto plants more generally.

Harvest your cucumbers as they ripen. Pick them young for a better taste. This will also encourage new growth.

CUCUMBERS – BEAUTIFUL DIVERSITY

Cucumbers are great characters. They can look completely different to one another. Embrace variety! Growing cucumber plants is incredibly rewarding.

The cucumber belongs to the gourd family, Cucurbitaceae – also home to melons, pumpkins and squash. A distinction is usually made between greenhouse and ridge cucumbers. The ordinary plastic-wrapped kind we buy from the supermarket is a greenhouse cucumber. As the name suggests, these are best grown in greenhouses. Ridge cucumbers are the pickled ones you see in glass jars.

A CUCUMBER'S WISH LIST

One thing all cucumbers have in common is a preference for sunny, warm and comfortable conditions. The soil should be light, nutrient-rich and permeable. Since the cucumber plant will produce large fruits, it needs plenty of water and nutrients, particularly potassium and phosphorous. Fertilise using farmyard manure and compost. Give a little boost with wood ash, rock dust and/or bone meal if necessary. Cucumbers also like calcium, so a little calcified seaweed also wouldn't go amiss.

Take care with nitrogen, because it will encourage foliage rather than fruit setting. If the plant turns pale and weak, you can top up nitrogen levels using liquid fertiliser (diluted urine, Biobact, etc.) or by adding a mulch of grass cuttings. If the problem is acute, add blood meal.

SOWING CUCUMBERS

Sow cucumber seeds in the warm indoors (ideally 25°C/77°F) and move outdoors in 4–6 weeks. They can be sowed directly into 8–10 cm (3¼–4 in) wide pots, then planted outdoors once acclimatised.

Don't plant them out too early. Frost means almost certain death to a cucumber. And remember not to plant them deeper into the soil than they were in their sowing pots.

GROWING IN A GREENHOUSE OR OUTDOORS

Greenhouse cucumbers will prefer a greenhouse or hot bed, and want a draught-free environment with high atmospheric humidity – though with good ventilation. Try to position the cucumbers as far from the doors as possible to avoid draughts or chills. They also like to have plenty of air around them, so plant at least 50 cm (20 in) apart.

If you're growing both tomatoes and cucumbers in the same greenhouse, as many people do, give the cucumbers more moisture and the tomatoes extra ventilation.

Cucumber plants like to grow in raised beds. Greenhouse cucumbers will need to be trained onto a string or cane. Pinch out the shoots as the plant reaches the roof. Gently shake the plant while in bloom, and this will help with pollination. During particularly warm spells, you may need to water the plants more than once a day.

Cucumbers grown outdoors are slightly easier to keep healthy. Here, among others, you'll find garden and lemon cucumbers.

They also like to grow in raised beds of loose, nutrient-rich soil. Certain varieties will thrive when allowed to grow up a trellis. Protect the plants with a fibre cloth after planting outdoors until they bloom. Mulching is particularly good for cucumbers since they prefer a damp soil, but leave the root crown free. Water often!

SQUASH, PUMPKIN, MELON

These weighty monster plants will literally grow until they burst given half a chance. They have similar appetites and requirements to cucumbers, so they are grown in roughly the same way.

Give them a good dose of fertiliser and even more water than cucumbers. Add top up fertiliser as necessary in summer. You can grow squashes and pumpkins outdoors. Melons need to be grown in greenhouses or hot beds.

FERTILISER – SHORT AND SWEET

CUCUMBERS:
Apply farmyard manure and compost to the soil if growing outdoors.

Top up with bone meal, wood ash or calcified seaweed.

Mulch, ideally with straw, to retain moisture.

Top up fertiliser levels with organic liquid fertiliser.

HERBS AND SPICES –
A WORLD OF FLAVOUR

If you don't have the space or feel hesitant about growing, but have for some reason read this far and feel a tiny, tiny bit interested, then herbs and spices are a great place to start. A few fresh herbs in the kitchen window will soon turn into more! Herbs are easy to grow and give a lot back, and quickly, if you buy good plants.

If you have a garden of your own and enjoy food, then naturally you'll want a herb garden, in pots if nothing else, and that isn't half bad. These plants will be equally happy on a balcony or a porch. Keeping them close to the kitchen is a practical move, almost like an easily accessible fresh spice rack, but allowing your herbs and spices to grow among the perennials and other plants will also work very well. Herbs don't necessarily need a room of their own in your garden.

Most herbs are relatively undemanding. That isn't to say they don't need fertiliser and water, just a little less than other plants. It's also important that the soil and the light meet their needs.

HERB BOYS & SPICE GIRLS
The classic image of a herb garden is a sun-drenched patch of land with poor, lime-rich soil, where bees and butterflies flit and buzz madly about. Something like Provence. Many of the herbs we grow today originate from such regions, and as a result we have to try to replicate that environment.

If the location and soil where you want your herbs to grow aren't optimal, you may need to improve conditions. Mix the existing soil with gravel and sand, add lime and calcium-rich fertilisers like bone meal, rock dust and calcified seaweed. Build a wind shield and make sure the soil is well-drained. Then pray to the sun gods for good weather. Certain sun-worshipping herbs like things to be extra dry around their feet, not least in winter. As a result, a raised bed or a slope of some kind can be the perfect well-drained spot for them to live.

There are, however, those herbs that prefer shade and a more nutrient-rich, deep and humus-rich soil. So if you have a garden, porch or balcony which has alternative spots to offer, it may be a good idea to split your herbs up. Because it's not just in terms of light and soil that these plants' needs differ, even their nutritional demands can vary.

Herbs like parsley, cicely, angelica, mint and bog myrtle prefer shade and like soils containing more moisture and more humus. Thyme, oregano, sage, lavender and wormwood, to name but a few, can't get enough sun. Different tastes, different needs.

As usual, organic fertiliser is a sustainable way of building up a good soil in the long term. But no overdosing, please – and remember the plants' possible lime needs, too.

SOIL AND FERTILISER SUGGESTIONS
The majority of herbs like the same type of soil as vegetables. That means porous, moisture-retaining soil. In fact, a humus-rich, sandy soil is perfect for almost all herbs. Many like their soil to be extra lime-rich, and this means that calcium-rich fertilisers are great. Think calcified seaweed, bone meal and rock dust.

Almost all herbs will do badly in soil which is too damp – this can actually be the end of them during winter. As a result, you should hold back on watering them in summer. If conditions are very hot and dry, all plants will need extra water, however. Covering your herb garden with pine needles or leaves during winter can also be a good idea. A thin layer will do wonders for frozen roots.

Fertilise your herb garden in spring in accordance with the type of soil you have. Add a little compost, a tiny amount of farmyard manure and calcified seaweed, bone meal or rock dust. Top up doses will rarely ever be needed. Just remember to take care with the nitrogen! When planting for the first time, you can buy special commercial soils for herbs/spices – this will often have the same composition as 'sowing soil'.

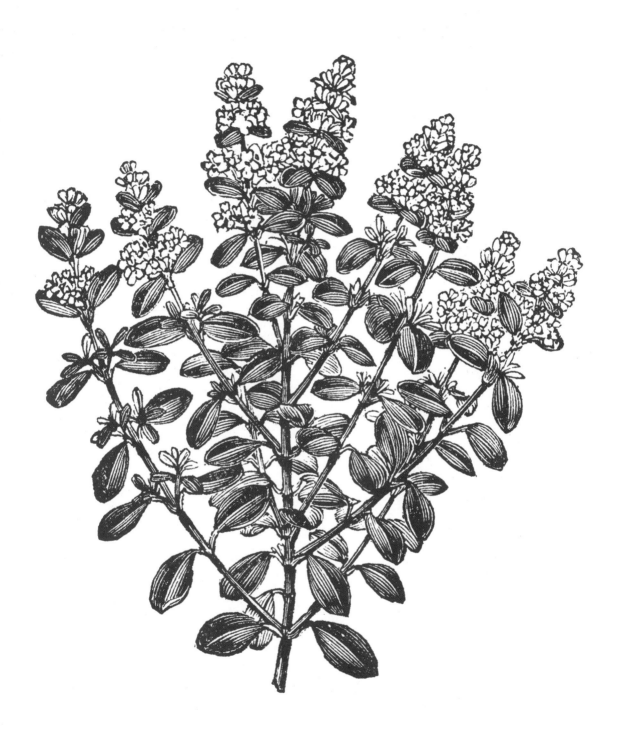

225

A general rule of thumb: the more you harvest your herb garden, the more fertiliser you need to use. If your herb scissors have been getting a lot of use, compensate for this by topping up fertiliser levels.

Planting herbs from the supermarket? These have been rapidly grown and will rarely be of the best quality, but if you replant them in good soil, they can last for a while. Bank on quality plants if you want to stay on the safe side.

Rosemary (which will rarely survive winter outdoors) is one herb which is particularly suited to growing indoors. Mint will spread wildly, vastly, but can be kept contained in a pot. All herbs can, of course, be grown in pots. It's unlikely they'll survive winter outdoors, but they can always be brought in. Otherwise, dig them into the soil in your garden – pot and all.

HERBS IN POTS

When you grow herbs in pots, roughly the same rules as growing outdoors apply, albeit cubed. The difference with growing directly in the soil is that you need to be even more attentive and vigilant. The sun worshippers need to be placed in the sun, and the shade lovers in the shade.

You also need to be extra careful with the soil, fertiliser and watering. Though many herbs like poor conditions, they can't live on nothing if the soil is empty. But over-fertilisation, particularly of nitrogen, will produce tasteless plants. Using organic liquid fertiliser or nutrient sticks sparingly will usually be enough. Diluted manure in a herb garden may not be the best idea, given that we usually pinch off a leaf or two here and there. Covering the bare surface of the soil with grass cuttings is, of course, good, but it will also provide a lot of nitrogen.

FERTILISER – SHORT AND SWEET

Distinguish between the sun and lime lovers and the shade and humus-loving plants.

Apply fertiliser carefully – using compost and possibly a small amount of farmyard manure (cow/horse).

Lime lovers can be given a small dose of calcified seaweed or bone meal and rock dust.

ANNUALS

A SUMMER FLING

They flower in summer and then wither away to become sweet memories. Summer blooms provide quick results and immediate enjoyment. And given the nutrients and water they need, the romance will be a long, happy one. Treating your annuals right can make them last long into autumn.

Summer blooms can be sowed or planted in pots, urns, hanging baskets, flowerbeds or garden plots. Cosmos, mealy cup sage and French lavender in a pot? A classic like marigolds or cornflowers in a vegetable patch? A row of golden marigolds or wandering nasturtiums between the cabbages? Choose varieties that will thrive wherever you want them, in sun or in shade.

Summer blooms are often referred to as annuals: plants which manage to sprout, grow, bloom, go to seed and wither away in the space of a few short months. Many will self-sow and live on through their offspring. Gather the seeds if you want to keep things a little more controlled. You can even move self-sown plants to a location of your choosing. Plants with a two-year lifespan are also available, known as biennials. They will grow leaves the first year and bloom the next. Unlike perennials, annuals don't need to overwinter. This means you can continue to fertilise these summer blooms in late summer and even early autumn. They need nutrients throughout their lifespans.

SEEDLINGS IN PLASTIC POTS
Many different types of 'garden ready' summer blooms are available for purchase from garden centres, not just daisies, lobelias and marigolds. Once you take your selection home, these seedlings will need to be planted in good soil. Choose a ready-fertilised soil meant for pots and urns if you'll be growing the plants in containers. The soil you had last year will be 'used up' and no good as a home for your new plants – throw this old soil onto the compost heap. Choose the biggest pots you can. They will retain nutrients and water better.

After a month or so, the nutrients in even the best of commercially available soils will be depleted. Liquid fertilisers tend to be the easiest method to top up nutrient levels, but there are a number of alternatives: granules, nutrient sticks, discs, etc. Either apply liquid fertiliser once a week, or dilute to create a weaker mix for use every time you water. It's a question of preference which you choose and what you use: diluted urine, nettle feed, liquid chicken manure or shop-bought liquid fertiliser.

And don't just give them a quick spritz, water properly. It's the roots which need the water. Dig a finger deeeeeep into the soil and have a quick feel. Allow the pots to dry up between waterings, but don't let them dry out.

FERTILISER – SHORT AND SWEET

Summer blooms need nutrients throughout their lifespans.

Plant in well-fertilised, shop-bought soil or boost your existing soil with compost and manure.

Top up with liquid fertiliser like diluted urine or shop-bought mixes.

SOWING SUMMER BLOOMS

One of the best garden activities over winter is studying the next year's seed catalogues. It can be hard to stop yourself. Later, next spring, when you can't move for all the seed packets from floor to ceiling, it's a bit too late. Then it's just a case of finishing the job, realising that we never learn, and making the same mistake the next time the catalogues arrive.

Read the packets to distinguish between varieties and types. Certain seeds can be sown straight outside in early summer, and others are better sown indoors a little earlier. When sowing directly outdoors, in a flowerbed or similar, the soil should be loose, free from any weeds, and have been fertilised a few weeks before.

For seeds planted indoors or in greenhouses, you'll need a nutrient-poor sowing soil to begin with, subsequently increasing the amount of humus and nutrients as well as light and water, repotting the plants in larger and larger pots. Growing plants from seed indoors will give you a head start: you'll have flowering blooms in your garden earlier than you would otherwise.

Concrete flowers

It's an ordinary weekday morning just after midsummer – warm enough, early enough, and with just enough people around. By the gates to Zetas Garden in Huddinge, not far out of Stockholm, a handful of lively customers are already waiting for the nursery to open. Victoria Skoglund greets us with a wide smile and a warm embrace, just back from midsummer celebrations on the island of Öland. Tanned, rested and fresher than a daisy.

'Wonderful! I love manure! We need to talk more about the importance of fertiliser! It's the base of all growing and a necessity for all plants. I like that it smells, that it's a bit dirty and messy. Definitely not something to wrinkle your nose at. I mean, I live with the benefits and effects of manure, so for me a bit of cow poo is just great,' Victoria says enthusiastically.

Ha! Appearances can be deceiving. This particular daisy isn't afraid of a little bit of muck beneath her nails. It comes with the territory as a head gardener. With the help of her staff, Victoria has developed Zetas Garden into one of Sweden's foremost nurseries, going under the slogan: 'the connoisseur's garden'. This doesn't mean it sells nothing but exclusive and rare plants; it means a large range, enthusiastic staff and an aesthetic approach. The place has knowledge, experience and taste, not just when it comes to plants but to growing in general. And even in relation to fertiliser and plant nutrition in all its forms.

'Knowing about soil and nutrient content is vital for any gardener, it's the basis of all forms of growing. Just because a plant is a connoisseur's plant doesn't mean it has to be difficult, particular or need any special diet. It's almost always the opposite, actually. I like robust, tolerant plants, and there are plenty outside of the "standard" assortment which work well in our climate. But regardless of where you are and what you're growing, your plants will need nutrients. Not just when you plant them, but continuously.'

Zetas Garden has become something of a destination for those interested in gardening from all over Sweden. The core group of customers are Stockholmers, however; those with gardens, inner courtyards and balconies. Allotment garden or castle grounds – everyone seems to find their way here.

'Interest in growing has definitely increased among people in cities. In the past, it used to be mostly villa owners from the suburbs buying things for their gardens, but now it's just as common for people to come here and buy plants and decorations for their inner-city courtyards and balconies. We get a lot of questions about growing in pots and containers. Growing for use has also increased. From having a few fresh herbs on their kitchen window, lots of people now want to grow tomatoes, chillies, beans and other edible things in town,' Victoria says, offering another piece of lemon cake.

Victoria Skoglund, Zetas Garden in Huddinge —
the head gardener with chlorophyll in her veins

Growing in small spaces, micro-gardening, has slightly different requirements. Here, the addition of nutrients is even more important. No matter how big the pots, containers or balcony boxes you have are, access is limited. The soil will dry out and the nutrients will be used up or leach away more quickly. In addition to that, winter-chill and winter-dampness are a greater threat. And if the nutrient and water balance is wrong, susceptibility to pests, disease and even to the weather will increase.

'Yeah, that's true,' Victoria says, her face suddenly serious. 'Never, ever skimp on the quality of the soil! Drill a few holes into the bottom of the pot so that any excess water can drain away. I don't usually bother adding any leca balls, but lots of people do. Make a good base mix of soil, fertiliser and compost – ideally adding both biochar (see page 54) to help retain nutrients and water, and bokashi (see page 46), which gives a good balance to the soil and helps increase its resilience. That's a particularly good mix for roses and clematis. During summer, I use diluted urine or Rika, which is an organic fertiliser, in my pots. If I go away and have to leave my kids or a neighbour in charge, I apply the fertiliser in advance, I use Chrysan, to make things easier for them.'

Ahead of winter, it's a case of protecting your pots against chill and damp, isn't it? So what do you do in terms of fertiliser in autumn?

'No more fertiliser then, the plants need to rest. But insulating them is good. I usually use cheap sleeping mats and top dress with 1–2 cm (½–¾ in) of cow manure. A large pot of perennials can stay that way for three to four years, but after that you'll need to split the plants, change the soil, etc. Nothing's eternal, unfortunately, no matter how hard we try.'

VICTORIA'S GREEN FINGERTIPS:

'Everyone should grow at least one bee-friendly plant, even if it's just in a pot on the balcony. Herbs like oregano, basil and lesser calamint are all popular with bees. Or garden heliotrope, which is a great pot or balcony plant.'

'Practically anything you'd grow in a garden can also be grown in pots or boxes, on balconies or any outdoor space. Just make sure the pots are big enough and filled with good soil, nutrients and water. Choose tolerant, robust plants. Ask at your local nursery!'

'Remember that a warm, dry summer means more nutrients are needed. When it's hot, you'll have to both water and add fertiliser more often. Give the plants a good watering so that their roots are damp. Better lots infrequently than too little too often. When it comes to nutrients, I do the opposite: I give the plants a little diluted liquid fertiliser every time I water them.'

'People need physical contact with nature and our cities need more small oases. Grow more!'

PROVENANCE PROVENCE

Ah, a sun-warmed stone terrace on the hills above the sea. Maybe a long lunch beneath the wisteria-covered pergola? Patinated terracotta pots of agave, laurel trees and geraniums. The scent of thyme, rosemary and lemon trees in bloom. Ideally with one foot in the pool and a cool glass of light rosé in one hand . . . It's not hard to understand our longing for the Mediterranean.

Often, it's that very feeling we Swedes want to recreate back home in the north: that fantastic sunlight and warmth. And it's precisely the warmth part which can lead to complications. Not during summer, but during or after winter. There are plenty of Nordic alternatives to the Mediterranean plants, the willow-leaved pear for example – 'Scandinavia's olive tree'. But if that won't do, make sure you choose the hardiest plants possible. Treat them like precious jewels, gently and carefully.

The atmosphere, materials and method of growing in large pots and raised beds can, of course, be applied directly. There are even some mediterranean plants which will accept the more southerly parts of Sweden, when placed correctly. Lavender, thyme and other herbs, for example. Even certain grapes and figs can be grown in the right place. But lemon trees will need to be brought in during winter, no excuses.

FOREIGN-BORN SWEDES

The plants we typically refer to as Mediterranean don't always have their origins there – citrus plants and African lilies, for example. The lily's origins are obvious, but that the lemon and its relatives originally stem from South East Asia isn't quite so clear. That said, they do well around the Mediterranean, along with rosemary, agave, olives, laurels, figs and bougainvillea, to name just a few of the plants which are popular in Sweden.

In an ideal world, our focus would be on vegetation from countries at roughly the same degree of latitude as Sweden – Canada, the Baltic States, Russia, Japan and so on. Plants from those countries could thrive, even in our climate. Otherwise, we will always have to make more of an effort to satisfy the plants' environmental needs. In this particular case: the hot, dry Mediterranean summers and cool, damp winters.

SUN WORSHIPPER SOIL

Ordinarily, we grow these warm-blooded plants in pots. Commercial soils for pots and urns are a good choice here. You can even buy special citrus/Mediterranean soil. It's vital that the soil you choose is permeable and loose.

It's also possible to create your own mix from rhododendron and ordinary soil, possibly adding a little gravel and clay. You could also add micronutrients, iron sulphate and rock dust (ideally basalt), for example. The simplest (and most expensive) method is, however, to buy ready-mixed, specialist soil from the garden centre.

Specialist citrus compost often contains a small amount of clay, is well-fertilised and has a low pH. Certain manufacturers also add lava gravel, coconut fibres and micronutrients such as iron. Adding iron will lead to beautiful green leaves, and yellow foliage (common in citrus plants) can indicate a deficiency

of the micronutrient. Re-plant your Mediterranean friends every second or third year, using completely new, fresh soil.

MEDITERRANEAN DIET

The thing that usually separates these plants' appetites from others is that they want more micronutrients, and in greater quantities. In addition to that, they also need nitrogen, phosphorous and potassium like any other native plant. Some, citrus plants, for example, like to grow in slightly acidic soils. Blooming varieties in particular need a lot of nutrients and a lot of water.

If you use specially mixed shop-bought soils in pots, you won't need to add anything in the way of fertiliser for the first few weeks. After that, you can use a weak nutrient solution every time you water the plants, or a slightly stronger one every other week. Special fertilisers for citrus, olive and other Mediterranean plants are available. You can also buy nutrient tablets and sticks, which can be pushed directly into the soil. Diluted urine and nettle feed will also work well, but they contain fewer micronutrients. One easy way to provide iron is to push a rusty piece of metal into the soil.

Start giving your plants small amounts of nutrients as the days get lighter after winter, and gradually increase the level as the sun climbs higher in the sky. Continue until the middle of summer, and then cut back drastically so that the plants wind down and save energy for winter.

EVERY OTHER WATERING

Many Mediterranean plants like a lot of water, but don't like to grow in wet soil – something which does sound contradictory. In practice, this means it's important that your pots drain well, with plenty of drainage holes and porous soil, possibly mixed with leca balls or gravel. Tall, narrow pots are better than squat, wide ones.

When you water your plants, make sure not to just give them a quick spritz: give them a real soak. The soil shouldn't stay wet for too long, so let it dry up – but not dry out completely. Rainwater is best. It's also a good idea to cover the bare soil so that the moisture doesn't just evaporate, using stones, shells or whatever you prefer. In winter, the plants should be watered only sparingly. Those which keep their leaves, like olive and citrus plants, will need more water and light than those which drop their leaves, like figs. Don't give them any nourishment, they're meant to be dormant. That said, they will be grateful for a refreshing shower every now and then.

HIBERNATORS

The majority of Mediterranean plants have roughly the same desires in life. They want a warm spot in summer, shielded from the wind, and they want to overwinter somewhere bright and cool indoors. If you experience problems with these southern treasures, it will usually be to do with their overwintering. Simply put, we have trouble finding a good spot for them. As a consequence, mites, scale insects and other nasties can sometimes take over.

Take care in early summer when moving plants out into the sun again. Place them in a shaded or half-shaded spot to begin with, so they have time to adjust. Bring them back in at night for a few days until they are acclimatised.

FERTILISER – SHORT AND SWEET

Use special fertilisers for Mediterranean/citrus plants when topping up nutrient levels. Diluted urine is also good.

Push a piece of rusty metal into your pots for an extra iron boost.

LODGERS

Just like plants outdoors, houseplants need water, nutrients and oxygen. Since their pots contain a limited amount of soil, it's important that you stock up the pantry more carefully than you would in the garden. Plants need both macro- and micronutrients, of which nitrogen, phosphorous and potassium are most important.

Nitrogen is important in ensuring that your plants grow as they should, but excessive amounts will see the foliage increase to the detriment of any flowers. Too much nitrogen can also make the plant more susceptible to disease. Phosphorous affects budding, which is particularly important in plants which flower. Potassium helps the stalks and stems to develop properly.

Pot plants also need micronutrients, albeit in smaller amounts. All nutrients have an impact on your plants, and both deficiencies and excesses can have consequences.

LIGHT, WATER AND SOIL

Find out about your plants' needs in terms of light, and satisfy them. Check that the soil is suitably moisture-retaining and water in line with individual plants' needs. Some like a constantly damp soil, whereas others like to dry up properly between waterings.

The vast majority of plants like to be given just *enough* water, which is obviously difficult to give an exact amount for. Very few plants can cope with standing in water for longer periods without starting to rot. In fact, one of the most common killers of pot plants is drowning!

After a while, once the roots have grown too big for their pot, your plants may need new soil. Replant in a larger pot of new, fresh soil. Ordinary compost from a bag is probably easiest. Many different varieties are available. Just remember that certain plants such as azalea, hydrangea, gardenia and camellia are lime-averse. Soil with a lower pH can also be bought for such plants.

Cacti and succulents have different needs again. They like sandy soils with low levels of nutrients, and this type of soil can be bought from garden centres.

...AND THEN THE NUTRIENTS

Different pot plants have such varied demands that it's difficult to generalise. Read up on specific varieties if you want to develop real green fingers.

Usually, flowering species will need more nutrients to be able to bud than those which are 'only' green. The vast majority of pot plants will need regular additions of nutrients during the lighter months, roughly from early-/mid-spring to mid-autumn. Either mix a weak nutrient solution and use it every time you water, or apply a stronger dose once a week.

There are a huge number of different nutrient solutions available from garden centres: liquids, powders, granules, soluble tablets and nutrient sticks to push straight into the soil. Read and follow the manufacturers' recommendations. Ordinary, homemade diluted urine will work just as well.

SYMPTOMS OF NUTRIENT DEFICIENCY OR EXCESS

A nutrient imbalance can reveal itself in different ways, depending on the type of plant and which nutrient(s) are missing or in excess. In general, a nutrient deficiency will lead to poor growth and an unhealthy appearance. The plant might also lose its lower leaves as new leaves develop, because it lacks the energy to support more foliage.

Too much nitrogen can cause symptoms such as dry leaf edges or excessively luxuriant foliage without any blooms. A lack of nitrogen will turn the plant pale, sallow and grumpy. It will become sparse, thin and weak.

Phosphorous binds to the soil and doesn't leach away as easily as the other nutrients. Deficiencies are therefore less common, but can present as an excessively green shade – almost verging on purple.

For the majority of plants, a potassium deficiency will cause brown, withered leaf tips and edges. Potassium is particularly important for plants which bloom, because it affects the colour.

POT PLANT 'REHAB'

If you suspect your plants have had an overdose of nutrients, it's best to change the soil completely. Replant in nutrient-poor soil (sowing soil, for example) and hold off on fertilising the plants until they seem to have recovered. You can then replant them in ordinary soil, starting over that way.

If it seems that your plants are suffering a nutrient deficiency, it's just a case of fattening them up, but carefully – so that they have time to adjust and absorb the nutrients.

GREEN AIR FILTERS

Houseplants contribute to better atmospheric humidity. Dry air can have a negative impact on our mucous membranes. Damp air also counteracts static electricity. Many plants will help (albeit to a small degree) to clean dangerous elements and particles from the air. As your plants convert carbon dioxide into oxygen through photosynthesis, they also absorb and bind any harmful particles in the air. Benzene,

formaldehyde, xylene and toluene are all things we don't want to breathe in but which are hard to avoid. Even the soil in your pots will help to clean the air.

Remember to wipe or wash the dust from your plants so that they can carry on their air cleaning work unhindered. Examples of good air filters are: gerbera, ivy, peace lily and mother-in-law's tongue.

HOMEBREW IN YOUR WATERING CAN

Diluted urine is perfect for watering and nourishing your beloved plants. Mix one part pee with nineteen parts water. Pour the mix onto the soil, not the plant. Diluted urine can easily replace shop-bought products containing synthetic nutrients. Even old aquarium water can work well as a source of nourishment!

DILUTED URINE
FOR POT PLANTS

50 ml (1¾ fl oz) pee

+ 950 ml (1½ pint) water

1 litre (1¾ pint) of
nourishment

FLORAL TIPS

Fruits such as apples, pears, peaches, etc. (even tomatoes) emit ethylene, a type of gas which can affect your flowers and cause them to wither more quickly. Remember to keep your fruit bowl away from your vases! Even conifers (Christmas trees, for example) emit gas.

Flowers don't like cigarette smoke or draughty locations. Strong sunshine can cause them to droop more quickly than if they were in a shaded location.

Put your flowers somewhere cool overnight, in the basement or similar, and they will last longer. A balcony will work well providing it isn't too cold outside. Even the fridge can work if the vase will fit.

PURE JOY

Fresh flowers are one of the more reasonable luxuries in life. Something beautiful, romantic and sensual to reward yourself or spoil others with, particularly during the winter months when the garden outside is resting. But the wonderful is often much too fleeting. And even though withered can also be beautiful, we want to extend the lives of our flowers. With the right care and a little nourishment, that task becomes just a little bit easier.

Choose fresh flowers while shopping or gathering. When you get them home, your bouquet should be put in the right temperature water as quickly as possible. Always cut the stalks, even if this has already been done in the shop. Cut with a knife or razor blade to ensure a clean, straight cut. If you use scissors, the channels in the stalks can close up, meaning that the water and nutrients have trouble moving up them. It's important that your flowers are as full of water and as healthy as possible.

A LONGER, HAPPIER LIFE

If a florist put together a bouquet you like, don't loosen the tie. Flowers with weak stems like Persian buttercups and daffodils should ideally be left to stand in water with the paper still around them for a while. Doing this means that the stalks have slightly more support while they're taking in water, and that they will then stay straight for longer.

Take away any leaves which end up beneath water level (not so important on flowers with softer stems). The leaves contain polyphenol, which can cause a build up of micro-organisms in the water. Not harmful, but this can mean that the water quickly loses its freshness.

Make sure the vase is clean. Fill with the right amount of water at the right temperature (see below). Sometimes, you'll be given a sachet of powder feed from the florist – use it. You can also buy liquid feed from the garden centre. The alternative is a mix of the usual things from the pantry (see below). Change the water often, and cut the stalks again if necessary.

MORNING FLOWERS

The best time to pick flowers, whether they're wild or grown in your garden, is the morning, before the air gets too warm. This is when they will be most turgid from the night's dew. It's best to cut the stalks with a knife or razor blade – don't use scissors or shears. Otherwise, cut the flowers as late as possible before putting them in water.

Once the flowers are full of water again, you can arrange them. Take away any leaves below the water level. If you want more greenery in your vase, it's better to have separate leaves or strands. Then change the water often, ideally every day.

SUSTAINABLE PURCHASES

Cut flowers from shops are often grown rapidly and sprayed heavily. Don't throw them onto your compost heap when they wither, particularly not if you use your compost to grow vegetables. Many flowers are also grown in countries where wages, working conditions, etc. aren't always the best. In addition to that, the flowers are transported both long distances and quickly, often on planes, so that they can be sold while they're at their best. Your flowers will likely have come either from the other side of the world or from a heated greenhouse in Europe – both options are energy-intensive and burdensome on the environment.

In other words, buying cut flowers isn't particularly good for the environment. That isn't to say you should stop doing it. You can always ask if your shop has any environmentally friendly, certified or organic flowers. There is some confusion around the markings – sometimes they refer to the environmental impact, sometimes the working and social conditions. Keep an eye out for organic, Fairtrade and Fair Flowers, Fair Plants labels.

The Swedish Society for Nature Conservation uses the 'Bra Miljöval' (Good Environmental Choice) marking, and has developed criteria for the flower trade. With higher levels of awareness and greater demand from customers, both the flower trade and the growers will eventually change.

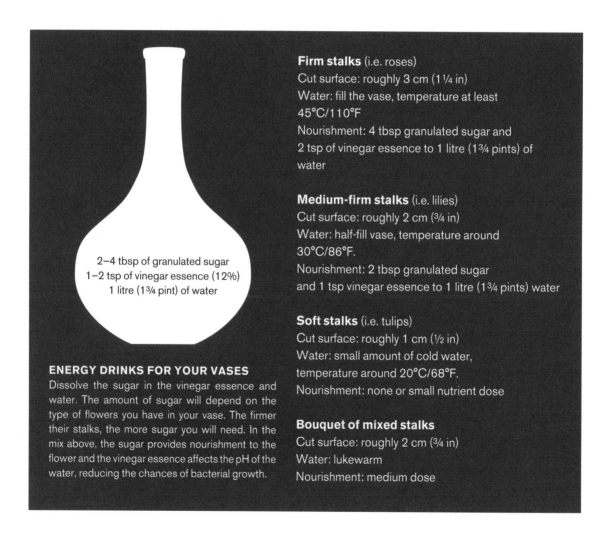

2–4 tbsp of granulated sugar
1–2 tsp of vinegar essence (12%)
1 litre (1¾ pint) of water

Firm stalks (i.e. roses)
Cut surface: roughly 3 cm (1¼ in)
Water: fill the vase, temperature at least 45°C/110°F
Nourishment: 4 tbsp granulated sugar and 2 tsp of vinegar essence to 1 litre (1¾ pints) of water

Medium-firm stalks (i.e. lilies)
Cut surface: roughly 2 cm (¾ in)
Water: half-fill vase, temperature around 30°C/86°F.
Nourishment: 2 tbsp granulated sugar and 1 tsp vinegar essence to 1 litre (1¾ pints) water

Soft stalks (i.e. tulips)
Cut surface: roughly 1 cm (½ in)
Water: small amount of cold water, temperature around 20°C/68°F.
Nourishment: none or small nutrient dose

Bouquet of mixed stalks
Cut surface: roughly 2 cm (¾ in)
Water: lukewarm
Nourishment: medium dose

ENERGY DRINKS FOR YOUR VASES
Dissolve the sugar in the vinegar essence and water. The amount of sugar will depend on the type of flowers you have in your vase. The firmer their stalks, the more sugar you will need. In the mix above, the sugar provides nourishment to the flower and the vinegar essence affects the pH of the water, reducing the chances of bacterial growth.

Apply fertiliser when the soil is ready (drier and workable).

Rack your memory or check your notes to see what you served up to your plants last year.

Vary the fertilisers you use to ensure a balanced diet. Think of the bigger picture.

Bring your garden compost to life, dig it over and air.

Improve the soil using a shop-bought compost.

Spring is a good time to begin a new compost heap.

Think about whether you need to add anything other than compost and manure to the soil – rock dust, composted bark, peat or lime?

Remove or push back any crop covers so that the soil can warm up in the spring sunshine. Apply fertiliser before re-covering.

Remove any organic material that has not decomposed or been eaten by worms (dig it into the soil or add to the compost heap).

Continue to apply fertiliser. Depending on the quality of your soil and the type of fertiliser you are using, the nutrients from the first application will last 3-5 weeks and will then need to be topped up.

Fertilise your pot plants. As light levels increase, growth will pick up and subsequently so will the need for nutrients and water.

- Top up the fertiliser! Continue to do this for the most demanding plants. Grass cuttings, diluted urine, liquid manures, nettle feed or similar. Apply a weak dose once a week, or a very weak dose every time you water. An alternative is a slightly stronger dose every other or every third week.

- Pick nettles, field horsetail, comfrey, etc. and create your own liquid fertiliser.

- Water your compost if the summer is sunny and dry.

- Sow green manure crops.

- Reduce the dose of fertiliser from mid-summer onwards, so that those plants which will overwinter have time to go into dormancy. During late summer, your plants will not need any more nitrogen because growth will drop off.

- Continue to give nourishment to those plants which will not overwinter. Vegetables and summer blooms, for example. They need nourishment for their entire life span.

- Gather/fetch fresh farmyard manure if you can, place it in a pile and leave to decompose so that it's ready for use in spring.

- Apply fertiliser to the soil and to those plants which really need it during late summer, but not otherwise.

AUTUMN

- Don't apply nitrogen fertilisers to those plants which will be dormant over winter.

- Continue to apply to summer blooms and vegetables for as long as they live.

- You may want to apply a little bone meal when planting spring bulbs.

- Dig your green manure crops into the soil, if they are still there.

- Clay soils at cold latitudes can be fertilised so that the nutrients are ready when spring arrives.

- Gather leaves and cuttings for composting.

- Rake leaves beneath bushes and into flowerbeds.

WINTER

- Collect ash from the winter's log fires

- Be sparing with water and nourishment for your pot plants. Frequently shower or spray them with water. Increase the dose as the days become brighter in late winter.

- Prepare a fertiliser inventory – plan and get hold of anything you will need.

THANK YOU
AND GOODBYE

Growers are probably a bit better than everyone else. They're warmer, kinder and more generous than people in general. A little calmer and a little smarter from having their feet firmly in the mud. Or at least that's how it feels after having met so many wonderful gardeners, hobby growers, farmers, scientists, fertiliser manufacturers, growing nerds and animal owners. We bow down to all the kind souls who opened up their stables, gardens and hearts to us. This book wouldn't have been nearly as fun to write without you. So, hats off to:

Karl-JohanBergstrand, PhD Agronomy at The Swedish University of Agricultural Sciences (SLU) in Alnarp
Göran and Margareta Hoas, organic growers at Lilla Bjers in Västerhejde
Luqaz Ottosson, chef at Lilla Bjers Gårdskrog in Västerhejde
Lars Krantz, head gardener and source of inspiration at Wij Gardens in Ockelbo
Lasse Pettersson, head gardener at DBW botanical gardens, Visby
Victoria Skoglund and her staff at Zetas Finsmakarens Trädgård in Segeltorp, Huddinge
Filip Älfvåg, Tony Ottosson and Claes Gyllensten, photographic assistants with Ewa-Marie Rundquist
Anna Bauer at Broms Karlaplan, Stockholm
Benny Jansson and Eva Leijon from Östergårda, Tofta – plus the boar, Magnus and young pig, Lillgrisen
Bengt Stenberg from Stora Källstäde, Lärbro. Special thanks to the five northern
Swedish mares and the beautiful donkeys!
Jenny Andersson and Kjell Nilsson from Graute Gård, Hejnum. Thanks to all the animals!
Rosendals Trädgård, Djurgården in Stockholm
Stefan Trolle Lindros, Tyresö
Niklas Frisk, grower at the Stora Skuggan allotment association, Stockholm
Catarina Volle from LEVA Kungslador, Visby
The Norman family, Ekerö
Niklas Vestin from Rölunda Gård, Bålsta
Mikael Albertsson and Eric Lagerberg from Algomin AB, Linköping
Lovö Prästgård farm, Drottningholm
Sara Nyström and Astri von Arbin Ahlander for believing in this book.

We'd also like to give heartfelt thanks to our editor, Susanna Eriksson Lundqvist, our publisher, Per Wivall, and to all the other fantastic publishing people at Bonnier Fakta.

LITERATURE

Campbell, Stu *Improving Your Soil* (Storey Books, 1999)

Chatto, Beth & Steven Wooster *Drought-Resistant Planting: Lessons from Beth Chatto's Gravel Garden* (Frances Lincoln, 2016)

Dowding, Charles *Charles Dowding's Vegetable Course* (Frances Lincoln, 2012)

Flowerdew, Bob *Organic Gardening Bible: Successful Growing the Nature Way* (Kyle Books, 2015)

Jenkins, Joseph C. *The Humanure Handbook: A Guide to Composting Human Manure* (Jenkins, 2006)

Kopecky, Mark *Managing Manure: How to Store, Compost, and Use Organic Livestock Wastes* (Storey, 2015)

Lodgson, Gene, *Holy Shit: Managing Manure to Save Mankind* (Chelsea Green, 2010)

RHS Plants for Places: 1000 Tried and Tested Plants for Every Soil, Site and Usage (Royal Horticultural Society, 2001)

Riotte, Louise *Carrots Love Tomatoes: Secrets of Companion Planting for Successful Gardening* (Storey, 1998)

Scott, Nicky *Reduce, Reuse, Recycle* (Green Books, 2007)

Shepherd, Allan *The Organic Garden: Green and Easy* (Collins, 2009)

Steinfield, Carol *Liquid Gold: The Lore and Logic of Using Urine to Grow Plants* (Green Books, 2004)

Thompson, Ken *An Ear to the Ground: Garden Science for Ordinary Mortals* (Eden Project Books, 2006)

Thompson, Ken *Compost: The Natural Way to Make Food for Your Garden* (DK, 2007)

Thun, Matthias *The Maria Thun Biodynamic Calendar* (Floris Books, annually)

Waldin, Monty, *Biodynamic Gardening* (DK Publishing, 2015)

INFORMATION ONLINE

ahs.org

algomin.se

biochar-international.org

biodynamic.org.uk

biodynamics.com

bokashidirect.co.uk

charlesdowding.co.uk

compostdirect.com

dalefootcomposts.co.uk

doctorgreenfingers.co.uk

envocare.co.uk

essentialgardenguide.com

gardeningknowhow.com

gardenorganic.org.uk

gardenzone.info

gcamerica.org

greatgardeninfo.com

growmore.com

howtocompost.org

ifoam.bio

johninnes.info

manurematters.com

miraclegro.com

ngb.org

rhs.org.uk

soilassociation.org

wij.se

Behind the book *Good Soil* is an unusually creative trio. Three authors, all of whom happen to be women: a copywriter who also designs gardens, an art director who gets excited by recycling and an incredibly down-to-earth photographer. What links the three is a passion for gardens and a love of manure.

Tina Råman (centre) uses virtually everything mentioned in this book, other than fecal matter and synthetic fertilisers. Not to say that she uses everything at once. Ewa-Marie Rundquist (left) uses a bit of everything, usually cow manure and Algomin. Justine Lagache is enthusiastic about diluted urine and bokashi, but she uses cow manure as a base.

Frances Lincoln Ltd
74-77 White Lion Street,
London N1 9PF

Good Soil
Copyright © Frances Lincoln Ltd 2017
First edition BonnierFakta 2016

Printer: Livonia Print, Latvia 2016
ISBN 978-0-7112-3872-5

Text © Tina Råman 2016
Photographs © Ewa-Marie Rundquist 2016
(except pp. 22-23: 123RF.com and pp. 25, 50, 58-59, 73, 76, 123, 125, 139, 142, 147, 196, 212-213, 222: Shutterstock)

Drawings pp. 5, 7, 40, 45, 47-49, 88, 109, 251, 256, back cover: © Christina Drejenstam/ Agent Molly & Co 2016

Other drawings: Shutterstock
Graphic form and identity: Justine Lagache
Editor: Susanna Eriksson Lundqvist and Hanna Jacobsson

Fact checker: Karl-Johan Bergstrand, SLU
Repro: JK Morris Production AB, Värnamo

Quarto Knows

Quarto is the authority on a wide range of topics.

Quarto educates, entertains and enriches the lives of our readers – enthusiasts and lovers of hands-on living.

www.QuartoKnows.com